THE STRANGE DISAPPEARANCE OF JIM THOMPSON

And Stories
of other Expatriates in Southeast
Asia

Harold Stephens

Wolfenden

Wolfenden Publishers
P.O. Box 789
Miranda, California 95553
Voice/Fax: 707 923-2455
e-mail: wolfen@northcoast.com
http: wolfenden.com

Cover designed by Robert Stedman
Edited by Austin B. Berry

Far East Trade Press: First printing January 1979
Travel Publishing Asia, Ltd.: Second printing March 1983
Travel Publishing Asia, Ltd.: Third printing September 1983
Travel Publishing Asia, Ltd.: Fourth printing Jun33 1984
Travel Publishing Asia, Ltd.: Fifth printing July 1995
Wolfenden Publishers: Sixth printing September 2003

Printed in Thailand

The Strange Disappearance of Jim Thompson, and Stories of
Other Expatraites in Southeast Asia / by Harold Stephens.

ISBN: 0-9642521-7-1

USA $14.95
CANADA $22.95

CONTENTS

Living in Asia over the years has given me the grand experience of meeting many fascinating and interesting people, many of whom should have been included in the chapters of this book, but for one reason or another have been omitted.

To one such person this book is dedicated:
To John Willoughby of Port Dickson, Malaysia, whose keen interests in Asian studies have had a great influence on me.

H.S.
June 2003
Bangkok

Also by
Harold Stephens

Discover the Orient
Malaysia
Destination Singapore
Singapore After Dark
Turn South at the Equator
Asian Adventure
Asiam Portraits
Motoring in Southeast Asia
(A Guide)
At Home in Asia
(Expatriates in Southeast Asia)
Three Decades of Asian Travel &
Adventure
The Last Voyage
(The Story of Schooner Third Sea)
The Tower & The River
(A Novel)
Who Needs a Road?
(The Last Motor Trip Around the World)
The River of Kings
(A Guide)
Return to Adventure Southeast Asia
Take China
(The Last of the China Marines)

FOREWARD BY DENIS GRAY

The fires of youth may have burned down low. We may have reached mid-life or even beyond. But moments come when we still dream about it: an emerald green cove in the South Seas with our own yacht lilting at anchor; throbbing, libido-unleashed ports-of-call; a life free of niggling bosses and nagging children and nasty bill collectors. Yes, many people dream about it, but Harold Stephens does it.

Once upon a time, pre-1959 to be exact, Stephens was just another one of us tropical dreamers, a teacher of English in a Washington, D. C. private school with a wife, children, dogmatic principals and mortgage payments. But that year he cut loose. He headed first through Latin America and eventually found himself in that ultimate of escapist havens: Tahiti. He had $24 to his name.

Life since those days, Stephens recalls, could not have been better, richer in experience or denser with excitement. Stephens can't remember how it feels to wear a necktie, has not had to say "Yes, sir" to anyone when he really was thinking "No way, you son-of-a-bitch," and he has remained a sailor-trim, handsome, mustachioed bachelor who at 50 plus looks at least ten years younger.

How does he do it? Let's take a year in his life, say from July 4, 1981 to July 4, 1982. On the 4th, Stephens and his seven-man crew arrived in Tahiti after a 20-day passage from Honolulu. They spent three weeks and were given a Tahitian farewell by 65 island dancers who came aboard his 70-foot schooner, *The Third Sea,* for an all-night party. The schooner's 9,000-mile odyssey ended 215 days later under the skyscrapers of Singapore. En route Stephens and company made 21 anchor stops (Tongareva, Bora Bora, Rabaul and Zamboanga to name only a few), explored the still littered battle fields of World War II, dove on one wreck to bring up 2,000 silver coins, listened to tales of crusty, colorful South Pacific diehards, and even climbed a few volcanoes to keep in shape. North of New

Guinea a typhoon blew out their sails and nearly sent them to the bottom, and off Indonesia his schooner was riddled with bullets in a hair-raising, encounter with pirates.

No sooner had they anchored in Singapore and his sea legs steadied, Stephens was off by air through half a dozen Asian countries and the United States, looking into sumo wrestling in Japan, rodeo riding in Texas and the legacy of an old friend and Gauguin-type artist Theo Meier who was ill in Northern Thailand. (Chapter 5). The year ended with Stephens driving across the United States with his sprightly 82-year-old mother, a trip which ended on July 4th with an old-fashioned American Independence Day celebration in Bridgeville, Pennsylvania, his hometown of 5,000 which he had last seen a quarter century earlier and where the folks asked him, "Yes, that's all very interesting, Harold, but what do you do for a living?"

A fair question. How can Stephens, one may honestly ask, maintain his kind of life short of having a rich grandmother pass away or being on the payrolls of the CIA, KGB or the drug-smuggling Mafia? Stephens has neither rich relatives nor dubious paymasters. And he doesn't like to be called an adventurer, at least not in the cliched sense of the word. Stephens in fact is a very gifted, infinitely curious and highly disciplined writer with ten books and countless newspaper and magazine articles to his credit, and many more dancing in his brain. He has also managed—through a fertile imagination and the courage of acting on his dreams—to put his craft in the service of a lifestyle to which he has grown eminently accustomed—and vice versa.

Take his schooner for example. Writing magazine pieces, taking bit parts in Pacific-location movies ("The Mutiny on the Bounty" is one, although he didn't exactly star opposite Marlon Brando) and even signing up as a hand on island trading boats, Stephens managed to scrape up enough money to start building *The Third Sea*. He put it together in the early 1970s at the bargain basement price of $50,000 after taking a crash course in yacht-building and persuading 30-odd friends to help out in exchange for future free berths. The schooner, which sleeps a dozen, has since saved him heaps in rent money and, more importantly, has served as a vehicle to as well as the subject of many of his books and stories. And when Stephens ventures from the water (he's driven a jeep across the Soviet Union and a Toyota land cruiser around the world, made frequent treks through the Malaysian jungles and has ridden ponies into the Himalayas), there are plenty of editors and travel business types ready to hand him a free airline ticket to just about anywhere.

With his "modus operandi" cleverly plotted, Stephens can roam the world. But his true beat and his real home is Asia and the Pacific. Asia, says Stephens, is the last great challenge, the last adventure—and it still yields the Asian characters a la Joseph Conrad and Somerset Maugham—romantics and soldiers of fortune, rebel souls with mysterious pasts, artists in search of paradise, men and women who like Stephens have found in Asia a niche, a life, a fulfillment of some personal quest.

"You often get people claiming that these characters have disappeared," Stephens likes to say. "But they haven't."

"In other times things moved more slowly so these people stood out. On a six-week sea voyage you got to know everyone on board. Today, you may be sitting next to the most amazing character on a jet plane but barely have the chance to exchange a few words."

Stephens takes time to know people. His lifestyle, again, allows it. He'll miss an airflight because he gets too deeply immersed in someone's story. He'll spend a few extra days at anchor in some remote outpost to catch up on what's been happening to an old friend.

Some of these peopleas exciting and romantic as the landscape of Asia—appear in Asian Portraits. Many, like Stephens, are expatriates because the writer can best understand their problems and longings. Some have become close, personal friends. None are portrayed without genuine empathy.

Stephens was working on this edition of *Asian Portraits* the last time I saw him—a rover turned disciplined writer, anchored to a typewriter for several weeks in the home of a Bangkok friend. From his writing table Stephens could look out over a lush, tropical garden and a pond filled with graceful Victoria lotuses.

"Listen, Steve, for this introduction I think I should put in something about where you go from here," I told him.

For a few moment Stephens fell silent and pensive. "From time to time I think about settling down and getting married. But after a while a woman will ask me: 'How long are you going to do it, Steve? I mean, how long are you going to live like this?'"

He soon answered the question. He was off again in his mind's eye, talking as enthusiastically as a youngster packing for his first summer camp about the vast, little-known stretches of the Indonesian archipelago, helping his game warden friend save the rhinos of the Malaysian jungle from extinction, about taking *The Third Sea* up China's Yangtze River . . . .

I can see it now. Stephens and I are meeting again in some corner of Asia years from now. I have dreamed my last dream of cutting loose and he's a little stooped, with much grey in his hair and a lot less robustness in his stride.

But the *The Third Sea*—*or* its successor—is being readied for another voyage. Stephens, like the aging Ulysses of Tennyson's poem, means to drink life to the lees until he casts his last anchor in the Happy Isles.

Denis D. Gray
Associated Press Bureau Chief
Bangkok.

WHERE HAVE ALL THE CHARACTERS GONE?

"Those were the days! They don't make people like that anymore." How many times have we heard someone say this after reading a novel by Joseph Conrad or a story by Somerset Maugham? Such fascinating and exciting people, today's world concludes, no longer exist. Before I came to Asia, I too believed the world of Conrad and Maugham was dead.

As a boy raised on a farm in western Pennsylvania, I spent much of my childhood alone, and as a consequence, I did a lot of reading. Joseph Conrad was one of my favourite authors. I read and re-read him and longed for something that was beyond my reach, but not beyond my hopes. Conrad's novel *Lord Jim* fired my imagination with vivid and romantic pictures of a adventure. The youthful Lord Jim was everything I idolized in life. "He saw himself saving people from sinking ships," I read with wild abandonment. "Cutting away masts in a hurricane, swimming through a surf with a line, or as a lonely castaway, barefoot and half-naked, walking on uncovered reefs in search of shellfish to stave off starvation." And when Jim died in Conrad's final pages, all the great adventures in the world passed with him. Or that's what I was told and made to believe. It was wrong to think otherwise. After all, my seniors insisted, Conrad was a writer who wrote novels, and novels are fiction. "Don't be a dreamer," they said.

It was the same with Somerset Maugham. I began reading Maugham in my late teens, and through him I was introduced to a world of rubber planters in Malaya, district officers in Burma, renegade trading boat skippers in the Celebes. I came to know and envy these people, and I thought I understood them, but again I was told that although Maugham's characters were drawn from real life they were much colored by his romanticized ideals of what life in the Far East might be rather than the way it really was. His short stories made good reading but they were not to be taken seriously. After all, could anyone in America or England really understand the logic behind the eccentric Englishman who died of hiccups because a curse was put upon him by a Malay woman he spurned? In Asia, where such things do happen, it is not such an outlandish plot.

But no matter who the teller of tales was—Joseph Conrad, Somerset Maugham or their contemporaries—the characters they created led adventuresome and romantic lives that are envied by many to this day. But were these people only the product of fiction? If they were real, what has happened to them? Could it be that the basic nature of man has changed? Is this because the world no longer has time for dreamers and romantics, for soldiers of fortune and adventurers? In other words, has life today with the rigors of modern society reconditioned and reshaped man and turned him into another less interesting kind of being?

I like to think not. After spending much of my life roaming around Asia and the South Pacific, I like to think man's circumstances have changed, but not his traits. He is still a seeker, a dreamer, but in different guises. A hundred years ago Jim was an energetic ship's handler in Singapore or a mate on a rusted tramp steamer chugging across the Indian Ocean; today Jim might fly a helicopter looking for oil in Burma or skipper a supply boat for the oil rigs in Indonesia. Jim's friends today might be anthropologists searching for lost cities or medical researchers living for years in the jungle working on a cure for filariasis. Regardless of who they are, what they are doing is different; it's challenging and, without doubt, exciting.

Often we do not recognize exciting people when we meet them. In our fast moving world we hardly get to know our next door neighbor let alone a person sitting next to us on a jet liner. Maugham had weeks and sometimes months to study his shipboard passengers. It takes time to find someone out, to learn if they have truly lead interesting lives. It takes time to separate the braggarts from the real. Today we don't have the time, or I should say, we don't take the time to do this.

And more often than not, we make hasty judgments about people. I recall years ago I took a job with the U.S. Geodetic Survey in the Choco Jungles of South America. A Piper Cub bringing in supplies crashed and we were forced to wait in a jungle camp several weeks for another plane. My sole companion during the long wait was a grizzled, bearded old-timer. We had open-sided tents, cots for beds and mosquito nets. There was little to do except read; when we tired of reading we talked. Or I should say, the old-timer talked. In fact, he did all the talking, from the moment we got up in the morning to long after the lantern went out at night. At first I found him interesting, all his antics and tales. He had done so much in his wild and adventurous life. I envied him. The third day the conversation was getting a bit heavy. No man could have done everything he claimed. By the fourth day he was boring, dreadfully so. It was all pure exaggeration, or maybe something he read in the heap of paperbacks he carried around. He talked about such things as Admiral Bull Halsey sending him into Guadacanal before the Marines landed; his covering an assassination plot in South America and saving the life of Vice President Nixon when he visited there; and his advising a young writer in the Pacific after the War to call his book *Tales of the South Pacific*. The writer was James Michener. I was overjoyed when the plane finally came and ended our jungle sojourn.

Several months later I was attending a reception in Panama where I met the American Consul. "You were in Colombia," he said. "Did you run across Bob Spensor by any chance?"

"Did I!" I exclaimed, and was about to tell him what I thought about old Bob, when he spoke up.

"Quite a character," he said. "You know, Admiral Halsey based an invasion on his decision and Nixon had him up for the Medal of Valor or something, and Bob refused it." Was I hearing correctly? Could he be talking about someone else? No, it was the same man. I missed a great chance and regretted it. Not only did I not believe Bob Spensor at the time, but after a while I had stopped paying attention to him. If only I could have seen him again. But I never had a second chance.

Through my wanderings in Asia and the South Pacific I've become acquainted with many such characters, characters who would have delighted Conrad had he met them. I find that nearly every expatriate who spends part of his life in Asia has something in common with his fellow countrymen living abroad. They both possess a curious trait the average person at home does not have. We might even call it madness, the madness Zorba the Greek said a man must have before he can be free.

After I began traveling to these far reaches of the world, in search of my own adventure, I found that many of the characters which Conrad and Maugham wrote about were, in essence, very much alive. Only their names differed. Whoever would think that the world has time for a South Sea Island trader today?

But the world does, most assuredly. I met one such trading boat skipper in Indonesia. He is a Dutchman. I saw him on several occasions around the Celebes while I was cruising there aboard my own schooner. He was not a talker and mostly what I did learn about him was information volunteered from his crew, after a night's bash in the seedy bars in Amboina and Kupang, and from others who happened to cross tracks with him in the course of their travels. He did not for certain make friends everywhere he went.

The only name we knew him by was Werner. He had to be pushing 45 but he was perhaps older, considering he was knocking around the islands during World War II. The story goes that he went to sea when he was seven or eight. His parents were planters on Java and were killed in a native uprising sometime in the 30's. Verner would have been murdered along with the rest of his family had it not been for an island trader who was loading cargo when he heard the gun shots. He rushed in to save the boy and dragged him back to his schooner *Ansar Puteh.*

When the smoke settled the plantation was burned to the ground. The boy had no place to go. Feeling sorry for him, the old man took him on as cabin boy. But young Verner was more like a son to him than a work hand. The old sea dog taught him everything and when he died from a stroke and too much boozing just before the War broke out, Verner inherited the schooner. He was only 16 or 17 then. In spite of his youthful age, he was able to play a successful game of hide and seek with the Japanese patrol boats. They never caught him. Some say he was a traitor, that he sold out to the Japanese, but I rather think not. The *Ansar Puteh* is still a sound and trim vessel after 60 or more years of service, and you can see her and her mysterious captain in the far and distant ports of Indonesia.

Another Dutchman I came to know rather well was Ben Raat. Born and raised on a tea plantation in Eastern Java, Ben was separated from his father, mother and younger brother when the war broke out, and he never saw or heard of them again. The Japanese sent him to an internment camp when he was only thirteen. They were lenient with him, until they discovered he was carrying messages for prisoners between camps. He was sentenced to be executed but at the last moment his life was spared, for the Japanese commander had another fate in store for him. Along with women and other children, he was herded aboard a Red Cross ship bound for Singapore. They were restricted to an area above deck in full view, exposed to the tropical rains and sun, while below deck a Japanese division was quartered. According to the Geneva Convention and the Articles of War, Red Cross and hospital ships were forbidden to carry troops.

Once in Singapore Ben was sent to the notorious Changi prison where he spent his next three years growing up. At the end of the war he migrated to New Zealand, earned a degree in engineering and is today a senior business executive in Singapore. Only recently, after more than 40 years, Ben made a visit to his family plantation. It was one of the most touching stories I ever heard, especially about an old Japanese overseer who thought Ben was his father returning from the war.

The Allied Prisoners of War in Changi Prison built a chapel when they were confined there. It was quite an accomplishment, considering what little they had to work with. A while back the Singapore Government opened the doors of the prison to ex-POWs who wanted to visit the chapel. When I heard this I requested permission to see the chapel and asked Ben if he would care to join me. His eyes narrowed and a strange distant look came to his nominally smiling face. "Changi Prison," he moaned. "You must be kidding. Not only do I not want to go near that place, I don't even want to hear about it." I visited the chapel alone.

Getting to know some of these fascinating people, of course, is not always easy. Often by their very nature, they tend to shun public attention. They are looking for neither fame nor fortune. Their reason for doing what they do is infinitely more complex. I met one such character in Singapore, an incredible yachtsman named Ed Boden. Ed was sailing alone around the world in a 25-foot boat. He was not insane nor was he a daredevil. He had, in fact, a degree in aeronautical engineering and left a high paying position with the U.S. Space Program to see the world in his tiny boat. After ten years of sailing he saw nothing unusual in it. It had become his way of life and a much appreciated one. "And I'm not doing it to write a book," he insisted. The last thing he wanted was publicity.

There is another individual I know who is very much like Ed. He does what he likes for the pleasure of it and nothing more. He's an American, Terry Sherwin from Chicago, and he lives in Japan. He speaks the language fluently and has studied Japanese culture and philosophy. He is mild mannered, quiet, almost shy. He is also a Yabusame, a mounted Samurai warrior. I first heard his name mentioned when I was visiting friends in Tokyo. A little later, I read in the paper there was a Yabusame tournament the next day in Kamakura in the south.

The sport, the news item said, dates back 800 years and in all its history no foreigner had ever participated. Now a young American had joined their ranks and was riding with them. The article gave his name: Terry Sherwin. I was on the next train to Kamakura.

What excitement! Before the tournament I walked the half-mile-long course the mounted Yabusame were to ride. From a charging horse they had to shoot at three targets, small round wooden discs a foot in diameter. Their weapons were long bows and arrows. It seemed an impossible task.

Just as the tournament was to begin, I found a position at the center target and waited. An announcement was made in Japanese and then in English. There would be a dozen riders, with the American archer, Terry Sherwin, riding last. Immediately following the announcement the mounted Samurai archers paraded by in front of the judges. It might have been the setting for a Japanese movie.

Here was the world of the gallant Samurai. They had the stance and the poise of knights in armor and they rode with the certain arrogance and pride of manner that only the proud Japanese have and respect.

Finally the tournament was ready to begin, with everyone stretching far out over the rope barrier to catch a first glimpse. Suddenly a distant gong sounded and a Samurai came thundering down the course. It was a moment of awe. He seemed to appear out of infinity, at full gallop, legs wide apart, bow drawn. The horse's nostrils were wide. The Samurai's face was drawn into an expression of fury. In that instant one experienced the full terror of how an opponent must have felt centuries ago when a mounted Samurai came charging down upon him.

One by one the Samurai made their charges, with all the beauty and form that can come only from long practice and generations of tradition. There was something almost magical in the way they moved, in the way the archer 'flowed.' Oftentimes it mattered not if he missed his target for the crowd

17

was enthralled more by his grace of movement than by his actually hitting the disc.

It was now Terry Sherwin's turn. The crowd grew silent and tense. The gong sounded and we knew he was off. Shortly after came the sound of shattering wood. He made good at his first target. At that moment I saw him, his arrow notched and ready for the second target, and he was bearing down rapidly on it. The arrow flew and the sound of the splintering wood was almost lost to the cheers of the excited crowds.

Now the spectators pushed beyond the rope barrier as he passed making it impossible to follow him down the course. Nor could I hear if he struck his final target, but there was no mistaking his victory. By the chorus of cheers and the wild ovation, we knew the American Samurai from Chicago had shattered all three targets.

It took me better than an hour to push through the crowds to locate the stables, which, I was surprised to find, were relatively quiet. Riders were putting away their equipment. I found Terry grooming his horse, almost pensive. "A fine horse," I said after introducing myself. He did not bother to look up.

"It's not mine," he answered. "They are on loan for these tournaments."

I complimented him on his fine shooting and asked how he placed. No sooner had the words come out than I knew I had said the wrong thing.

"Please don't ask how I placed," he said. "Yabusame is not a sporting competition as such. It is more of a tradition, a ritual." It was my first meeting with Terry, and others followed. We had some fine meals together in Tokyo, and his experiences in the world of Japanese culture never ceased to fascinate me. He is still at it, living in his house with paper sliding doors and doing his thing. He never talks about being a modem-day Samurai, but he is.

And there are more. Rubber planter, soldier-of-fortune, treasure diver, jungle doctor, sailing boat skippers, belly-dancer, hotel entrepreneur, artist, sumo wrestler. In the pages that follow you will meet these people, as I have, all old Asia hands, all with something interesting to tell.

I once read in a biography of Joseph Conrad that not long after he left Asia for the last time he had to give up the sea he loved so much for reasons of health. He had developed crippling arthritis. It was then he took up the pen and began writing. When his books appeared in print and were read around the world, some people in Singapore recognized themselves. A bar keeper at Tiffany's tea room remarked, "Why, who would believe it? I didn't even think he knew." But Conrad did know, and through his writing the people he met and wrote about have been kept alive down through the years. They may be no different, however, from the person you sat next to on the jet that brought you, or the person you bumped into on the terrace at the Oriental Hotel in Bangkok. Lord Jim is still alive, well and living in Asia.

Thomson deemed alive

Moonlight Cottage - the Cameron Highlands vacation spot of Mr Thomson - was the place where he was last seen alive.

JIM THOMSON, the silk magnate who vanished in the Malaysian jungles two years ago, is still regarded as alive by the Thai Silk Company and is still drawing a salary.

The Manager of the company Mr Charles Sheffield, today said that Mr Thomson would be officially regarded as dead in another five years. Until that time. he would still be regarded as alive.

Thai silk king disappeared two years ago today

TWO YEARS ago today Mr Jim Thomson, the man who made Thai silk the popular luxury, disappeared in the jungles of the Malaysian "

Indian and ...

Thompson reward now 500,000 baht

by Post reporters

... search for Bangkok silk king Jim

US general joins Thompson search

KUALA LUMPUR, Friday—Two mediums and an US general today joined in the bizarre hunt for Delaware-born millionaire Jim Thompson, missing, feared dead, in the Malaysian Cameron Highlands hill resort for the past six days.

Brigadier-General Edwin Black, Commander of United States Support Forces in Northeast Thailand, told reporters by telephone that he had come to the Cameron Highland as a friend and old time schoolmate of Thompson and not as a US government representative.

Black was accompanied by his 'de-de-camp' and an American, rasche, business associate of the Thai silk Company, empowered by the company to pay a 5,000 US dollar about 100,000 baht) reward for information on Thompson's whereabouts.

The reward today attracted a Ialay medium from the plains amed only as "Dato of the Datos" Dato is a Malay honorific title).

second medium to join in the hunt for Thompson, who went out for a walk from a holiday bungalow on Sunday and has not been seen since.

The local Cameron Highlands medium, 39-year-old Chinese house painter Thong Weng, has already gone into three trances to check Thompson's whereabouts and come up with the conclusion that he is lying in a hole at the base of a large tree, unseen by nearby searches and possessed by evil spirits.

Thompson: Interpol called in

Jim Thompson's sister beaten to death in US

MRS KATHERINE THOMPSON WOOD, 74, prominent in Delaware and Philadelphia society, was beaten to death Wednesday in her secluded home in Centerville, Delaware, news services reported here yesterday.

Authorities here were wait on the violent death of the elder millionaire Jim Thompson befor terious events surrounding the

Two giant watchdogs, the reports said, were present

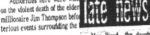

late news

Mrs Wood, the daughter of Delaware socialites Mr and Mrs Henry B Thompson was

Jim Thompson reward extended

KUALA LUMPUR, Tuesday – The 28,000 US dollar reward for finding missing American millionaire James Thompson, better known as the "Thai silk king," has been extended, police announced today.

A police spokesman in Ipoh, 100 miles north of here, said the police reward of 3,-

in 300 US dollars was being extended for three months while the 25,000 US dollar reward by the Thai Silk Company of Bangkok was being extended "indefinitely."

...

Jim Thompson
The strange disappearance of the Thai Silk King

In Bangkok today, among friends, acquaintances, people who meet for the first time, new arrivals, tourists—wherever they are, at cocktail parties, embassy receptions, Patpong Road, hotel lobbies, restaurants, elevator lifts or in taxis and planes—any place where two or more people gather you sooner or later hear the question, "What do you think happened to Jim Thompson?"

Jim Thompson is by far the best-known postwar legend in Asia. Whenever his name is mentioned it is liable to be prefixed with "the millionaire American" or else "the Thai silk king." When someone wants to act knowledgeable and mysterious they might say, "Thompson, the ex-OSS agent." But to his friends, to those who knew him best, he was something else. He was a warm and sensitive person; he was a master architect and designer; and he was one of Southeast Asia's foremost art collectors. To these people Jim Thompson was a charming host who lived in grand style. And he was always a friend.

Indeed, Jim Thompson was successful, rich, world renown, and to all outward appearances, contented with life.

Then on Easter Sunday in 1967, at the height of his career and when visiting friends at their mountain retreat in central Malaysia, he disappeared. He vanished completely without leaving a trace, not one single bit of evidence behind. His disappearance led to the largest and most thorough search and investigation ever conducted for an individual in this part of the world.

Immediately rewards amounting to more than US$30,000 were offered for information which would establish his whereabouts, either dead or alive. The rewards produced only disappointment and charlatanism. Cranks, soothsayers, witch doctors, clairvoyants and crystal-gazers of half-a-dozen nationalities came forth to claim the reward. One of them, a well-known Western seer, attracted serious attention for many weeks because of his detailed vision of the missing man's whereabouts. He meticulously described a house surrounded by palm trees in Stung Treng, Cambodia, where he 'saw' Mr. Thompson being held prisoner by agents of a hostile power. Others reported seeing Thompson in Singapore, Tahiti, Canton, on a ship bound for Indonesia, and in a gambling casino in Macao where he was employed as a croupier. To further add to the mystery, six months after his disappearance his older sister, Mrs. Katherine Thompson Wood, was found bludgeoned to death in her lonely house in Pennsylvania. Her desk had been rifled and papers strewn on the floor; her valuables and money untouched. Had it anything to do with Thompson's will which had failed to turn up after his disappearance?

Rumors, exaggerations, opinions, they continue to multiply with each passing year. And until there is definite proof to establish Jim Thompson's death, there will always be the lingering hope that one day he will return from the shadows. There are some, although I must admit, fewer each year, who believe that he is still alive. One person who does so is his faithful houseboy, Yee. Yee continues to manage the house, and he patiently awaits the master's return. The reason that Jim Thompson is alive, he firmly believes, is that he has not returned to haunt the house. He cannot be dead then.

I met Jim Thompson briefly in 1965, two years before his disappearance. I was invited to lunch at Mizu's on Patpong Road by the editor of the *Bangkok World*, Bob Udick, and Roy Howard, the Advertising Director of Thai Airways International, to discuss a writing contract they had prepared for me. Thompson was at the next table, and as he was leaving he stopped at our table and chatted for a minute or two. I knew nothing about him other than what Bob and Roy mentioned after he had gone, that he was a business man and had something to do with the Thai silk industry. I do remember him mentioning his Thai house, and that we should come by for a visit. He was extremely polite and gentle mannered.

There appeared to be nothing about his character that made him stand out from the others at Mizu's.

After his disappearance I tried to read everything into the brief luncheon, his character, his personality, but, of course, it was pointless. In the years that followed I did, however, come to know many people who were close to him. Through Joanna Cross I met her mother, Connie Mangskau, Bangkok's legendary hostess and a long-time friend of Thompson, and one of the three people who was with him on that fateful Easter Sunday. I spent many wonderful days at Connie's beautiful Thai house, one that Jim Thompson had built for her, rehashing the details of the disappearance. I came to know Barrie Cross, Joanna's husband, very well. Barrie was the first person Connie phoned in Bangkok when Thompson disappeared. It was Barrie who immediately alerted Brigadier General Edwin Black. General Black was in charge of all US forces in Thailand, and it was he who had been instrumental in having Thompson transferred into the OSS, forerunner to the CIA, during the early days of World War II.

I had the opportunity of co-authoring a book on Malaysia with writer Star Black, daughter of General Black. I worked with the general's wife, Coby Black, who was a columnist on the *Bangkok World*. Through Star and her mother, I got to know General Black, and in time we became friends. I later visited the Blacks at their home in Hawaii. There was Prince Ajavadis Diskul who, one afternoon at lunch at his private residence, explained his version of the "missing" will. I worked with Denis Horgan who became editor of the *Bangkok World* a few years after the disappearance. In 1967 Horgan was a lieutenant in the U.S. Army, and an aide to General Black. When Thompson failed to return, Black and Horgan immediately went to Malaysia, where Horgan personally investigated one of the soothsayers involved in the case. Horgan later had some amusing stories to tell about the incident.

Not long after I had that meeting with Bob Udick and Roy

Howard at Mizu's, I began writing a weekly travel column for the *Bangkok World*. When Jim Thompson mysteriously disappeared, and all Bangkok was alive with rumors, I convinced the editor that a travel piece on the Malaysian highlands where Thompson disappeared might be appropriate. He agreed. I went to Penang and followed the same route that he and Connie Mangskau took to reach the hill station.

Cameron Highlands was a circus when I arrived, with half a hundred people trying to out smart one another. Nevertheless, I did see the cottage where Thompson was staying. I walked the grounds around the cottage, and hiked the jungle trail that led to the cottage. I talked to investigators, including jungle experts. None of it made any sense, not then.

In the years that followed I kept adding to my files on Jim Thompson. I came to know scores of people who were close to him, but more important than all of this to me was the feeling and mood I captured by living in the Jim Thompson compound at Soi Kasemsan. The compound had several private residences for rent, all in the Thai style of Thompson's house. General Black and his family had one residence, and my friend, Robin Dannhorn, had another. Whenever I went to Bangkok for a visit, Robin invited me to stay. Many evenings we sat with dinner guests on the verandah overlooking the klong, and we could hear Thompson's white cockatoo calling in the night, and conversation would stop. "Do you think he will return?" someone would whisper, and soon opinions were voiced and an eerie, somber feeling would settle over the gathering, until Robin changed the subject. But when the guests had left and I had retired to my bedroom, lying there under the mosquito netting, I almost expected to hear footsteps on the gravel path outside. And eventually, that wonderful first feeling of staying in the Jim Thompson compound turned from satisfaction to uneasiness.

It has been more than ten years since Jim Thompson has disappeared.* Over the years rumors and speculation about his strange disappearance have continued to increase. They

*This was written in 1978

only seem to add to the confusion of Jim Thompson.

Who was this man, Jim Thompson?

Jim Thompson was born in Delaware, USA, in 1906. He came from a wealthy and well-established family. There was nothing unusual about his childhood. He was a better-than-average student, was interested in sports and never missed a Saturday-night party. His favourite uncle was a general in the Union Army during the American Civil War, and was later sent by the president to China to survey

Thompson family in 1906

the building of a railway across the country. Thompson was sixteen when the general died, but he must have been influenced by the Asian tales the old gentleman had to tell. Thompson entered Princeton University and graduated in 1926. With his family and friends he travelled widely throughout Europe. It was from these trips to the continent,

University Student

when he was in his '20s, that his interest in lively colors and costumes began to take shape. On one trip to Europe he saw the famous Diaghilev Ballet which was then in its prime. He was deeply impressed by the scenic effects rather than by the dance itself. He was amazed at the brilliant costumes and designs. He returned to America and furthered his studies in architecture and design at the University of Pennsylvania. He began practicing professionally in New York, but when World War II broke out in 1941 he closed his office and enlisted in the army.

Thompson entered as a private but was later commissioned, and soon after he met Captain Edwin Black, he transferred to the Office of Strategic Services. Their friendship was to continue until Thompson disappeared in 1967.

Captain Black's influence upon the 36-year-old lieutenant was profound. First, he convinced Thompson to transfer to the OSS, and second he introduced him to a talented and attractive ex-Powers model. After a whirlwind court-ship, the couple were married a few months later. They had but a half a year together, for Thompson was transferred to North Africa with the French Forces.

Thompson in the US Army

Thompson served in North Africa, France and Italy, and following Germany's defeat, he trained as an OSS agent on Catalina Island off the California coast. His next assignment was in Ceylon where he formed a special unit whose mission was to parachute into the northern Thai jungles and join forces with the Free Thai undercover there. The Free Thais were opposed to the pro-Japanese government in Bangkok. Two days before the operation was scheduled to start, Japan surrendered. Colonel Thompson arrived in Bangkok as U. S. Embassy military adviser.

Thompson's visions of the Orient, as first seen through the eyes of his uncle, passed from the quixotic to the real, and he liked what he found. He fell in love with everything Thai, the culture, the architecture, the art, the customs, the easy way of life, the people. He travelled widely up country to the borders of Laos and Burma. Sometimes, he was away from Bangkok for weeks. He made many friends, some of whom were in influential positions.

Although he was still in the service and attached to the Embassy, Colonel Thompson began to make plans to return to Thailand after his discharge. He looked for any opportunity that might bring him back and seized upon the idea of getting into the hotel business.

Bangkok in 1946 had few accommodations for foreign travelers. There were only one or two decent hotels, and apartment houses and flats were unknown. Thompson was living with other staff officers in the Oriental Hotel, an old converted royal palace on the Chao Phraya River. The Japanese High Command had used it as their headquarters during the war and it was in much need of repair. The Oriental was owned by the government, but in 1946 it was offered for sale to private investors. Thompson jumped at the opportunity.

He was most intrigued with the scheme for it would give him the opportunity to use his talents as architect and designer. He entered into partnership with five others to purchase the hotel, each putting up $250 to form a new company. One of the partners was Germaine Krull, a French journalist for a Paris magazine, who was to become the hotel's famed manager. She later wrote an enlightening book about her experiences at the Oriental.

Since he was still in the army, Thompson could not take an active part in the partnership. He returned to the U.S. for his discharge and to convince his wife to return with him to Thailand. Mrs. Thompson had no intention of returning with her husband to a distant land, nor did she intend to remain married to him for long. The wartime separation had had its effect. She greeted him with a divorce suit. It was a harsh and unexpected blow. If there were any remaining doubts about returning to Thailand, they were now dispelled. He had nothing to keep him in America. He returned to Thailand with renewed determination to begin a new life.

Jim Thompson was now past 40, and it was not usual for a man of his age to change so completely his lifestyle and profession. Furthermore, he was relocating to a distant and little-known country, far removed from the business world he knew in New York. But his mind was made up. There was no turning back.

One author who wrote about Jim Thompson compared him to the characters made famous by Somerset Maugham. "For some deeply private and often inexplicable reason," Maugham wrote, "he suddenly deserts his ordinary, secure world and starts a new life in totally alien surroundings." Maugham found such characters as Jim Thompson "mysterious and romantic, and perhaps enviable," and in story after story he sought explanation for their strange behavior. It's interesting to note that Maugham did visit Jim Thompson at his house on the klong when the author was visiting Bangkok.

On his return to Bangkok, Thompson moved back into the Oriental but his dreams and expectations of making his mark in the hotel business were short-lived. He had a disagreement with Madame Krull and resigned from the partnership. There are differing versions of the story. In her book, Madame Krull wrote that she and Thompson did not agree on the architectural design which he drew up for a new wing. He resigned from the partnership,but he continued to live at the Oriental for another year.

Left, Jim Thompson sitingin a sampan while inspecting raw silk hanging on racks to dry along a klong. Right, Thompson checking a weaver's piece of new silk for quality. He provided the dyes and specifications.

Thompson's attention now turned to Thai silk. Since he had first come to Bangkok, even long before he had considered the hotel business, he had become fascinated by the odd bits of locally-made silk he had seen up country in his travels. Textiles were not new to him. It had been the family business and it was only natural that when he traveled around Thailand he became deeply intrigued by Thai silk and the methods by which the weavers produced the cloth. Jorge Orgibet who had been with Thompson in the OSS and traveled with him in northern Thailand, recalled that Thompson was very much interested in the dust-covered looms they saw in villages. He was sad to learn that weaving had all but stopped. It was an ancient industry in Thailand but one which had almost died due to competition from cheap fabrics imported from Europe and Japan.

After the war there were a mere handful of silk weavers left in Thailand. These few worked at home, barely making a living. Weaving for them was more a side line than a money-making profession. Thompson sought them out, invested $100 and brought up a suitcase full of colorful samples. In 1947 he took the suitcase with him to New York.

In New York, Thompson was introduced to Mrs. Edna Chase, the authority on American high fashion and editor of Vogue. When Mrs. Chase saw the samples she was so impressed she called in her staff. They had seen nothing like them before. She persuaded Thompson to leave the suitcase with her for a few weeks. The glowing colors and quality of silk greatly impressed designers and decorators alike. Mrs. Chase persuaded a top New York designer to make a Thai silk dress which was photographed and appeared in Vogue, giving credit to Jim Thompson's silk of Thailand.

The success of Thai silk was immediate. Thompson was promised big orders if he could produce. He flew back to Bangkok and formed the Thai Silk Company. After he sold shares he had a working capital of little more than $10,000.

"He was so excited," said Mrs. Ankana Kalantananda of

the Oriental Hotel. She recalls Thompson's enthusiasm when he returned. "He brought me a beautiful Italian silk scarf and he said, 'Ankana, I'm going to make Thai silk even more famous than Italian silk.'" Jim Thompson kept his word.

Thompson had lived in Thailand long enough to know he could not get the Thais to work under pressure. What he did was search out the weavers in their homes and give them the raw silk and dyes. The colors he introduced were high quality, non-fading Swiss dyes that eventually replaced the vegetable ones. He gave the weavers specific measurements which they had to follow before he could market the cloth successfully. He insisted on quality and encouraged many old weavers to begin again their trade, which they had abandoned because they could not sell small lengths of various shapes and sizes.

"The weavers thought I was crazy," Thompson said. "They said no one would wear silk in the country. Ladies of fashion in those days wore rayon and nylon. I explained the silk was not for the ladies of Thailand but for the ladies of America and Europe.

In a few months Thompson had 200 weavers working for him. It is interesting to note that by 1967, the year he disappeared, there were more than 20,000 weavers in Thailand. The part-time plumber who wove the first few lengths of cloth which Thompson took with him to New York had, 20 years later, 400 looms in operation and employed 500 weavers.

The real impetus to the success of Thai silk came in 1951 when New York designer Irene Shareff used Jim Thompson's Thai silk for the entire wardrobe for the famous Rodgers and Hammerstein musical "The King and I." What had been a vanishing craft in Thailand suddenly became big business. In a few short years silk was one of Thailand's major exports. It was being used for dresses, shirts, drapery, even upholstery, and was sold by leading stores around the world. Thompson, on his way to becoming a millionaire, established two big mulberry plantations in northern Thailand to feed the silkworms, and he gave many Thais a share in his business.

The silk industry became so profitable that by 1960 the Thai Silk Company had 140 competitors. The Thai Silk Company alone had over 2,000 weavers on contract working for it.

Jim Thompson's background with the OSS and his position made him a slightly mysterious person. Rumors were that his business was merely a cover up and that his main interests were still intelligence work. His closest friends, who knew him intimately, disregarded the rumors, and Thompson ignored them himself.

Thailand was Jim Thompson's spiritual home and he was happiest living there. He had two interests that occupied him full time: his work in the silk business and his art collection. The two are paradox to the Jim Thompson story. He came to a little-known country, never learned the language, and yet built up a lucrative and competitive business that brought him riches and fame. Then he became an authority on Asian art which was totally unfamiliar to him before he came East. His interests in art, as his interests in silk weaving, were not planned.

Thompson liked to explore the villages in northern Thailand, and on such trips he began to take a collector's interest in Thai art, mostly old temple paintings on silk, wood carvings and Buddhist sculpture. When his collection grew he no longer had room to house it all, so he built himself a house which is one of Bangkok's most famous private residences.

The house on the klong

Jim Thompson's museum-like home soon became the show piece of the Thai capital. What he did was buy six old Thai houses and reassemble them on property he purchased along a small klong in the heart of the city. He used traditional Siamese architectural forms which had not been used for years. The houses were constructed of carved teak. The changes he incorporated into these 19th century buildings were interior corridors, a staircase and modern bathrooms, but he retained the high ceilings for the free flow of air. He had open but screened porches, spreading verandahs with flowers and Chinese porcelains and lush green gardens. In the gardens were henna trees, hibiscus and gardenias. Brilliant lorikettes and white cockatoos gave magnificent color to the place.

Not all the art collection was Thai. There were Burmese lacquerware, Cambodian bronzes, Ming pottery, Belgian glass and Victorian crystal chandeliers, set off against warm teak walls and red painted ceilings.

Thompson lived alone in his grand house on the klong, but he rarely dined alone. His nightly dinner parties became the talk of the town. Ambassadors, heads of state, actors and actresses, playwrights and novelists—they all came to his house on the klong when an invitation was extended. Such personalities as Lyndon Johnson, Prince Michael of Greece, Tennessee Williams, Barbara Hutton, Anne Baxter, Ethel Merman and Somerset Maugham whom I have already mentioned. With the flickering glow of candle lights on the tables and torches burning in the gardens, guests dined in the open on the lower terrace. The mood was always gay, and reached a high point when the soft sounds of a native orchestra filled the night and from out of the shadows nymph-like classical Thai dancers appeared. In their elaborately jewelled costumes and gold-flaked head-dress they danced for their spell-bound guests. It was more illusionary than real, and often when guests left they wondered if it happened at all. A night at Jim Thompson's was never to be forgotten.

It was after one such dinner party that Somerset Maugham sent a thank-you note to Thompson. "You not only have beautiful things," he wrote, "but what is rare, you have arranged them with faultless taste." Maugham was on a sentimental tour of the Far East at the time. He was then 86 and had he been younger, I'm sure, Jim Thompson would have been the subject of one of his stories.

Thompson's intention was to leave the house and its art collection to the Siam Society. However, two years before he disappeared he had a disagreement with the members of the Society over the rightful ownership of several pieces in his collection, and rumor had it that he had changed his will, leaving the Soi Kasemsan property to his nephew.

By the middle of the 1960's the Thai Silk Company had outgrown its original quarters. Thompson drew up plans for a new building which was completed in March 1967. He was overworked and tired. He was also suffering from gallstones and had agreed to have an operation later in the year. He carried pills to kill the pain whenever the need arose. He felt the need for a real rest. And the opportunity came when his good friends, Dr. and Mrs. Ling, invited him and Connie Mangskau for an Easter holiday to their mountain retreat at Cameron Highlands in central Malaysia. Dr. and Mrs. Ling were old friends of both Thompson and Connie Mangskau.

Mrs. Mangskau is English and Thai by birth and had married a Norwegian rubber planter who had died suddenly leaving Connie with their three children. Thompson had met her in 1945 when she worked as an interpreter for the Allied Services in Bangkok. They had become good friends. He had helped her open her first antique shop in the Hotel Trocadero, and later

Connie and Jaqueline Kennedy

drew up plans for her exquisite Thai home which was patterned after his own. Thompson was very proud of the house and often said everything he did wrong on his own house he corrected on her house.

Dr. Ling, a Chinese business man from Singapore, and his American wife, Helen, had invited both Jim Thompson and Connie Mangskau to their Cameron Highlands home at Easter three years before. Thompson liked the British hill station and was fond of the Lings and they had common interests. Helen Ling was an art collector and had an antique shop in Singapore. When the Lings extended invitation for Easter 1967, Thompson changed his plans and accepted.

It is interesting to note the entries in Connie's diary: *Tuesday, March 21, 1967. Celebrated Jim's 61st birthday. Wednesday, March 22nd. Scheduled Qantas 752, 4:50 PM to Singapore but changed flight as Jim decided to go along.*

Since Thompson had a lot of last-minute details to organize due to the moving of his office, he asked Connie to make the travel arrangements. Her diary reads: *Leave for Penang, ML 521, at 12:30 PM.* When they met at the airport Thursday afternoon, Thompson had neglected to get his cholera shot and had forgotten to validate the required certificate showing that his income taxes had been paid. Connie knew the airport officials and smoothed over the difficulties.

The incident was minor, but it underlines the fact that Thompson had not made previous arrangements to leave Thailand, nor did he intend to remain away for any length of time. He only had approximately $100 in cash with him when he left.

Jim Thompson and Connie Mangskau took off as scheduled and flew direct to Penang. The events that then took place have been the subject of endless debate. Connie was very helpful in letting me piece the story together by letting me read her diary that she kept on the trip. Parts of it were kept in shorthand which had to be translated.

Connie had been to Penang many times, but it was Thompson's first visit and he was anxious to see the island. They hired a car and were driving around the island when Thompson suddenly decided he wanted to return to town to get a haircut. Connie was mildly annoyed but agreed and dropped him off at a barber shop while she returned to the Ambassador Hotel where they had booked two rooms. When Thompson returned he commented that he would rather have stayed at the E&O Hotel, since it was an old colonial establishment, much like the Oriental in Bangkok. Had he for some reason gone to the E&O Hotel?

The next morning they hired a private taxi to make the day-long journey to "Moonlight Cottage," as the Lings called their Cameron Highlands home. The taxi picked them up at the hotel but parked at a taxi stand down-town and kept them waiting ten minutes while the driver went into the office. A different driver came out and took over the wheel. When

Thompson inspecting new silk

they reached the halfway mark at Tapah, the driver pulled into a taxi station and announced that they would have to change cars, as he was having engine trouble. He led them to another taxi in which two Chinese men were sitting and waiting. Connie was irate. She said they had paid for a private car and didn't see why they had to share with anyone. After a few words the driver agreed, the two Chinese got out and Connie and Thompson continued their journey. Had Connie foiled a kidnap attempt? They arrived at the cottage only minutes after Dr. Ling. When Mrs. Ling arrived later in the evening, they had a quiet dinner at home. Connie's entry in her diary read: *March 24th. Good Friday. Arrived in Cameron Highlands.*

The next morning Dr. Ling announced that he had found a new trail that led to the golf club where they were to have lunch and asked Thompson if he would like to join him on the hike. Thompson was fond of long walks, especially into the jungles. He had made several jungles treks three years before when he was there, and he cheerfully accepted Dr. Ling's invitation. The women would drive ahead and wait for them at the club.

When the men failed to return at noon the women became upset, and Mrs. Ling considered informing the police. But finally at 1:00 the two men strolled into the club, a bit tired and worn. It seems they had become lost in the underbrush. Dr. Ling had pulled a ligament in his leg and was a bit shaken up but Thompson was in great spirits. It gave him the chance to practice his jungle training. They had found their way by finding a small stream which they followed until they came to more familiar ground. Thompson had obviously enjoyed the adventure.

The next morning was Easter Sunday. It was the Lings' custom to attend mass in a small church in the village. Both Mangskau and Thompson accompanied them, but Thompson announced that he felt like a walk and set out before them down the road. There was nothing unusual about his decision to walk ahead, but it did bring out two interesting points during the investigation. Firstly, it was one of the few times he was alone, and it is possible he could have kept a secret rendezvous with someone. Secondly, if there had been a kidnap attempt this certainly would have been the time to strike. Whether or not he met with someone is questionable, but there was no attempted kidnapping. Thompson arrived safely at the church.

After they resumed from the service, Thompson wanted to remain at the cottage, but Mrs. Ling had packed a picnic lunch and insisted that he join them. They drove to a broad plateau on a military reservation three-quarters-of-an-hour from Moonlight Cottage. Thompson, everyone recalled, seemed uneasy. He wasn't relaxed and was anxious to return to the cottage. Joanna Cross, Connie's daughter, thought it could be because he had an appointment at the US Embassy in Singapore the next evening, Monday, and hadn't mentioned it to anyone. This wasn't brought out until much later. Anyway, whatever the motive, he began putting things away before everyone was ready. They returned to the cottage at 2:30 PM.

Connie suggested they rest before dinner, to which everyone agreed, except Thompson. The last time anyone there saw him he was sitting in the living room. A few minutes later, when Dr. and Mrs. Ling were in their bedroom on the ground floor, they heard the scraping of an aluminum deck chair as it was dragged across the verandah. They assumed that Thompson intended to rest in the sun, but minutes later they heard footsteps on the gravel path beneath their window. Perhaps Thompson had decided to take another of his afternoon strolls. Had they looked out the window they may have had another story to tell the investigators, but of that they didn't.

At 5:00 PM Thompson had not returned. It was their first cause for concern. They checked his bedroom and saw that he had not used the bed, but more importantly, he had left his cigarettes and pain killer pills for gallstones behind. Thompson was a chain smoker, and he would not willingly have gone far without his cigarettes or medicine.

When Thompson failed to return at sunset, Dr. Ling called the police and was asked to make a report, which he did. A dispatch was released and the Highlands were alerted to look for the missing man. If he had not returned by dawn a full-scale search would be launched.

But Dr. Ling did not wait until morning. He phoned a friend who had a tracking dog and asked for help. The friend arrived with a British Army colonel who was on leave, and the two men with the dog set out on a trail which led to the 'Beehives.' Three years previously Thompson had taken the trail, and only the day before mentioned that he would like to do it again. It was their only clue. The men returned at midnight. They had searched along the trail with flashlights and called out into the night, but there was no sign of Jim Thompson, no response. They ventured forth a second time, and again returned unsuccessful. That night, before retiring, Connie phoned her son-in-law Barrie Cross and gave him the news. "I immediately called General Black and alerted him," Barrie said.

At dawn, the police arrived and combed a radius of five miles around the cottage. When this brought no results they called for reinforcements. The Bangkok press was notified, and within 24 hours, General Edwin Black and his aide, Lieutenant Horgan, joined in the search. More than 1,500 people were involved. The most thorough manhunt in local history had begun.

After 48 hours of fruitless search, with still no trace of Jim Thompson, there was speculation that he had not simply gone on an aimless walk and become lost. It opened up endless alternatives.

The foremost question was, whether or not he was still in the jungle. A number of things might have happened: (1) He had become lost; (2) he had fallen into an animal pit; (3) he had been eaten by a tiger and (4) he had died of an accident, perhaps a heart attack or gallstone seizure. All these possibilities were ruled out when Richard Noone—one of the best qualified authorities on the Malay jungle—was called into the case. He not only knew the terrain, but he also knew the aborigines and could speak their half-dozen dialects. That Thompson had merely become lost was ruled out, due to his jungle training and the fact that only the day before he had proved his ability to find his way out of the jungle. That he had fallen into an animal trap also was not accepted, nor could he have been eaten by an animal. Noone pointed out that pits were illegal, and if he had been killed by a tiger or any other animal there would have been obvious signs which would not go undetected by the aborigine trackers. Likewise, if he had had an accident or died of an ailment, his body would have been found. "I am convinced that Jim Thompson is not in the jungle," Noone confirmed when he resumed after several days.

Did Jim Thompson's connection with the OSS have anything to do with his disappearance? Some believed that he might have been negotiating with Ho Chi Minh, or undermining a coup in Cambodia, or attempting to quell the communist disturbance in North Thailand. Many reasoned that he could have agreed to a rendezvous in a neutral area, such as the Cameron Highlands. The fact that Thompson was so disorganized when he left Bangkok proved that he had not made plans to leave Thailand until Connie Mangskau invited him, and besides would not busy Bangkok have been the less obvious and easier place to have arranged a clandestine meeting? Had kidnappers made off with him in the hope of collecting a large reward, but when they realized the bombshell they had in hand, immediately murdered him? Was the change of taxi drivers part of a plot? Exhaustive investigations proved that it was common practice for taxis to change at Tapah, and the switching of drivers at Penang was due to the fact that the first driver did not have a valid license for Malaysia. Also in all the years of kidnapping in Singapore and Malaysia, the victims were mostly wealthy Chinese; never had an attempt been made on a Westerner. Suicide was considered, but there was nothing in his character and personality which gave the slightest indication that he would take his own life. And even if he had, by what extraordinary method had he disposed of his own body?

The last known photo of Jim Thompson taken on that fateful Easter Sunday on the morning he disappeared. Photo was taken by Connie Mangskau.

There was the question of his art collection, and the changing of his will. When the time came it was found that the will had vanished as completely and as mysteriously as its author. The possibility that the missing will might have had something to do with the murder of his sister in her home in Delaware was considered by the police, but they later concluded that there was no connection between the two. The possibility of relating the two circumstances evaporated when Prince Ajavadis Diskul found the document.

"The Siam Society wanted to act and take over the property," Prince Diskul explained to me during lunch at his house. "They reasoned that since there was no will it was their property. But Thai law says a man cannot be presumed dead until after seven years. Also, Thompson's nephew arrived from the States. He knew about the new will but nothing more. It was almost two years later, when I was unrolling some blueprints for the extension of his house, that I discovered the will. It was true, he had made a new will leaving everything to his nephew."

In the hope that someone would come up with information leading to Thompson's whereabouts, the Thai Silk Company offered a $30,000 reward, and the Malaysian police offered another $10,000. Instead of concrete evidence, the supernatural entered the Thompson case. The first bomoh, or witch doctor, arrived and after going into a trance announced that Jim Thompson was alive and being held by tree spirits in the jungle. In the days which followed the public was to be fed tales which could add another volume to Grimm's Fairy Tales. One Chinese lady had a vision in which she saw Thompson board a Norwegian ship bound for Hong Kong. An Indian astrologer decided that the Silk King had been drugged and abducted by mysterious enemies, who were keeping him captive in Indonesia.

Members of the Thompson family in Delaware engaged the services of a famed Dutch clairvoyant, Peter Hurkos, a sort of Western bomoh, who had developed his powers from a fall from a ladder. He arrived at Moonlight Cottage with Lieutenant Horgan, General Black's aide in Bangkok, and set his psychic powers to work. "Thompson is alive," he announced, "but he is not in the jungle here. He has been abducted to another country."

Hurkos went on to explain in graphic detail that Thompson had been picked up by thirteen members of an underground communist organization who had arrived in five cars, bearing Thai license plates. "What they want him for, I don't know," he said. "They are not holding him for ransom." He mentioned the name of the town in Cambodia where he was being held, and wanted to go there immediately but Lieutenant Horgan wisely suggested that they return to Bangkok first and consult General Black who was back at the U.S. Embassy. For obvious political reasons it was thought best that Hurkos' involvement in the case stop where it was.

Before Hurkos even returned to Bangkok, details of his story were thoroughly checked by the Malaysian CID. No five cars with Thai license plates had entered the country according to the border authorities.

Denis Horgan had some interesting tales to tell about Hurkos. "Peter Hurkos was a mind-reader," he said, "who supposedly got his powers after falling off a ladder. A very unpolished guy, he had been involved in a lot of high profile crimes — most notably the sensational Boston Strangler Case." As a cub reporter for a Boston newspaper, Horgan covered the case. "Some people said he was a wizard. Some people said he was a fraud. I tended toward a benign version of the latter. I think he thought he was real, and he was certainly a celebrity. Probably as much to keep him out of trouble as to assist him, I had to tag along with him and watch him play his games which were quite fascinating and challenging. Later at the home of Maxine North, Hurkos gave Horgan a painting he had done. "Probably it's only value," Denis said, "is it's ugliness with all its dark brooding colors."

Years have passed since Jim Thompson disappeared, and

still the public knows nothing more than it did on that Easter Sunday in 1967. But the theories continue. He was reputed to have been kidnapped by a lovesick aborigine girl; swallowed by a python, eaten by a tiger {thus eliminat-ing all evidence); lost in a cave inhabited by wild boars; felled by a silent dart from an aborigine blowpipe; kidnapped by mistake (Dr. Ling was the objective); and had a discreet love affair over the years which was discovered and he was done in. One Hindu palmist insists that Jim Thompson is still alive, since his stars say that he will not die until he is past 80.

Thompson with his pet bird

The fact remains that Jim Thompson did vanish from the Malaysian Highlands on March 26, 1967, and has not been seen or heard of since. Yet some logical explanation must exist. In the meantime, the Thai Silk Company continues to do business, and Henry Thompson Jr., heir to the Thai estate, has established a foundation to maintain the house and art collection. A friend of Jim Thompson's, Bill Riley, has rented the house on a caretaker basis and maintains it more or less as Thompson would have kept it. Many evenings, when I visited my friend Robin Dannhorn in the Thompson Compound, Bill Riley invited us for drinks in the main house. We sat in the large open living room surrounded by the priceless collection of art, and Thompson's houseboy, Yee, brought us drinks.

Nothing in that house has changed. Even in Thompson's bedroom, opened books are as he left them.

And as we sat there, I almost expected Jim Thompson to come walking in and say, "How nice of you to come," and then call to Yee to bring him a drink.

(Note; for an update on Jim Thompson, see the epilogue.)

Chapter 2

R.V. Perkins
The last of the great planters

Anyone who travels by road through Malaysia today will see endless miles of lonely rubber estates. Rows upon rows of supple rubber trees, sometimes wind-bent, stand solemnly in dark forests, and, in places where the road narrows, they form an arch overhead and blank out the sky. A tropical day can suddenly turn into twilight. The trees seem to belong to the land, but it was not always this way. Not many years ago the land was jungle, dense and tangled. The world's sudden need for rubber brought the early planters, English, Dutch, Australian, some French; singly and together they hacked clearings from the jungle, which they planted with rubber saplings. They called the clearings plantations. The trees remain but the men have long since gone, and with them a way of life. Rarely does the casual traveler see one of their great plantation houses, and chances are if he does come across one, it has been turned into a club house of sorts or else is in total ruin.

They don't call them plantations anymore, either. They are referred to as 'estates,' and most of them are corporate owned and run by a board of trustees elected by shareholders. That romantic role of the plantation manager as depicted by Maugham is not too different from today's manager of a department store or bus company. Instead of sipping whisky sodas on his verandah in the heat of the afternoon, he sits in an airconditioned office, drinking coffee, checking ledgers, writing reports and cursing the paperwork piled on his desk. It is not exactly what Maugham had in mind.

But there are exceptions. There is a great plantation house high on a hill near the famous Richardo Lighthouse south of Port Dickson. Its owner is a rubber planter who has been in the business for more than half a century. But there is also a certain mystique about the place and its master. The rumors are many.

You might hear it said that Mr. Perkins, the old planter, keeps his wives chained up inside his watch tower that faces the sea. There are other stories that he runs his plantation as planters did 50 years ago, that he is the supreme master over his indentured laborers from India. And there's a whisper that he controls half the rubber yield in Malaysia, secretly, of course. And everyone agrees, he is very rich, indeed.

Now if there is anyone who needs no rumors to make his life appear more interesting, it is Mr. Ronald V. Perkins, a Welsh ex-mining engineer and surveyor, who left the comforts of England 50 years ago to sail to a distant land called Malaya to become a rubber planter. When the British domination and colonialism ended with Malay independence in 1957, and other planters went home, Mr. Perkins stayed on. Other than becoming a Malay national, little else in his life-style changed. He's one of the last of his breed in Malaysia today.

I first saw his plantation house years ago when I sailed my schooner *Third Sea* up the Malacca Straits. The place stands out so prominently that it is marked on the sailing charts as a navigational aid. When I later visited Port Dickson and inquired about the house, everyone said it belonged to an Englishman. The house they merely referred to as 'Perky's Place.'

Out of curiosity I wanted very much to meet Mr. Perkins and to see his house, for I thought I might learn something first-hand about Malaysia's colorful past. But how can one

Perkins in his plantation house garden

invade another's privacy? Mr. Perkins was not a public figure, and after all, this might be the very reason he was living in Asia, to maintain the privacy of his life. So as time passed I listened to the rumors and wondered. It was a few years later, and quite by accident that I had a chance to meet him. I was spending a weekend with friends, John Willoughby and his family in Port Dickson, when I learned they had been invited by Mr. Perkins for a social visit the coming Sunday. "Do you want to come along?" John Willoughby asked. He didn't have to ask a second time. He phoned and Mr. Perkins extended the invitation to include me.

Although the house and gardens stand out at sea, from the coast road it is difficult to identify the estate through the dense tropical growth. Once you pass through the gate at the bottom of the hill, it all changes. Lawns and gardens appear. The drive winds its way upwards. The view is magnificent, with the islands of Indonesia shimmering on the distant horizon. A stone wall guards the seaward side of the drive. With potted plants every few yards it takes on a sort of Mediterranean appearance. I had to concentrate hard to realize I was not on the Riviera but in tropical Malaysia.

Dogs barking warned us we were near. We rounded the last bend and there to greet us was Mr. Perkins, at the edge of the walk leading from the house. It was suddenly like opening the pages of Maugham. "He was sitting on the verandah waiting for his guests to come to luncheon," Maugham had written 50 years before. "The Malay boy had drawn the blinds when the morning lost its freshness. Then he heard his guests' steps on the gravel path and rose up from his chair to greet them."

The planter wore shorts and his shirt was open at the throat. He pulled a handkerchief from his hip pocket to mop his brow. Although he was not deeply tanned his skin was hardened from years under a tropical sun. Judging from the stories I had heard about him, he had to be nearing 70, yet I have known men of 40 who did not look as trim. He carried himself well.

We were introduced. He spoke with a Welsh accent. He seemed genuinely pleased that we had come and bid us follow him into the house. My attention quickly switched from Mr. Perkins to the grand house he had built for himself.

If Mr. Perkins' house was representative of planters' houses of old, then they certainly lived splendidly and in total comfort. It had every desirable luxury, and simultaneously it reflected the personality of this strange man.

The house was English manor in style but without the closed-in architecture of Europe. It actually opened on three sides to let in the sea breezes.

"I didn't plan it that way," Mr. Perkins later explained. "When I first came on the hill I knew I had to build my house here, so I designed it and laid it out. I had the contractors begin, but when I returned to the site a few days later, it was all changed. They had consulted the village bomoh, the local witch-doctor. It was unlucky the way it was, and I had not considered the seasonal winds. I followed their advice and have never regretted doing so."

The house was built on two levels and followed the contour of the land. We entered through the study, an impressive paneled room with shelves lined with books. Beyond a double-arched doorway was the dining room. A grand staircase led to sleeping quarters on the second level. High above the house was a watch tower with a winding stairway to the top. Mr. Perkins sooner or later takes all his guests to the tower for a panoramic view of the Straits. It was here I learned that at least one of the rumors they tell about Perkins was not true. He does not keep his wives chained up inside the tower.

The view has to be one of the finest in Southeast Asia. Up and down the coast great fingers of land reach out into the sea and mighty palms bend to the changing breezes. But perhaps the most phenomenal sight is the Straits themselves. Not far beyond the base of the cliff where the house stands, two of the great oceans of the world meet—the China Sea and the Indian Ocean. As the tide changes you can actually see them clash.

We spent most of the afternoon in the study, while Mr. Perkins's faithful servants brought us drinks. (His gardener had been with him for 30 years.) I played my role and had gin and tonic in a tall glass, the way they did in all the Maugham stories.

The room had a cozy, lived-in feeling. There was one worn leather chair. No doubt Mr. Perkins's favorite. On all the shelves were old, often rare books: *The Naval side of British History* by Cullener. *The Southern Gates of Arabia* by Freya Stark. Even *The Complete Works of Shakespeare* in miniature. All the volumes were old, and except for Shakespeare, written mostly by long-forgotten authors.

Mr. Perkins caught me looking at the titles. "Care of books in the tropics is a problem," he said. "Each week they must be aired. Every day my servants take down certain shelves and place them in the sun. Let one week pass and insects get into the binding. Seems they go for the glue."

He went on to explain how a vast part of the library came from his uncle, J.A. Sanderbrook of the *Calcutta Statesman*. Later when we were in the vestibule he pointed to a framed photograph of his uncle, in full uniform, with epaulets, medals and sword. The same sword lay on the table beneath the photograph.

A long way from plantation life in far-off Malaya, a young Perkins, front row left, poses with family for a wedding photograph in England..

That was my first meeting with Mr. Perkins, but over the next few years I stopped often to see him. I spent time at his house on the hill, engaged him in long chats, and wandered through his plantation when he went out to oversee its operation. Little by little his life's story unfolded. The more I listened, the more fascinated I became.

It wasn't by plan or design that Perkins came to Malaysia, or Malaya as it was then called. It was by chance. He was a young graduate mining engineer in Wales. During the depression of the late 20's, when times were difficult for everyone, he was visiting relatives when a letter arrived from a distant cousin. It came from the other side of the world— from Malaya.

The sender wrote about such things as rubber plantations, riding motorbikes through the forests of rubber trees, and watching tigers and elephants. "It seemed romantic," recalled Mr. Perkins, "but what really got to me was when he said they were forming a rugby team and needed players."

The young, aspiring mining engineer from Wales traveled up to London to see about the job, was hired immed-iately and two weeks later was on a steamer to the Far East. The ship took six weeks via the Suez Canal to reach Singapore. There the young Mr. Perkins booked into the old Europe Hotel, then world famous, but which has long since been torn down.Crowded pulsating Singapore was exactly as he imagined it would be. "To read Maugham then," he exclaimed, "would be like reading a contemporary travel novel written today." Two days later Perkins left by train for his new home, a rubber plantation in Negri Sembilan.

Perkins was hired along with another young man from England. As was customary, the manager had organized a gala dinner party at the plantation house the night they arrived, and with eyes wide they listened to all the exciting tales about life on the plantations, while beyond their verandah they heard strange and fascinating sounds from the forest. It was real now, and not a story in a letter read in England. Whisky and gin flowed until the wee hours of the morning.

When they finally retired to their quarters, they were told there would be no muster or tapping if it rained in the morning. They awoke at dawn to the pleasant sound of the rain falling on the roof. "What a blessing!" Mr. Perkins said joyfully. "It had been a late night, and one of heavy drinking. Now we can remain in bed." Perkins rolled over and soon fell asleep. But not for long! They were abruptly awakened by an angry plantation manager.

"Why haven't you been to muster?" he demanded. Then with all the dignity of the English gentleman, he added, "I presume you came here to work, didn't you?"

"Yes, Sir," they replied. "But you said not if it rained."

What they had heard was not rain but dew falling. The manager quietly walked out of the room. The incident was never again mentioned but it was the first and last muster Mr. Perkins ever missed.

Life in those days on a plantation was not easy. The white proprietors and overseers held musters before dawn, seven days a week. Their life-style became regimented, a pattern they dared not break. A planter had to learn discipline to survive, or go mad if he didn't.

There were other requirements. Planters were required to take their daily dose of quinine and never go outdoors without wearing their solar topees. Their uniform was shorts, long sleeved shirts with red sweat bands around their collar and walking sticks.

In those days an ambitious and energetic young man could carve for himself a rubber plantation from the jungle, but there were no fortunes to be made unless he could survive the sweltering heat, the disease, and the pressing loneliness.

Overcoming loneliness was the most difficult task a young planter had to face. He might spend days, even weeks on end, without seeing another planter, and when he did want to visit another plantation, the distances were vast and road conditions poor. It was not often that they got together.

But when planters did meet it was always with great gusto. There were occasional dinner parties on birthdays, to send someone off or to welcome others, and, without fail, their annual functions and celebrations. At least once a year Mr. Perkins gathered with fellow planters at Fraser's Hill, a cool mountain resort patterned after the British hill stations found in India. Forty years later he still recalls who went that year, what they drank and how much.

Every four years a planter was eligible for six months' home leave, and it was usually during this time that a young man was expected to find himself a proper wife and return with her to take up their new life in Malaya. "I don't know if I was lucky or unlucky," Mr. Perkins jokes. "I never found a wife."

Mr. Perkins has kept several photo albums that depict life on a Malay plantation prior to the war. There are group shots of plantation rugby teams; a photo of a handsome young Perkins with a foot on the running board of a fashionable roadster; another of a group of young planters, all leaning over the handle bars of their sturdy motorcycles; and still others of weddings and social functions. But the good times were doomed although at the time it seemed unlikely that the Japanese Imperial Army would dare challenge the might of the British empire.

It was when Mr. Perkins was returning from home leave in

It was the thought of playing Rugby that brought Mr. Perkins to Malaya.

England that the war in Europe broke out. He reached Singapore and was commissioned into a Malay regiment in the British Army. "Even after Pearl Harbor was bombed," he said, "and the battleships *HMS Repulse* and *HMS Prince of Wales* were sunk by Japanese dive bombers off the Malay coast, we never believed the Japanese could take Singapore."

The military still believe had the Japanese attempted to take Singapore from sea, they might not have succeeded. Singapore was prepared for any surprise attack by sea. Instead the Japanese landed on the Malay East Coast near Kota Bahru and made their famous attack on Singapore by land, charging down the peninsula on bicycles. "We were at a dance and could hear artillery fire across the Straits in Johore," Perkins recalled. "We continued dancing half the night, still not believing."

Within 24 hours Singapore fell. Perkins was taken prisoner along with 140,000 others. What remains today in the memories of those who survived the ordeal is interment in Changi Prison or an excruciating journey up the Malay Peninsula by train, an agonizing and seemingly interminable march into the mountainous jungles of Thailand, a primitive camp, sadistic Japanese and Korean guards, starvation, disease and death. These are the black years in Mr. Perkins's life, when he was sent as a POW to build the infamous Siam-Burma 'Death Railway.'

To Perkins it is the memory of monsoons and malaria; of cholera and corpses; of pain and torture and despair. For every mile of its useless track, the railway cost the lives of approximately 393 men, 47 of whom were officially prisoners of war.

The picture we have of the railway today is very different than that the survivors hold. Ours comes from the much publicized film, "The Bridge over the River Kwai." It is Alex Guiness locked in a hot box by an insane samurai; it is hundreds of well-fed extras whistling 'Colonel Bogey,' it is a bridge that never was.

There were bridges, of course, that had to be constructed,

hundreds of them, if the Japanese were to succeed. For them the decision to undertake such a formidable engineering task, to push a railway through a tropical rain forest with fast-flowing rivers and the old hard rocks of a mountain range, was not made lightly. But in a sense, Japan had no other choice. Her limited naval resources, especially her merchant marine, were under heavy strain. It was becoming increasingly difficult to furnish the shipping lanes of her new empire with an adequate supply of vessels, and nowhere was this more keenly felt than on the long haul to Rangoon. Allied submarine activity in the Malacca Straits began to play havoc with their merchant vessels. The Siam-Burma railway became essential. The switch to Bangkok as the terminus of sea traffic to Burma was consequently a logical decision. The only difficulty was that Bangkok was separated from the well-developed Burmese railway system by 250 miles of rugged terrain. Japanese engineers who examined the railway project estimated it would take five to six years to complete, a time span much too lengthy for the immediate demands of war. There was another factor, however, that made the Siam-Burma railway a realistic possibility. There was a ready labor force of 140,000 allied prisoners of war in Singapore and Malaya. A target date was set and the wheels began to turn.

The first leg of the journey of the POW labour force was by rail from Singapore up the Peninsula to Ban Pong in South Thailand. Thirty men were crammed into small, steel, boxlike cars. They were so overcrowded that lying down was impossible, and it was equally impossible for everyone to sit at the same time. In some of the cars rosters had to be devised by which each prisoner had a period of time sitting and a time for standing. The nightmarish journey took five days and nights. At Ban Pong they disembarked. Perkins recalls the last one hundred miles was a forced march to Kanchanaburi where they began their work on the railway.

The first advance parties of POWs arrived in Ban Pong in May 1942. The target date for the completion of the railway was for November 1943. Two hundred and fifty miles of track in eighteen months. Perkins was assigned to No. 2 Group under the command of Lieutenant Colonel Yamagita. The group's duties were to construct bridges. The work required some prisoners to spend the whole day waist-deep in swirling waters, moving logs into place or holding timbers whilst they were secured. Others in groups of a dozen or more operated a mechanism of crude pile drivers, pulling or releasing the ropes at the chanted command of the gang leader, like so many slaves of old.

One bridge which No. 2 Group completed over the Mae Khlong River was several hundred yards in length and about five stories above the river. Construction was accomplished without the benefit of machinery. Everything was done by hand, from hauling and sawing timber to cutting gorges through solid rock and actually moving mountains. By May 1943, the Japanese had assembled a labor force of 161,000 Allied prisoners and almost 300,000 Asian workers and were determined at all costs to complete their railway by the given target date.

But what the Japanese did not take into account were the crippling forces of nature that befell the project. The monsoon broke early that year, washing out bridges and miles of track. A month later cholera struck, an epidemic that spread unchecked. The apparent hopelessness of the situation did induce quite a few men to attempt escape, despite the daunting obstacles in the way of success. One early bid was made by a group of eight Australians in an advance party, but they were quickly recaptured by the Japanese and shot soon afterwards, while kneeling in front of a pit dug by their comrades. The same fate met three Dutch escapees, and further south near Perkins's camp, three British officers enjoyed three weeks of freedom before they were recaptured and brought back to camp. After a short questioning, they were bayoneted. Perkins recalls another incident where four English prisoners escaped from the tyrannical command of Captain Neguchi of No. 5

Group only to seek protection in No. 2 Group under the benevolence of Lieutenant Colonel Yamagita. The commander tried to protect the unfortunate men but his harsh subordinates forced him to return the prisoners who were later bayoneted.

There are no known records of successful escapes by European POWs from the railway camps and most attempts ended in execution although there were cases of recaptured prisoners being sent to civilian camps to a fate which has never been recorded.

Ultimately even the single-minded Japanese had to admit they could not meet their target date for the completion of the railway. The date was extended by two months. The Japanese commanders pushed even harder than before. At one particularly difficult cut through solid rock, known as 'Hellfire Pass,' one Allied official who had eventual access to medical records and reports estimated that 68 men were beaten to death by the Japanese in an attempt to 'hasten' the work. At another bridge all the engineering skill and improvising known could not prevent lengthy delays. The bridge, almost a quarter of a mile long and eighty feet high, collapsed three times during construction. It claimed the lives of 31 men in falls, and as many men again were reported to have died from beatings while working on it. Nevertheless the long working hours and the slave-driving force of the Japanese produced the desired results. The railway was finally opened to traffic.

The question that remains is: why? Why the suffering and death for so many thousands, not only Allies but "Asian friends of Japan" as well? To Perkins the explanation lies in the deep rooted martial philosophy of the Japanese armed forces which considered the concept of death in battle as the only alternative to victory. This belief was so accepted by Japanese society that when a solider left home to join a combat unit his departure was often no more nor less than a funeral rite, for he could return alive only as a conqueror. The military regulations promulgated by the Japanese Minister of War in January, 1942, actually stated that each man must die if unable to carry out the task assigned him. As a result few Japanese were taken prisoner. At the end of the war there were 6,400 Japanese prisoners compared to nearly 200,000 Allied POWs. The point is, the Japanese did not expect to capture 140,000 men at the collapse of Singapore, at a time when they had scarcely enough food and supplies to support their own advancing armies.

After 35 years Perkins can recall with precise detail the events which took place during those frightful years. And, in part, he has a further explanation for Japanese brutality. The International Rules of War agreed to at the Hague Convention laid down in general that prisoners should be accorded the same treatment and enjoy the same living conditions as those of the forces who captured them. The result was that the POWs were subjected to discipline and punishment almost medieval in nature, to a medical system that was almost non-existent, and to living conditions that would be totally unacceptable in any other army. Not only Allied prisoners were beaten, but Japanese soldiers as well, including officers. Torture was an accepted part of the order. One junior Japanese officer who had failed to carry out an order was sentenced by his commanding officer to a "month in prison and bodily torture." Some soldiers were driven even harder than the prisoners themselves. Prisoners sometimes felt obliged to give food and water to wounded Japanese soldiers who were ignored by their own compatriots. The Japanese tended to regard sickness in general as shameful.

When the railway was completed and traffic began to move, the prisoners' work was by no means over, for now Allied bombers made daily sorties and blew up bridges and whole sections of track, all of which had to be hastily repaired. An air raid late one afternoon sent the prisoners scurrying for cover but it was not bombs that rained from the skies, it was pamphlets which proclaimed that the Japanese forces had surrendered unconditionally. The war was over.

"Everyone was too stunned to react. We all longingly awaited this day," Perkins said, "but when it finally was confirmed, and we accepted it, the real agony began. We were instructed to remain in camp. It took weeks for rescue to come." No. 2 Group traveled by rail to Bangkok where they were given medical treatment and then shipped to Burma and finally India. "It was frustrating," Perkins stated. "I wanted to return to Malaya and I had to go to India. I took my discharge and returned to Singapore as quickly as I could arrange a ship."

Perkins arrived in Singapore when the Japanese high command, consisting of three generals and two colonels, were being tried for war crimes. One of them was Colonel Yamagita, the commanding officer of No. 2 Group to which Perkins had been assigned. Against the protests of his friends but acting as his conscience dictated, Perkins appeared at the trial and testified in defense of the colonel.

"The Japanese were strict disciplinarians," he said, "but they were no harder on us than they were on their own men." He went on to explain that the prisoners were given medical treatment whenever it was available and their rations were the same as those given to Japanese soldiers.

As a result of Perkins's testimony, Colonel Yamagita's sentence was commuted from death to fourteen years in prison. After three years he was released and returned to Japan. Colonel Yamagita's family wrote to Mr. Perkins, thanking him for what he had done. For years afterwards, Perkins corresponded with the Yamagita family.

The post-war years brought many changes. Before the war, owners managed their own plantations. They were up at 5 AM and supervised their Indian tappers who labored seven days a week, fifty-two weeks a year, with three days off a year. A laborer's wage then was fifteen cents a day.

"Times change and progress will surely come," Mr. Perkins emphasized. "But science has yet to design or develop a machine that will replace a good tapper."

The art of tapping a rubber tree is exacting. Too deep a cut and the tree's fragile pulp is injured. Too shallow and the tree won't yield its true capacity. With the skill of a surgeon the experienced tapper knows precisely how to make incisions with his hooked implement called a 'gouging knife.'

When Perkins arrived there were about a million acres of rubber trees in Malaysia. Today there are over four million producing about forty percent of the world's natural rubber supply.

The tappers' lives have changed greatly since Mr. Perkins first arrived. They now receive today's prices and wages, are provided with free housing and medical care and many can now afford a TV set and even a small car.

It's a rewarding experience to go out at dawn with Perkins when he oversees his tappers. His solar topee has long since disappeared, but in the best English tradition, he never ventures out into the tropical sun without a hat. He slipped behind the wheel of his Land Rover and with his faithful German Shepherd dogs, Whiskey and Soda, in the back seat, he thunders down the road to his forest of rubber trees ten miles distant. He parks and begins his inspection. He may walk for several miles in the course of an average day.

In the distance appears the shadow of a lone tapper, and when you stop to listen you can hear the scrape, scrape of his razor-sharp knife as he cuts into the life bark of the tree. It's a sound that could be part agony.

Perkins now speaks in another language, unfamiliar to untrained ears. "Those rows are PB 86," he says waving his walking stick to the right. "They are not high yielding. Don't really like them." He points to the left. "Now those, they are RRI 600. They are the highest yielding," and soon he is telling you about the PBIG No. 2 and some of the more recent developments of the Rubber Research Board in Kuala Lumpur.

He puts in a good eight hours and his work is usually finished by 11:30 am, and now he has the leisure to enjoy fully his house. He has a long lunch and perhaps a swim in the ocean in the afternoon. If it's an extremely hot day he may take a nap. Usually on a Saturday he goes into Port Dickson to play golf with his pals. If he does not entertain friends at his home on weekends, he goes to the Port Dickson Yacht Club for dinner.

Does he ever plan to retire?

"And do what? Certainly not leave my house for a place in cold England. I should say not. Going back once a year for a visit is quite enough."

Were Somerset Maugham alive he would be at ease with Mr. Perkins, and he would be pleased that times have changed so little.

Chapter 3

Connie Strickland
Lady doctor from the jungles

There can be few more engaging ways to spend a leisurely afternoon than with a few old-timers listening to their tales of times past in Asia. After a few drinks their stories may become wild and exaggerated and it is difficult to separate the imagined from the real, but fair enough, the conversation is always good. This is especially true when the old-timers are retired civil servants and planters. It was on one of these abandoned afternoons that I first heard the name Dr. Strickland. I was sitting at the bar in the Selangor Club in Kuala Lumpur with a few friends, amongst whom were two planters. For most of the afternoon they kept us amused, with one story following another, and then one mentioned the name Strickland.

"What ever happened to her?" someone asked.

"She's still around," one planter replied. "I hear she's running a clinic on one of those god-forsaken islands in the Klang Estuary."

Dr. Connie Strickland at her clinic on Ketam Island in the Klang Estuary on the west coast of Malaysia

My interest was immediately aroused. "A lady doctor living on the islands off Klang?" I asked.

"You don't know about her?" the second planter inquired. "She's one person you should know. Now there's a story!"

Quite often when people learn I'm a writer, they approach me with suggestions about people and places I should write about. Sometimes they have a secret scheme whereby we can both become rich. They explain that although they cannot write they have a story that is absolutely certain to make a fortune. It's simple. They will tell it to me and all I have to do is write it up and we split payment down the middle. It is a sure thing.

There is not much to say to such people, other than that everyone's life is worthy of a book, if they just knew how to put it down in print. But with the planters and their discussion on Dr. Strickland it was not the same. There was no question about it, even with all their exaggeration, she seemed indeed, a very unusual person. I asked more about the lady doctor from the jungle. For the next hour or two, accompanied by many more rounds of drinks, they told stories about the Dr. Strickland they knew or had heard about. Bits and pieces of disjointed information came from everyone present, that she was born in England, India or Australia. That she became a medical doctor so that she could work aboard British merchant vessels during the Second World War. That she gave her British passport up to become a Malay citizen. That she could stand up to the best sea captains and hold her own, drink for drink. The only thing that they could not agree upon was whether it was brandy or whisky she drank.

And there was more, about her taking up flying, studying judo, trekking through the jungles, living for two years with aborigines, and now working with the poor on some lonely offshore island. "Only Dr. Strickland could do that," everyone agreed and the conversation finally moved to other topics.

After I heard about Dr. Strickland at the Selangor Club, I found that her name kept coming up everywhere I went. It was like listening to a Bartok concerto for the first time, and then, seemingly hearing it wherever and whenever I listened to music. And inevitably when the name Strickland was mentioned, I would be asked: "You mean you haven't met her?" I was beginning to feel something rather important had been left out of my life. I made several attempts to meet her but each time I visited Port Klang over the following two years, the ferries were not operating to Ketam Island or I heard she was on a visit to one of the other islands.

The question that puzzled me most about her was why she chose to settle on one of the most inhospitable islands of the Klang Estuary? They are all as forbidding as any island can be. But then, had she had a practice or operated a clinic in Kuala Lumpur or any town on the mainland, she might not have been the person who fascinated everyone who heard about her. She obviously was not out for publicity, nor to make a name for herself. Everyone certainly knew of her but when it actually came down to it, few people had ever met her.

Regarding the islands in the estuary, I had sailed in and out of them many times, aboard coastal steamers and on two occasions when I navigated my own schooner through the tricky passageways. Depending upon the tides, the currents can run swift and strong.

The estuary is formed by the Klang River which empties its muddy silt into the Malacca Strait. The islands number more than a dozen. For the most part they are really little more than mud flats rising up but a few feet from the sea. You get the feeling that a neap tide might wash them clean of all life and being. Undistinguished blots of land, thickly blanketed with mangled mangrove trees, they appear to be uninhabitable.

Less than a hundred years ago they were just that: uninhabitable. Sir Frank Swettenham, British Regent and one of the founders of Kuala Lumpur, had a devil of time attempting to construct a port at Klang which would serve as Kuala Lumpur's link to the sea. Even after he had successfully established a rail line in 1886 between the capital and Port Klang there was little hope of success, for fever and pestilence ruled the day. Of the original 86 tin miners who poled up the Klang River and founded a settlement at Kuala Lumpur, all but nineteen died of fever within the first month. It was not until the turn of the century that construction finally resumed, after Dr. Malcolm Watson, a government surgeon, took over. Watson had previously worked in the Americas on similar projects and had experienced enough medical breakthroughs in malaria to tackle Malaysia's mosquito problem. Despite objections that he was spending too much time and money on his experiments, he drained the swamps around the towns and made living in Klang and on the other islands possible. And now, a more than half century later, there was an English lady doctor living in the islands. But why?

A chance meeting with a Mr. Fernandez, the manager of the Selangor Royal Yacht Club, finally gave me my introduction to Dr. Constance Strickland. I was sailing my schooner up the Malacca Strait to Penang when I decided to stand off Ketam Island for the night, but with adverse winds and the channel in front of Dr. Strickland's clinic too shallow for deep-keel vessels, I moved on to the yacht club. There I met Mr. Femandez. He knew Dr. Strickland well. He was serving as a sergeant in a Malay regiment in Borneo when he first met her. "She was Medical Officer on a Government troop ship," he explained. "She was nobody's fool. She'd knock you flat if you had something bad to say about her, and then she'd doctor you up in the sick bay. She was a good doctor."

"So you want to meet Dr. Strickland," he continued. He thought for a moment. "Come back and check in the morning."

The next morning I was in his office and found him waiting. "The ferry leaves in an hour," he announced. "Disembark at the second landing. The second landing, mind you. Dr. Strickland will be there waiting for you."

The ferry was one of those ancient contrivances, the type that had plied the coastal trade for the past hundred years. Since there was no wharf, both cargo and passengers boarded by small sampan. Once on the ferry, passengers sat on hard benches athwart ship, and when these had filled, they crowded the rails and all available empty deck space, including the top of the engine hatch. The bulky cargo consisted of sacks of grain, wicker baskets filled to the brim with fruit and potatoes, and on top of these were bunches of green bananas. There were stacks of unwrapped bread fresh from the bakery in Klang.

A half hour after our scheduled departure time, the helmsman sounded a bell, the engine chugged and fumed over and, to everyone's relief, the ferry slowly backed itself out by kedging off on other boats at anchor. Suddenly the engine stopped and the ferry came to a halt. All 86 passengers strained to see the cause of the delay. Two more passengers and more cargo arrived in a sampan. The gunners now were barely six inches above the water.

The current ran swift in the heavily-silted river. In the roads great freighters and tramp steamers and tour ships pulled at their anchor chains. They had exciting and mysterious names painted on their bows: *Orchid Garden* from Singapore, *Jaladharma* from India, *Hana Maru* from Japan and the luxury cruise ship *Rasa Sayang* churning slowly through the waters en route to Penang.

The ferry left the roads and entered a narrow channel. It twisted and fumed around endless bends, with every mile of shore line exactly as each mile that preceded it. The monotonous roar of the engine deadened any possible sound of animal or bird life from the jungle. 'the channel began to widen and soon, a mile or two ahead, was a village low to the water, built on stilts. Some roofs were tin; others were attap. Occasionally there was a high sloping roof of a temple. The village occupied a clearing at the edge of the jungle.

The ferry made one hurried stop and at the next landing dropped anchor; sampans sculled passengers ashore. In the crowd on the deck, a head taller than the Chinese surrounding her, was Dr. Strickland. When she pushed forward there was no mistaking her. She wore slacks and a jacket. Her hair was grey and closely cropped. She wore glasses, through which she strained hard to see if a stranger was sitting in the sampan. Suddenly she saw me and began waving frantically. Soon I heard her shouting: "Mr. Stephens, Mr. Stephens, over here!"

Dr. Strickland has one of those personalities one finds too rarely nowadays. She's in love with life, and everything interests her. "How nice of you to come visit me," she exclaimed. "You must be tired after the ferry ride." But before I could answer she insisted we go directly to the clinic. I met her 24-year-old Chinese assistant, and Jimmy Lim, the post master who stopped in to see who the stranger was.

"Now, we will all have lunch," she said with ceremony and began clearing a table in the examining room. "But first we must have some cold beer while we wait. " Quart bottles of Tiger Beer suddenly appeared. So far the stories about her were running true.

"And where are you from, Dr. Strickland?" I asked as we awaited lunch which was being delivered from a local restaurant.

"I refuse to answer unless you call me Connie," she said, and when I did, she said she was born in Australia. Her father was governor of Western Australia and when she was six the family moved to Malta. It was difficult to get information from her. Not that she was secretive or evasive about her past, but she was more interested in what I was doing and what was happening in the outside world.

After lunch it was back to work. Her patients were lining up in the hall outside her door. She asked Jimmy Lim to show me the village until she could see me later.

Jimmy was able to fill in some of the background on Dr. Strickland as we walked through the village. In addition to his position of post master, Jimmy, as a black belt Tae Kwon Do master, spends three evenings a week teaching martial art to the islanders. "Dr. Strickland," he proudly announced, "is one of my pupils. She comes to class whenever she can find time."

The village is entirely built on stilts, with all the streets' walkways made of boards. There is a peace and tranquility about the place which is hard to find in our modern world, and even after a few hours, I could understand why Dr. Strickland chose to make the island her home. Here certainly she was needed and loved by all. Jimmy explained that at first she came on periodic visits to the island by her own boat which she skippered. But often the winds and seas made the passage treacherous. There was one unfortunate episode that occurred when her boat boy was washed over board in a storm and she had to dive into the black water to save him from drowning. They both barely escaped death. During the rescue she swallowed so much sea water she was confined for a week to the hospital in Klang. After she left she decided to move permanently to Ketam. I was curious that a foreign national should set up practice in Malaysia. Another rumor was confirmed. Dr. Strickland gave up her British passport and became a Malay citizen in 1960. She speaks fluent Malay but is somewhat handicapped with her lack of Chinese, since 90 percent of the island people are in fact Cantonese. Fortunately many of the younger generation speak Malay, and she is progressing in Cantonese.

Later that afternoon I met Connie Strickland at her new clapboard house on the waterfront. She shares it with her two pets, a hound dog named Pedro and a white talking crow, Snowy. From her balcony she has a sweeping view of the wide channel and the ferry landing.

Little by little the fascinating story of Dr. Strickland began to unfold. Most of what I heard was true. She had taken up flying and her love for the sea was the reason she became a doctor. When she learned I had a schooner in Klang, her eyes grew wild and she clapped her hands as a child might when handed a present. "You must bring it here, you must," she said. When I explained the channel was probably too shallow for my vessel, she thought for a moment, then said, "I will go to Klang when you are there again, if I can only get away."

Connie Strickland craved adventure as far back as she could remember. When she lived in Malta with her parents during

World War I, she recalls putting aside her dolls in the nursery and taking up the volumes of G.A. Henty's *Adventure Stories of Boys*. One volume she remembers especially well is *With Clive in India*. Thereafter her dream was to go to India and the Far East. She became particularly good at geography of the Orient in her school days.

Connie Strickland spent her youth in Malta and took up her education in Dublin. Her first real adventure, the first of many was when she sailed in a 30-foot yawl across the Irish Sea with two boys one summer holiday.

Her dream of going to sea became reality when the War in Europe broke out in 1939. Having studied medicine in Dublin she was assigned to a convoy, and after the War when she graduated from medical school she became a ship's surgeon with the Blue Funnel line. She made four voyages to the Far East, and on the last one signed off in Singapore.

Singapore with the Malay Peninsula to the north opened up new avenues for a lady doctor looking for adventure. The fact that she was approaching middle age did not stop her. "Never think of your age and you will always feel young" is her philosophy. She spent her first year in Southeast Asia in government service as Medical Officer in Johore State. She later transferred to the Department of Aboriginal Affairs. This new position took her into the depths of the Malay jungles and in contact with indigenous tribesmen who had never seen the outside world. For three years she trekked through the jungles, forging her way far up river, calling on jungle outposts seldom visited. It was a hard and difficult life, and in all probability she might have stayed on several more years but policy prevented her from extending her contract.

When her tour with the Department terminated she returned to Singapore to become a general practitioner only to give that up again when the call of the sea became too great. This time she signed on as ship's surgeon with the Malaysian Armed Forces where she spent the next three and a half years. It was during this period that Mr. Femandez at the Port Klang Yacht

Club got to know her.

Most likely Dr. Strickland would be still at sea but she had to resign when it was discovered she had breast cancer. She was operated on in Singapore, under local anesthetic, without spending a single day in the hospital. After many long months of radio-therapy she returned to her profession. By this time she had developed a most unique scheme which she hastened to put into motion. She bought her own boat and began a medical service for merchant seamen of all nations in Port Klang. She eventually gave this up when her services were needed more on Ketam Island. She moved there permanently in 1974.

Aside from many of her friends and patients on Ketam Island and neighboring islands, Dr. Strickland has set up a youth club, she attends the various Chinese clan meetings, practices Tae Kwon Do, does body building, and spends hours teaching Snowy, her white crow, adding new words to his vocabulary. She's proud of the crow which occupies a cage half the size of her living room. "A maharaja in India," she will tell you, "sent a pair of white crows as a gift to the Sultan of Selangor. The crows escaped and now their descendants

Dr. Strickland with her pet dog Pedro rests between patients on the verandah at her clinic on Ketam Island in the Klang Estuary.

67

can be seen in the banana trees around Klang. Snowy was picked up by some Malay boys. The poor thing had its wing injured. I nursed him back to health, and he has dominated my life ever since. That's been five years now."

We shared two more quarts of beer at the Chinese shop before the last ferry of the day departed for Port Klang. "It was so nice of you to take the time to come and visit me," she said. "Do come back with your schooner. I'd love to come aboard. You could anchor right out there at high tide. I'm sure," she pointed to the channel in front of her house. "You know, I suppose I've told you, but I do love boats."

I watched her waving as the ferry pulled away with its full cargo of passengers and crates of chickens and eggs.

I have since received a number of letters from Dr. Strickland, one by special delivery via the harbor master in Penang where I was anchored. I could see her excitement as she scratched the information on a medical pad. "I spoke to the captain of a trading boat," she wrote, "and he is certain you can come up the channel in your schooner." She then carefully laid out the coordinates and fixes I would need, and made notation of the water depth at low and high tides. She told me exactly where to anchor and which direction I would swing with the changing tides. "I do hope you will come now," she concluded. I did not stop on that trip down the coast, but I did wind my way up the channel another time, while my entire crew and passengers thought I was mad to follow a sketchy scrap of paper scribbled no doubt by one more mad than I. But the direction was accurate, and when we anchored the schooner swung exactly as she said it would. We hoisted up all our signal flags, and eagerly I scanned with my binoculars the waterfront and the balcony of her house for some sign of activity. She was perhaps at the clinic. I sent word ashore with a sampan, only to have an answer from her assistant that she was in town for a few days buying medical supplies.

There will be another time, but time is not really important. Dr. Strickland, lady doctor from Ketam, will be there.

Chapter 4

Doug Tiffany
Treasures beneath the Southeast Asian Seas

The most engaging and successful adventurers in the Far
East today are marine salvage divers. Theirs is a profession
that is relatively new to this part of the world. In Conrad's day
men seeking adventure, and a purse, might have dared to
skipper tramp steamers through uncharted reefs, or to trade
with hostile savages up untamed rivers, or, as in Lord Jim's
case, to serve as ships' chandler in distant forgotten ports. But
such occupations, those that still exist at any rate, are no longer
available to Europeans. There are exceptions, of course. I know
one tough, grizzled Welsh captain who has skippered coastal
freighters and passenger ships for the Straits Steamship Company
for 35 years. He has the Port Kelang-Singapore-Sandakan run
today. But as I said, this is rare. Our modern-day adventurers
have turned to other fields, one of which is salvage diving.

The advent of the diving lung after World War II and the
high stakes offered by oil companies has brought divers to the
East by the score. In a few short years, those who have lasted
have made both names and fortunes for themselves. But the
risks are high, and the demands placed upon them are great.

What sort of people are they? It takes great courage and
daring to do what they do. Do they dive to the depths of the
oceans of Asia for profit alone, or is there some secret mystery
beneath the Eastern seas these men will not or cannot share
with others. Most often they do not talk about it. But why do
they dive at all?

I often ponder these questions when I meet a commercial
diver. And since I live aboard my own schooner as much as I
can, I meet my share of seafaring men, many of whom are
divers. Once I get to know a diver, he can be rather pleasant
company. He is never dull. But then suddenly one day out of
the blue he will mention he is going away for a few months.
He has perhaps signed a contract to dive on a pipeline in the
Bay of Bengal or work on an oil rig in the Philippine Sea, at

depths of up to 700 feet. He goes and in time his name eludes me, until months later I hear it mentioned, and I ask, "What happened to him? I haven't seen him around." There is silence, and the answer comes "Haven't you heard. It was on the east coast of Borneo . . . ."

When you visit places like Singapore and Jakarta, and sit in one of the lounges or cafes where oil men hang out — you can't miss them with their heavy Rolex wristwatches and their penchant for spending money — you'll hear them talking about salvage divers on their rigs. Salvage divers always make interesting conversation, and soon these oil men will start throwing out names like Pat Hamilton, Bill Mathers, Sandy Lentz, Ian Chamberlain and Doug Tiffany. Even the oil men have to admit, divers have one thing in common. They possess a zest for living shared by few other men. They learn to feel life to the tips of their fingers. Maybe that's the way it is when you live close to death, when adventure is your business.

Take Pat Hamilton. He's one of the old timers. He began diving about the time Jacques Cousteau developed scuba after World War II. He has been with it ever since. Pat is the true professional every young diver respects. They listen when he talks. I have seen him come ashore in Singapore and drink a case of beer before the bumboat lands, and be standing after a night's bout of heavy drinking when everyone else has left. "What's happened to this younger generation?" he shouts and a few hours later is first on the job. Pat has explored the bottom of oceans from Mexico to Indonesia, and unless oil becomes obsolete he will continue to dive as long as companies will hire him. There is not a diving job he cannot do, or will not do.

Then there's Bill Mathers. He's an ex-U.S. Navy diver, 32 years old and holds a degree in engineering. Discharged from the services in 1970, after a hitch in Vietnam, he was not ready to go home. Instead he headed out to the Philippines to look for a sunken Spanish galleon, which he never found. He later became salvage adviser for the recovery of a Chinese junk with a valuable cargo of Ming Dynasty porcelain. They did locate the junk, but when they brought the cargo to the surface they found the pieces marked "Made in England." Realizing he would probably not obtain his fortune immediately, he went to work in the off-shore Indonesia oil fields as a diver and geophysical surveyor. Since then he's been involved with various diving operations in East Borneo, along the Malacca Straits, the Java Sea and the Indian Ocean.

Between periods of work Bill managed to explore Krakatoa, the volcano that shook the world when it exploded and caused fallout in London two years later; he has photographed the breath-holding Filipino shell divers; and has located World War II wrecks along the Malay coast.

For several years Bill fought fires on tankers, rescued stranded seamen from fishing vessels hung on reefs, laid moorings for large drilling rigs and raised sunken tugs and vessels, including the infamous pilgrim ship *Malaysia Kita* which rolled over on her side in the Singapore Harbour after a fire gutted her. And Bill joined me as master diver on an expedition I led into the Malay jungle to search for a lost city at the bottom of Lake Chini, in spite of unpleasant rumors the lake was infested with leeches, white crocodiles and a Loch Ness-type monster. We found remnants of a Chinese trading post of sorts but no indication there was a mighty walled kingdom as suggested in 7th century Chinese chronicles.

Today Bill is managing director of a marine consulting firm based in Singapore. On clear days he can often be caught gazing hopefully over Singapore's main anchorage knowing well that each of the hundred-odd vessels there is a potential client. His future plans are to handle salvage operations and survey work on marine archaeological sites. His real goal is to find a Chinese trading junk over two thousand years old.

One of the youngest divers in the business in Asia is Ian Chamberlain. A few years ago, when he was nineteen, Ian arrived in Singapore aboard a sleek yacht cruising around the world. But the skipper was a misplaced airline pilot with an airline hostess wife twenty years his junior, and they were becoming bored with the life. They decided to sell the boat and when that failed, they shipped it back to Boston at an astronomical price and left Ian high and dry on the beach. He had no where to go, so I signed him on as crew. He soon became intrigued with the diving world, whereupon Bill Mathers hired him to assist in retrieving a six-ton anchor lost in the harbor. Ian not only located the anchor but single handily brought it to the surface. Bill then hired him as salvage diver to work on the Malaysia Kita, the sunken pilgrim ship. The ship was raised and Ian moved on to another company. Now you can see him, whenever a ship is in distress, dashing out to sea in a salvage vessel, leading his own crew. Give him a few more years and Ian will be one of the area's top salvage officers and divers.

Sandy Lentz towers six feet five and began his career at sea as a fisherman on the California coast. He had considerable experience as a hard-hat sponge diver and when he heard about money to be made in Asia he packed up and came East with his pretty wife. He was a natural in the business, moved up to top diver and was sent to the North Sea for a year to lead a salvage team. When he returned to Singapore he had the cash for a new Taiwan-built ketch. He's retired today, and dives for pleasure. He, his wife and their two sons live aboard the ketch.

Doug Tiffany is a salvage diver, and like Sandy, he lives on his yacht when he is not on contract. Doug and a diver from Australia saw a fortune slip between their fingers. They located a World War II wreck in the Rhio Straits and discovered its cargo was Malaysian tin. They got the salvage rights, hired a barge with a crane mounted on deck and in two weeks salvaged close to three quarters of a million dollars worth of tin. "The Indonesian navy came," Doug sighed. "They said, 'Thank you' and took everything, including the barge. There was nothing we could do. But —" he begins waving his arms— "but that was only a drop in the bucket. We had located a Japanese cruiser and half-a-dozen wrecks in the same area. There's no limit I tell you, no limit."

When you talk to Doug, when you get to know him, you

have to admire him. Medium height, handsome, with searching blue eyes, he's the most determined man I know. Nothing phases him. And the fact that he is alive is nothing short of a miracle. He has survived one occasion at a depth of 500 feet when his air was cut off, and another when a steel plate dropped from a rig severed his hoses. He was blown off a bottom pipeline and carried into the Bay of Bengal in the black of night. He has outwitted pirates, fought tropical typhoons and sailed his ketch single-handed up and down the China Sea. But most remarkable, he once directed operations to remove a piece of heavy equipment which had turned over on him and had pinned his head beneath its twisted carriage.

Doug Tiffany is an incurable romantic who looks for the good life in Asia, and he will go to any extreme to find it. He has come close several times. You could say he has the soul and mind, if not the character, that makes men turn to the diving profession to make a living. He may not be entirely typical but he's a good example of what motivates these strange people.

Born in a small town on the California coast, Doug was a high school dropout. Like so many other dropouts, he found employment in a gas station, had his own beat-up car when he was sixteen and became intrigued with the exaggerated tales of two oil men up from Bakersfield, flashing dollars and talking big about money to be made in the oil fields. Impressionable Doug was sold. He would make his fortune early in life.

He headed for the oil fields, conned his way into a position as "chain-man" on a survey party and spent the next ten years working for the state. His only claim to riches was that he was a well-paid heavy road equipment operator. "I'd probably still be there," he recalls, "had it not been for two things. I saw the movie 'Mutiny on the Bounty' and I had an accident. Both changed my way of life." He tells his story as no one else can.

"I was working a highway job in northern California along the Oregon coast. It was steep country. I was operating an over-sized earth mover. We had big cuts with big fills to make.

It was the morning shift that started at 4 AM. I had a full load following a sliver made by a bulldozer. We didn't have lights. I did not realize it until it was too late. I had passed the cut and there was nothing to hold on to. We went out of control, over and over, down the mountain side. The first roll took the cab off right to the floor, crushing me in between. The seat broke off, the steering column, everything. She ended upside down at the bottom of the mountain with me underneath. The first roll knocked me out. I felt the initial crunch and remembered saying to myself, "Oh, no, Doug, you did it this time."

"I don't know how long I had been there when I came to," he continued. "It was light. No one knew about the accident. They didn't see me until the sun came up hours later. Then they came down the hill shouting but when they saw the wreckage they thought I was dead. I heard them say, 'He's dead. He has to be dead. We have to get this machine back on its wheels.' If they moved it I would be finished. I began shouting, 'Hey, man, I'm not dead.' Luckely they heard me."

Doug was aware that his head was pinned. Another inch and it would crush like a watermelon. He was in shock but his mind was still functioning.

"I wanted to live. God, I wanted to live. I wanted to see Tahiti, like in the movie 'Bounty', and all those places I read about. I realized there was only one way to get out of this mess and I alone would have to do it. They obviously could not turn the machine over, nor since it was upside down could they cut through the bottom. The only way was to jack the cab up, and I would have to direct operations."

The rescue team handed Doug wooden blocks and a portable jack with a long hose. He positioned the jack, and as they pumped it up, he kept moving the blocks closer and closer to his head. The blocks and then the jack. Very gently and very slowly. Finally they raised it high enough to free his head, but when they tried to drag him out, he was stuck. His arm was caught. It had gone through the windscreen which had buckled around it. He had no feeling; his shoulder was dislocated. They had no choice but to go in with an acetylene torch. They wrapped his arm in burlap and kept a waterhose turned on him while they cut away at the steel. Two more hours were to pass before they dragged him free.

"I remember standing up," he said. "They wanted me to lay down, to put me in the ambulance they had winched down the side of the mountain. I was not hurting, not yet. But I was a mess. Glass and diesel were ground into me. My head was open from my right eye to the back of the skull, and when I felt with my fingers I stuck them up under the eye to the second knuckles. My right ear was torn off."

Doug spent the next six months in the hospital. Surgeons pieced his ear back together, which took painful weeks of cutting away dead tissue. His left arm had no feeling. He underwent physical therapy for another six months. When feeling came to his finger tips he knew he would be all right. He made up his mind then that he would see those far-flung ports of the Pacific and Far East.

Doug's chance came soon afterwards when he was offered a contract to instruct South Vietnamese in the use of heavy equipment. He found himself based in Saigon with a war erupting all around him. One morning he reported to work to find two barges sunk in the river in front of his office. They

A group of divers on an oil rig in Indonesian waters pose for their photograph between dives. The pay is high, but so are the risks.

had taken rockets through the tops and out the sides.

"The C.O. called me," Doug said. "Can you raise them?"

"Sure," I said, "if you draw up a salvage contract." He agreed and I was in the salvage diving business."

Fortunately in California Doug had taken up scuba as a sport. He knew basically what he needed and borrowed the equipment from the Navy. In two weeks he had both barges raised. "Then they called me in to do underwater explosive work," Doug said. "I was in luck again. A few years back I had worked heavy equipment for the Corps of Engineers. We were putting in a tunnel. When they were drilling I had nothing to do, so I would go back into the tunnel and help the powder monkeys load charges. So in Vietnam I just applied this knowledge to underwater work. Everything I ever learned seemed to apply to underwater at one time or other."

After Vietnam Doug Tiffany earned big money as a salvage diver on pipelines, oil rigs and oil exploration. In the beginning it was mostly "hard hat." Hard hat is that romantic style of diving in which the diver is zipped up into a rubber suit and fitted with a heavy pair of lead boots that forces him to walk when on land like Frankenstein's monster. A huge brass headpiece called a "hard hat" is bolted to a chest plate. His air comes from the surface through hoses. John Wayne popularized the role of the hard hat diver when he went to the sea bottom, fought a giant octopus, recovered a treasure chest and came to the surface to the awaiting arms of Dorothy Lamour. Doug found it somewhat different. He joined his first rig and served as assistant to a tough old retired U.S. Navy diver. "They only had hard hat. No scuba," Doug said. "The old bastard didn't ask if I knew how to dive. He just zipped me up and threw me in. It was drown or survive. That first dive was ninety feet. The old man taught me the business. The hard way."

What is most remarkable about Doug Tiffany is that he has no academic background. He has learned to do everything himself, without benefit of formal training, university degree or foundation backing. But this does not mean he will let the absence of a piece of paper stop him.

Doug's learning process did not stop in the technical field. He has become self educated in many other ways. Even when sitting on the deck of a rig, waiting in a wet suit for hours—which every diver must do and dislikes—Doug uses his time wisely. He is an avid reader, delving particularly into history and the arts. He likes reading poetry, and I have known him to become attracted to a quite unattractive girl simply because she wrote lovely poetry. He has learned to appreciate fine wines and good music, and when drama and musical festivals come to the Far East, he may travel miles to attend them. When he's away from a rig, he surrounds himself with interesting people; he has little time for dullards. A long time ago Doug learned that although time is measured in biblical spans, life is also measured in minutes. It is precious, not to be wasted.

The fact that his life frequently continues to hang on the fine threads of chance makes him enjoy it more. "When you're doing bell work at 500 feet and come to the surface, you appreciate those things we take for granted. The colors that surround us. The warming feeling of sunlight. Or breathing air, nature's air. And all the glorious sounds. You become aware, and that is important, and that makes it worth it."

The bell Doug mentioned is used for transporting divers to the bottom, when they must work at extreme depths. "Once you reach the bottom you 'lock out'," he explained. "Then you leave the bell. It's the most difficult and dangerous diving."

Doug was working the bottom at 500 feet when surface control accidentally cut off his air supply. His self reliance and his attitude towards fear once again saved his life.

"When you once reach the bottom, you 'blow the bell down', which means pressurizing it." He described the scene with his hands, how the bottom hatch opens and the diver swims out on an umbilical cord fifty feet long. A second diver in the bell serves as tender; he plays the hose out as it is needed.

"I was out of the bell twenty feet when I began breathing

hard. I was on mixed gas. I called the surface to give me more pressure, not knowing they had cut my gas by accident. Surface kept jacking up the pressure until they could not give me any more. It was harder and harder to breathe. Then I got cold. My hands began to shake so hard I could not control them."

Doug signaled that he wanted to return to the bell, and would normally have had little difficulty doing so, but on this occasion the tender became excited and dropped the remaining thirty feet of hose on the bottom. It became tangled in the blow-out preventer.

"I knew things were serious and I had to get back into the bell. But the entire hose was fouled on the bottom. My immediate reaction was to cut out, rip off my hat and do a free ascent to the bell, which meant climbing at an angle of 45 degrees. But I knew I would be blinded, and locating the bell would be a gamble. Time was precious but I stopped to reason it out. I said to myself, 'Straighten out, Doug. Be cool! Get your act together or you are not going to make it."

To scramble back among the twisted hose would have been folly. Slowly and carefully Doug began bunching up the hose until he had it completely unfouled, and at this point he returned hand-over-hand to the bell. He was blue by the time the tender closed the hatch and they surfaced. For 22 hours he laid in a decompression chamber. When the chamber was opened and Doug stepped out he immediately got the bends, a decompression sickness caused by too much nitrogen in the blood. The bends, if not fatal, often cause paralysis. Bends are the deep sea diver's curse. Doug was put back into the decompression chamber for another 24 hours. After being confined for two days in a chamber not much larger than an over-sized sewer pipe, and not much more comfortable, Doug was a nervous wreck when the door was finally unbolted.

"Did you dive on that job again?" I asked him.

"No, I did not," he said. "I would have, but they fired me."

"They fired you! But it wasn't your fault."

Doug smiled. It was one of those victorious smiles you see

on people's faces when they sip a drink they have just mixed, and the drink is good. "I found out who the guy was who turned off the gas, and I basted him. I laid him out flat. And then I went after the tender, so they fired me. They had to. I can't blame them. You can't let guys go around punching people in the mouth. But I guarantee you he won't make that mistake again."

A few months later Doug found himself in another difficult situation which required cool thinking. He was changing valves on a blow-out preventer at 325 feet off the coast of Sumatra, working hard hat and with mixed gas. An Indonesian worker on the drilling platform above failed to secure properly the cable on a flat sheet of steel they were unloading. The steel slipped from the cable, dropped through the platform floor, and as it plummeted to the ocean below it severed Doug's hoses. He was on the bottom without air.

"I had come down on a stage," he said. "I immediately closed down my exhaust valve and then walked back to the stage and sat down. I had to conserve air. It all depended upon whether or not the stand-by diver could reach me in time."

Standard procedure in commercial diving is to have a stand-by diver ready when anyone is working below. Doug's stand-by saw what happened and was in the water in less than a minute. He did not

Doug Tiffany in a hardhat,

wait for a stage to lower him to the bottom. Instead, he slid down the cable fastened to Doug's stage and arrived with no time to spare. Doug was losing consciousness. Three minutes had passed since the hoses were cut. The stand-by took his hose and shoved it up the sleeve into Doug's suit. When the

79

suit filled with air, they came to the surface together, sharing the air, doing their decompression stops as they did. It took two hours to reach the rig. Meanwhile, the terrified worker who dropped the steel plate had locked himself in a tool room. He knew Doug's reputation. It took two days to convince him to come out, and only hunger and thirst obliged him to open the door. For days he walked around with a heavy wrench in his hand, and when the next supply boat came around he somehow managed to get on board and sail with it.

Since 1968 after turning to commercial salvage diving, Doug has worked the ocean bottoms around Singapore, Indonesia, India, Bangladesh, the Philippines, Burma and Thailand. Three years ago he bought a ketch in Hong Kong and he now seeks excitement with his own diving equipment and compressor aboard. Like so many other salvage divers in his field, he has turned to marine archaeology as an avocation. "There's no limit to what the ocean floors of Southeast Asia might hide," he insists.

How correct is Doug Tiffany? Are there no limits? What's really down there?

The truth is no one knows for certain, but current thinking is that there is far more than anyone realized. The millions of dollars oil companies spend on research and exploration have done little to advance marine archaeology in the area, but have succeeded in introducing scuba to Asia. The fact that it has been so long coming is no mystery. Since scuba is such a new field, a little more than 30 years old. It began after World War II when French explorer Jacques Cousteau developed the scuba diving lung. It opened up a whole new era of under-water exploration. It meant that the ocean floors were now attainable to anyone with the price of a diving lung and a bit of adventure in his soul. It has meant that divers like Doug Tiffany can branch out on their own without the need of financial backing from large salvage companies.

Another thing that scuba has done is to expand marine archaeology and put it into the hands of the student and weekend scientist. And it has introduced another very profitable pastime which has taken on new dimensions — treasure hunting. What actually started off with Cousteau in the Mediterranean as a search for Greek and Roman amphora-laden galleys has led to the quest for sunken gold-laden Spanish vessels in the Caribbean.

Incredible discoveries in the Caribbean have been made and are not uncommon. Records show that in the waters around Florida alone, Spain lost some 281 vessels in a span of less than 150 years. And every ship lost was carrying either gold, silver or precious stones, and in some instances, all three.

As new fields of marine archaeology and discovery are constantly being broadened in the West, such work in Southeast Asia is just beginning. The most significant realization of what lies beneath the sea in this region came when sunken Chinese junks were found by Thai fishermen off the Sattahip coast in the fall of 1975. No one ever gave much thought to old Chinese wrecks. They generally carried little gold and after a few centuries silver recovered from the bottom of the sea proved worthless. But when the Thai fishermen brought up precious porcelain and valuable Ming pottery, all perfectly preserved, the world took notice.

Historians were well aware long before the Sattahip finds that China sent her junk fleets on expeditions of trade and exploration to the far reaches of Asia over a period of some 2,000 years. And now divers like Doug Tiffany are doing their home work in libraries and archives and learning long before the Portuguese arrived in Asia the Chinese were actively engaged in trade. One Chinese admiral reached Malacca with a flotilla of 62 vessels and 37,000 men. His gift to the Sultan of Malacca was the daughter of the Emperor of China and 500 hand maidens to serve her.

Thus for perhaps two centuries or more junk traffic has been coming down from China. Their rich cargoes, no doubt, were destined for the palaces of India and later for the nobles of Europe. Chinese captains followed the coasts, along the fringes of the Gulf of Siam and southward down the Malay Peninsula, around Singapore through the Malacca Strait and finally on to India. Many of them did not make it.

Another and even more menacing threat than uncharted reefs was that of pirates, and their domain were the narrow straits near Singapore and Malacca. Rather than take their chances against this formidable foe, Chinese merchants began to ship their wares across the Malay Peninsula and Indian merchantmen collected them on the other coast. As a result several trading posts built up, as described in Chinese chronicles dating back to the 7th and 8th centuries. These have become lost with time.

Doug's research has led him to Admiral D'Albuquerque, the Portuguese conqueror of Malacca. "I'll find his ship," he swears, "I'll find it." If he does, it will be one of Asia's most noteworthy discoveries.

D'Albuquerque had his eyes on Malacca, and for good reason. For centuries the port had been a rendezvous for every seafaring nation. Indians, Japanese, Chinese, Bugis, Arabs, Burmese, Siamese—they all ventured into the harbor in search of profit through trade, piracy or plunder. And each in turn left something of his own culture behind to be forged and blended into a part of the world that had never been seen before. "Malacca was the richest of all ports," Doug likes to remind his listeners, "far greater than Venice or Genoa in their time."

Then came the Portuguese under the command of D'Albuquerque. He sailed his fleet up the Malacca River, which was possible then, and laid siege to the town. The Sultan fled and Malacca was sacked.

It is here when Doug really becomes excited. "For three months, for three months, mind you," he shouts, "they loaded the Portuguese fleet with the spoils of war." And then he tells how D'Albuquerque set sail, only to watch his vessels break up in a violent storm off the east coast of Sumatra. "His losses were never recovered," Doug concludes, "nor are there records to show that anyone has ever attempted to salvage them."

The biggest difficulty for treasure divers in Southeast Asia, obviously, is locating the wrecks, even after they have been documented as lost. Survivors from a shipwreck were less than accurate in fixing positions. Even more of a problem is the fact that most vessels go down on the windward side of reefs, where their bottoms are torn out by coral. Considering that coral can grow half an inch a year, only a few years are needed for a ship, its cannons, anchor and all its cargo to lose their distinctive shapes and outlines. And wooden hulls within a few years, unless protected by sand or mud, will be eaten away by worms.

And even more destructive is the seawater itself. Chemical action between salt water and iron objects eventually converts such objects as cannon balls into pure hematite. Wrought iron merely disintegrates. Silver, unless protected, becomes silver sulfide. Copper and brass are soon encrusted with patina. Pottery or earthware becomes overgrown with oyster shells. But oddly enough, and what makes diving in Southeast Asian waters so challenging and profitable is that the early Chinese packed their precious cargoes of porcelains and pottery in unprepared rice, which, when wet, formed a permanent protective coating. A perfect vase on the market might fetch as much as US$5,000 from a dealer. Even inferior vases might bring a few hundred dollars. Considering that a recent wreck in the Gulf of Thailand yielded more than 4,000 pieces, it is no small wonder that a new era of exploration is taking shape in Southeast Asia.

Southeast Asia has known civilization in some form or another far longer than has the West or Middle East.

One major key to that history is certainly marine archaeology, and names like Doug Tiffany, Bill Mathers and Ian Chamberlain are likely to be the ones who turn that key.

Theo Meier in his studio on Bali, with his wife/model looking out the window.

Chapter 5

Theo Meier
The private world of a South Seas painter

In 1932 when Theo Meier left Switzerland as a young man and went to the South Seas to paint, he knew precisely what he wanted from life. He found what he was looking for and has never looked back since. For an outsider it is not a simple matter to understand his motives, nor him. I doubt if anyone could ever really understand the complete Theo Meier, although I thought I did after having known him for ten years. Then one night when we were drinking, and the best of friends, he came up to me and knocked a glass of brandy from my hand, and began shouting, "Not in my house. Not in my house you won't." He was like an angered bull.

Shortly before, Theo and his wife, Laiad, moved into their new house in Chiang Mai. They were quite pleased with their new place, having re-constructed it from two old-style Thai houses they purchased up North, and they invited me up from Bangkok one weekend to see it. They chose a time when there was a festival in a village nearby. It was a colourful celebration, one you do not see unless you know the villages and people who live there, and after it ended the dancers and drummers and half of the village escorted us back to Theo's and we all sang and danced along the dusty road. We had a very late dinner that night on the verandah, and when Laiad and the servants retired, Theo and I sat up talking and drinking until three in the morning. I was getting too sleepy to enjoy any more drinks and suggested we turn in.

"A nightcap," Theo said and sat up, alert. "One more Mekong and soda."

"Thanks, Theo, but I have really had enough," I replied.

"Ah," he sighed. "Maybe something else. Whisky," he said and pointed to a cabinet. "There's whisky in there. I never touch that foreign stuff. People bring it as gifts."

The cabinet contained enough alcohol to make any home bar complete—rum, brandy, scotch, sherry, rye, vodka and

gin—some of it was expensive, such as a twelve year old
Chivas Regal. Then I noticed a bottle of Benedictine.

"Just one," I agreed and took out the brandy. Theo smiled
approvingly. I carefully poured a peg of brandy into a tumbler,
reached for the Benedictine and added an equal amount to
make an after-dinner drink.

"What are you doing?" Theo shrieked, in a tone so loud
that it startled me.

"It's okay, Theo," I replied. "I'm mixing a B&B."

"You are ruining good cognac," he cried.

"No, Theo," I insisted. "It's a drink they all take in Europe
now. Even in the best restaurants."

At that instant Theo charged across the room and knocked
the glass out of my hand. It shattered against a teak railing. I
fully expected his wife to come running into the room to see
what the disturbance was. Theo continued his harangue. "I
left Europe because, because this"—he waved his arms—"I
left because you were expected to do what proper people do.
Proper! What is proper? If you say you like to drink good
cognac mixed with rubbish, then I say okay. But not to say
you drink because that is what is proper in Europe." The rage
soon passed and Theo calmed down. A moment later he quietly
asked, "What would you like?"

"Not B&B," I said and he laughed and we were friends
again.

I have seen Theo lose his temper many times before, but it
was usually over other matters. He may become annoyed when
we are in a restaurant paying top prices and the service is bad,
but he never becomes aroused with bad service if we dine in a
food stall. Once he lost his cool when a reporter misquoted
him, and another time he became absolutely furious over an
incident he remembered that happened 20 years or so before.
That was when an island mistress slashed an unfinished canvas
of a nude he was painting. "She was jealous," he said angrily.
"Not jealous because the girl was nude. All women in Bali
went around half nude in those days. No, she recognized the

look in her eyes. When she saw that painting she knew I was making love to the model." From anger his mood changed to laughter.

Most people can get along with Theo providing they do not try to read meaning into his life. Never ask him why he reacted in a certain way. Never question him about such matters. His self-styled philosophy is simple enough—he came East, found a life for himself and has made the best of it ever since, without regrets. He has succeeded as a painter. Celebrities and people in the know make tracks to his door. His paintings and sketches hang in private collections and art galleries around the world. His murals adorn a hospital, hotels and many government buildings in America and on the Continent. He has and is what any inspiring artist would like to be. Theo leads a life that gives him freedom of choice, and he is one of the few men I know living in Asia who is completely at ease in his environment. He does not have the guilty compunction that he should be somewhere else, nor does he have that regretful feeling that one day he must return home and close the ledger, as many foreigners do who live for a long time in distant lands. Theo has not "gone native" as many white men do, by cutting himself off from the world. He is very much part of both worlds, East and West. Theo has enjoyed every minute of his life. I won't venture to say why he smashed my glass that night, but I will tell something about the Theo that I knew, from what I have seen and what he has told me about his life in the South Seas and Asia.

Actually I heard about Theo Meier long before I met him. I was crewing on a schooner that was sailing to Indonesia, with a scheduled stop at Bali—that was long before the island had an international airport—and was told a Swiss artist lived there who was worth meeting. I was just beginning my writing career then and Theo seemed like good story material. When we dropped anchor I set out to find this legendary character, but I was too late, by more than a year. Theo had left Bali and moved to northern Thailand at the invitation of a Thai prince.

I was also told that Theo had taken a new wife, a Siamese girl almost 30 years his junior. He already had two wives in Bali.

It was almost ten years later that I did finally meet Theo, and I must admit, I was a bit disappointed. When I arrived at his home, which was then near Wat Suan Dork in Chiang Mai, accompanied by a mutual Swiss photographer friend, I found not an eccentric South Sea island painter with uncut hair and a mad look in his eye, but on the contrary a very sober-looking gentleman in his mid fifties. He was clean-shaven and wore knee-length shorts and a bright batik shirt. Except for the strong Shan cheroot he was smoking he could easily have passed for a Swiss banker on holiday. He was very polite, and spoke in a distinctive German accent and immediately signaled for the servant girl to bring us drinks.

"We take Mekong," he said, looking at me. I nodded approval. "Not many foreigners like Mekong," he explained. "The trouble is they don't know how to drink it." A servant appeared with a bottle which he grabbed firmly with his left hand and broke the cap by tapping it with his right elbow. " Must have soda, lots of soda, and lime, lime and ice, very important." He held up his glass. "Salute," he said, and so began our long friendship.

At that first introduction Theo and I discovered we had something very much in common. As a young man, when he first left Switzerland to paint, Theo lived in French Polynesia. Twenty-five years later, when I decided to take up writing seriously, I went to Tahiti to live. But unlike in Theo's time, when I arrived beachcombers were not permitted to stay longer than six months. So for six months I would remain in Tahiti, or a neighboring island such as Moorea or Bora Bora, and the rest of the time I would travel the Pacific in copra boats or trading schooners, sometimes as far as Asia. Other times when I was more affluent, I would voyage by Massegeries Maritimes to Marseilles and then travel overland down to Spain for a few months. It was a satisfactory arrangement, for I never had that much time in the islands to become bored.

Although Theo had lived in Polynesia some years before me, there were places and still a few people left whom we both knew. "The McCullens, remember them?" he would ask.

"Yes, of course, from Moorea," I would reply.

"No, don't tell me they are still there," he would say, slapping his side and throwing back his head in disbelief.

"Then what about Bob McKitteridge, the Scot who ran a trading store in Nuka Hiva. Did you know him?"

"He's still there," I answered, and explained that Bob was a very old man now, and blind, and spent his time sitting in front of his store spinning yarns to anyone who had the time to listen to them. Then Theo would tell me tales about an island trader of whom I had not heard.

Whenever I arrived for a visit in Chiang Mai the routine was always the same. Theo would lead me to his studio, show me his latest work, generally two dozen or so canvasses, some as high as I could reach, and we would then

Theo's Thai house in Chiang Mai.

go to the verandah and slump down into comfortable cane chairs with Mekongs and sodas and we would start again about the McCullens and the McKitteridges. We would sit and talk and discuss people we knew and all the old times in the islands, all the old gossip nobody else could understand, but it was the breath of life to Theo. We were frightfully boring to anyone but ourselves. And poor Laiad, I do believe she dreaded seeing me arrive, although her reception was always very warm.

I learned more about Theo's early years from old photographs he kept than from our conversations. He has some grand photographs, literally hundreds upon hundreds of them, stuffed in envelopes and cardboard boxes which he keeps tucked away in drawers and on shelves in his studio. Sometimes, suddenly, when he would remember a name or a face, he would rush to the studio with me in close pursuit and would start pulling down boxes and dumping the contents on the floor. For hours we would thumb through them.

Theo's photographs are not the same "snap-shots" people generally keep, the slightly out-of-focus family album stuff of birthday parties and Christmas gatherings and weddings or of pets. No, Theo's photographs were taken by him and as an artist with an eye on composition. Many were scenic shots of a Tahiti that once was. Others were of people most likely long

Two photographs of Tahitian women taken by Theo in 1932.

since gone. They all tell of Theo's extraordinary story of a reckless, happy youth in the islands; of wild and savage dancing and drums in the night; of sitting cross-legged at great feasts with roast pig and baked bananas and poi and garlands of flowers around necks and wreaths of leaves on heads like Roman Emperors; of cane chairs pulled out on the verandah and Theo working on a painting in the cool shade; of shining mountain pools beneath tumbling waterfalls and beautiful women.

And, indeed, there are Theo's women. You cannot help loving these women as Theo loved them, especially when you saw them bathing under waterfalls and strolling on empty beaches and lying upon mats in grass shacks with bamboo curtains drawn.

If photographs can tell a story, these can. There is young Theo in his various moods—arrogant, happy, belligerent, drunk, serious. He made a handsome picture, standing in his white trousers, an open shirt, a wide-brim straw hat. And usually there was a native girl or two about.

"Ah, look at her! She was lovely," he would say, holding up a photograph of a Tahitian girl. "There was not another wahine like her in all the islands." He could lose himself completely in thought until he picked up yet another photograph and quickly forgot the previous one. "Now this girl, what was her name . . . ." and so it went.

Theo was 23 years old when he left his native Switzerland and set out on a steamer for the South Seas. He packed his easel and paints, and never explained exactly why he gave up Europe, except when he smashed my glass, but he was obviously searching. Like Gauguin he was discontent with Europe. The year was 1932.

He sailed through the Panama Canal and across the Pacific to Tahiti. "During the last few days the excitement began to build up." Theo was now the poet. "There were those hot days aboard ship when the sea was so blue and the flying fish dropped like falling rain on the smooth sea. Everything seemed so beautiful, so fresh. Then came a change in the weather, in the air, in the atmosphere and in the wind that brought the smells from land. It was difficult to discover which it

Theo in linen suit and solar topee bound for the South Seas

was, partly the land, partly the vegetation, partly the very rapid way dusk fell."

Then landfall—"The mountains, like the ridges of broken glass, falling down abruptly into the sea where the ocean rolled on black sand beaches and behind them the grass houses of the natives, and finally the buildings of Papeete, low to the ground with tin roofs, and rows of copra boats and trading schooners lined up stem to, along the quay. And that smell again, copra. The sweet, sometimes nauseating, smell of copra in dirty sacks. This mingled with the scent of fresh coffee. I felt happy that somehow or other I belonged here, that this was the place for me."

And Theo did fall easily into an idyllic island life. He arrived at a time when the white man was welcomed. He was there at a time when a man could remain as long as he wished, provided he did not cross swords with the local gendarmes, and to do this one had to do something really serious, such as commit a murder or desecrate the French flag. But Theo soon found Papeete not unlike Zurich or even Marseilles.

He went to live for a time in Tauteria, at the far end of the island. He stayed in the house where Robert Louis Stevenson lived and worked. And when he grew weary of visitors—there were tourists even then— coming to see where the author wrote Treasure Island, he moved on to Moorea, an island 10 miles from Tahiti.

There are many world travelers who argue which is the most beautiful island in the world—Bora Bora or Moorea.

Theo with a friend in Tahiti.

Theo held that Moorea was the most beautiful. "Bore Bora is spectacular, but not as breathtaking as Moorea when you enter Oponohu Bay," he sighed. He remained only a short time, however. He caught the trading schooner *Marechal Foch* and sailed to the Marquesas where at last Theo found what he had been seeking, or so he believed then. Unwittingly Theo was destined to follow in the steps of Paul Gauguin. Thirty years before, the French artist had captured the essence and soul of Tahiti on canvas, and, in a real sense, Gauguin was an albatross that hung around Theo's neck; for whatever Theo accomplished, he was likened to Gauguin. Theo felt a need to reach beyond the great master, and it was by chance that he did, not immediately but years later when he went to Bali. But I am getting ahead of my story.

Theo tells a story of how the three-masted schooner *Marechal Foch* ran into a storm three days out, and so severe was it that the half-breed skipper ordered a bishop who was aboard to make ready for their last mass. Also aboard was the wine-drinking, red-eyed and unshaven Monseigneur of Atouna returning to his mission. He and Theo never saw eye to eye. "Can you not behave with your language when I am aboard?" he shouted whenever Theo cursed at the habitually drunk skipper. The feud was not to end when the schooner anchored at Atuona, because Theo took a house on the island and remained for months. The Marquesas in those years was a penal colony with exiles sent from all the surrounding islands. The prisoners could take employment during the day, but at night they were required to return to their cells. Theo made friends with local gendarmes, who confiscated the island-distilled rum and drank it at their own parties, which Theo would organize. Theo had working for him one of the most infamous prisoners on the islands, Johnny Hamoi from Samoa. One afternoon Johnny got into the rum supply Theo and the gendarmes were hoarding for their Saturday night party. When Theo resumed he found Johnny had chopped up the house with a coconut knife. Fortunately by then he had drunk himself into a stupor and the gendarmes were able to carry him back to prison.

After months of painting and debauchery in the Marquesas, Theo was perhaps wiser but certainly no richer. He would have to return to the Europe to sell his paintings and then he could return to the Marquesas. He was at the dock in Hiva Oa, negotiating with the Chinese for passage on a trading boat to Tahiti when an old man, a gardener on a Catholic mission, approached him. The man explained he was moving graves and had in his possession Paul Gauguin's tombstone. Theo, of course, wanted to see it. The old man led him to a rickety horse-drawn cart, and there wrapped in sacks was the tombstone. It was roughly cut but bore the artist name and the date he died. "But I can't buy this," Theo said.

"Then I will have to dump it into the sea. The mission has ordered a new one, and this is of no use."

Theo thought for a moment. "How much do you want?" he finally asked.

"How much do you have?"

"Five hundred francs."

"Four hundred francs then."

"But I would only have 100 left. You can't do that."

"Then you cannot have the stone of the great one."

Theo knew it was useless to argue logically with an islander and paid the old man 400 francs and when the schooner came he loaded it aboard. But when he set sail for Tahiti he felt badly about it. The stone did not belong to him. It belonged to everyone. In Papeete he knew the curator of the museum and announced that he had a contribution to make. "The tombstone of Paul Gauguin," Theo stated proudly.

"We don't want it," the curator said.

"You don't want it! Paul Gauguin's tombstone!"

"That's the tenth Gauguin grave stone I've been offered in the last few years. No, my friend, you may keep it."

Theo returned to Switzerland, without the tombstone and 400 francs poorer. But he did have 32 paintings. He arranged for a one-man exhibition and it was a sellout. Solvent again, he made plans to return to the Marquesas, but this time he travelled by ship via the Suez to Asia and intended to continue eastward across the Pacific. When he arrived in Singapore he altered his schedule to enable him to visit the Dutch East Indies, which everyone claimed to be so beautiful. He reached Bali, allowing himself a week. He remained 22 years. Bali was the Marquesas and more. Bali was Theo Meier's advantage over Gauguin.

But why Bali? What made Bali special? For a painter there was Bali's natural beauty. She rose like a myth out of a blue, blue sea. Her smoking cone-shaped volcanoes gave the island an air of mystery. Her hills and valleys were perpetually carpeted in velvet green, her forests were deep and dark, her land was always bathed in bright sunlight, important for an artist working in oils, and her temperatures were kept cool by gentle sea breezes.

And there was Bali's man-made beauty. "I could not imagine anything so beautiful," Theo recalls. Trim fields and terraced rice fields gave the island a manicured look, as if by design they were planted for their beauty alone. Theo marveled at the island's 10,000 temples, on deserted hilltops, on beaches, among tangled roots of banyan trees, on barren rocks among the coast, in the market squares, in rice fields, in cemeteries. They varied from modest family shrines to extravagant ornate monuments. He found some hidden from sight in thick forests, while others with as many as 11 superimposed pagoda-like roofs could be seen from one hillside to the next.

He began painting the moment he arrived, fast and furiously, without thought of where he would live, as though it was all a mirage, or a dream which would end when he awoke. Indeed, Bali to the impressionable young artist had a strange loveliness; here was a tropical wonderland rich with temples, where monkeys played on stone gods and  goddesses and the night air was filled with the sounds of delicate music. "And there were the Balinese," Theo whispers,

Theo found subject matter on Bali.

nodding his head, "so much like the natives of the Marquesas."

The Balinese lived in primitive simplicity, in thatched huts close to the soil. Their artifacts, for farming and household use, were the same as those their ancestors used 2,000 years ago. They went half nude and bathed naked in the streams and rivers. They were children of nature. That was one side. The other was that these same simple people had highly-refined tastes. They gathered in elaborately-carved stone buildings to worship. They dressed in silks and gold and wore garments of magnificent colours. Their music and dances were highly developed and showed great technical skill. They were a serious people steeped in a mystic religion, and unlike the unfortunate Marquesians who had lost their culture a century ago, the Balinese could not be swayed by seamen's tales or tempted by nails pulled from yardarms to make fish hooks. Theo had found his island paradise and his subject matter — the island of Bali and the Balinese.

"Bali did not have the loneliness of the South Seas," he recalls. "And the Balinese are not ones to idle their time away like the Polynesians. They were active. They would do things. And the women," — he sighed — "It was frustrating in Polynesia. You could not get a girl to pose in the nude. She would not even take her sarong off. The Balinese were only

Artist Theo Meier bathing in a pool with two young women on Bali. He went to Bali expecting to spend two weeks and spent 22 years.

too happy to undress. Painting in Bali was natural. The painter is understood." It would be wrong to portray Theo's life in Bali as all cakes and ale. On the contrary, there were some difficult years, especially in the beginning. The supplies that he needed for his trade — oils, good quality canvas, brushes — all had to come from Europe and cost money, which he did not often have. The islands then had few tourists, thus few people to buy his paintings. But nevertheless in time his name became a household word in art circles. In addition to the many Balinese artists and craftsmen, other European artists lived in Bali. There was the Belgium painter, Le Mayeur, and the Dutchman, Rudolph Bonnet, and the German artist, Walter Spies. But Theo never was close with other Europeans. "I did not come to live with the Europeans," he often said, whenever I would ask him about these people. "I lived with the Balinese and I lived as they did."

And indeed he did. When someone came looking for Theo Meier, they had to search for him, which was not always easy. I recall I had gone to visit a remote village in East Bali, long after Theo had moved to Chiang Mai, and upon arrival I was greeted by the headman. "Welcome," he said through my interpreter. "You are Swiss and you are invited."

"But I am not Swiss," I said to the girl interpreting. "Tell

Left, Theo's wife on Bali presents him with his duaghter. Right, now three years old, his daughter peeks around a pillar in his studio in East Bali.

him I'm American."

"I cannot do that," she said. "He believes that you are Swiss, for once in this village lived a Swiss artist, and he told the villages that all the good people in the world were Swiss. They believed everything the artist told them. Now I cannot tell them you are bad." Theo Meier was the artist who had lived there.

Gradually his name became associated with Bali, like Gauguin with Tahiti, and soon anyone important who came to Bali also came to see Theo. Celebrities, such as Charlie Chaplin. Photographers like Ernest Hass and Henri Carter Bresson. There was the American novelist James Michener of *Tales of the South Pacific* and *Hawaii* fame, who later, following Theo's advice, married a Japanese lady. In later years there was President Sukarno, who acquired several of Theo's paintings and had the masterpieces added to the famous "Sukarno Collection." Several of these people have remained friends. James Michener is one. Whenever Michener visits the Orient he makes a point of contacting Theo. "That old reprobate," Michener said at a reception in Bangkok when I mentioned Theo. "Where is he now? I must see him."

Prince Sandith Rangsit, left, with Theo in Chiang Mai. Sandith and Theo were friends on Bali, and Sandith invited Theo to come to Thailand to live.

The Second World War disrupted the Indonesian islands and things were never quite the same. Much of the old charm on Bali was lost. Being Swiss, Theo did not have to flee as other Europeans did, nor was he sent to a concentration camp. But he did see the Japanese command confiscate most of his paintings, which they shipped back to Japan. "They liked the nudes mostly," Theo remarked. "Anything with sex." Although 1945 ended the nightmare, the Allied Forces did not arrive in Bali until 1946. But then came the war against the Dutch and Indonesia's long and bloody social revolution.

Fifteen years had passed since Theo had been back to his native Switzerland, and he decided to return. He arrived in the summer, and at first seemed quite contented, but when winter came with its long nights and bitter cold, Theo knew well that his love remained for the warm tropical climes of the Far East. He returned to Bali but knew he could never take up his life again there as he had lived it before the War. To complicate matters, he had met Laiad when he was visiting his friend of long standing, Prince Sanidh Rangsit, who had invited him to Thailand for a visit. In Chiang Mai in the north he found a gentle peacefulness, much as he had known in Bali. He decided to make Chiang Mai his home.

Theo's new house on the Mae Ping river, some eight kilometres north of Chiang Mai, is a masterpiece. I was most anxious to see it, and when I did, I thought it a painting come to life. A few years before Theo had shown me sketches he had done. Everything was exactly as he wanted it. The floor space had to be right, as well as the ceiling height. He needed light, plenty of light, yet he wanted to be surrounded by trees. He wanted a guest house and separate cook house, plus another for servants. Had he intended to build such a place from scratch it would not have been difficult to do. But what Theo wanted was to buy old antique houses and move them to a lovely bank on the river. After months of searching he found two one-hundred-year old houses that would fit his scheme of things. The fact that one was 300 kilometres away in the Mae

Taeng District did not bother him. He had them dismantled with care, marking each timber frame before transporting them all to their new location.

The river gives the house its mood. In the early morning at dawn soft mist rises up from the water and lends a feeling of mystery to the place. In the evening Thais on the opposite bank come down to the water to bathe and you can hear their gentle laughter.

Around the house are gardens with flowering plants and patches of bamboo as in Chinese paintings. The house is unpainted teak, suspended high above ground on huge poles. Statues and carvings are everywhere, and all seem to blend with the pattern. Balinese carvings make up the eaves at the edge of the roof and lintels above the doors. Most carvings are demons, the protectors and "good" demons from the Ramayana story. It is strange indeed to be invited by Theo to stay in his guest house and to awake in the morning and momentarily forget where you are. You look up at the rafters and ceiling overhead—there are carvings everywhere. It is weird and beautiful.

The whole experience of a visit with Theo is something not easily forgotten. You are surrounded by a dream that seems

Dinner with Theo at his home in Chiang Mai was always a grand affair. He enjoyed dining and drinking with his friends, with long conversations.

unreal. It's not only the house and environment he created, it's the overpowering dominance of the man. He radiates authority and you know immediately if you say something contrary to his belief, he is not going to let you get away with it. I recall taking a Japanese photographer to visit Theo one evening. The photographer made some snap remark about painters which no one took seriously, except Theo. Ten or fifteen minutes passed when Theo got up from his chair, walked across the room, and punched the photographer in the nose. I had to get the photographer out of there before Theo smashed him with a bottle.

I arrived at Theo's house another time just as he was putting the finishing touches to three large murals which now hang in Heidelberg. In some remote way the paintings might be the reason Theo punched the Japanese photographer in the nose that night. The three murals depicted the Balinese version of how disease came to earth and how it can be cured. Theo had completed a series of similar paintings on Bali, which were confiscated by the Japanese and put aboard a ship sailing to Japan. He watched the ship bombed in the Straits and go down with his art.

But art is not Theo's only field. He is interested in music and helped his friend, Ernest Schlager, write *History of Balinese Music*. He is also a gourmet, with an amazing knowledge of herbs. A meal at Theo's is another memorable experience. You start lunch at noon and at dusk you may still be eating. Theo supervises the preparation of all the dishes himself. It might be a special raw fish, a recipe that he learned in the Marquesas. Then there is *lawar*, raw beef made with sixteen different spices. And sausages from Chiang Mai and roast duck, and there will be sweet potatoes, hearts of palm in oil, red cabbage and a salad of six greens. And in the background when you dine, there will be the soft tones of gamelon music.

Theo stands out not only as a fine artist that he is, but also as a man who has not sacrificed principle for money nor for profit. He has done what so many men have wanted to do, but which so few have ever had the courage to try. His art reflects his freedom. Theo Meier paints as he lives. He is truly the last of his kind.

Theo Meier in later years at his home in Chiang Mai in northern Thailand. His painting, a scene on Bali, adorns the wall behind him.

Chapter 6

Zeina Amara
Travels with a belly dancer

Her name was Zeina Amara. The story told was that her father was Greek, her mother Turkish and that she was born in Morocco. Her press agent billed her as an "Oriental Dancer," which is another way of saying "belly dancer." She kept her dance traditional Arabic. The costumes she wore were the same as one could see on the dancers in Cairo or Istanbul, with all the bangles and flashing sequins. Her music was Arabic, right from the Bedouins. She always insisted that the musicians play her music correctly, and each time she signed a new contract, she spent days rehearsing the band until they captured the right beat, until they could build up to the fevered pitch she desired, at which time the audience went wild. I have watched her dance in a dozen cities in Asia, where I have seen men who at the end of the performance would give their soul to have her for one night.

Zeina was beautiful. I do not mean that she had the scrubbed athletic look of the university girl with rosy cheeks. She was more like the exotic women you see in *Vogue*, somewhat savage. She had masses of thick brown hair that fell over her shoulders like a cloak. She accented her features to make her look Arabic, her nose and high cheek bones, her large eyes and brows which she painted black. She wore so much heavy jewelry that she clanged when she moved. When she smiled at a man, she could make him blush; and when she loved, she destroyed.

Zeina always gave the appearance of helplessness, and men, even women, wanted to assist her in every way. They threw themselves at opening doors before her, they carried her packages, they volunteered to drive her around. They sent cars to take her to her hotel, and cars to pick her up. She had to mention something just once, and it was done.

What people did not know about Zeina was that she was a very self reliant and capable young lady who knew precisely

Clockwise: Sri Lanka, On stage, Korea, Tahiti, Morocco, Africa, Cambodia.

what she wanted. She had a sharp business acumen, a keen nose, so to speak, for making money. Whether it was precious or semiprecious stones, paintings or antiques, she knew what and when to buy, and most important, when and where to sell. In some things she invested. She studied her markets. Her dancing, I often thought, was only a side line.

For half a dozen years Zeina reigned in Asia. She was known from Tokyo to New Delhi. Promoters liked her because she could always command a full audience. And then one day, at the height of her career, she gave it all up and went to live in America. That was the last Asia saw of her.

I first met Zeina in Panama many years ago when she was just beginning her dancing career. I doubt if she would have admitted it later, but at the time she was innocent and inexperienced. She could not have been more than twenty and was rather proud of her accomplishments. She was going to see the world.

It was only by accident that I met her. I was in Panama City to arrange a private plane to carry me across the peninsula to the San Blas Islands off the East Coast. I checked into the Colon Hotel, a tiled Spanish-type hotel with an inner courtyard. When I leaned over my balcony to look down upon the fountain in the yard, I noticed a very pretty lady sitting on the balcony below. She had her arms resting on the railing, reading *Time*. I could only see part of her face when she leaned back her head and brushed aside her long hair. Her arms were long and slender, with smooth white skin. Her nails were well manicured. She wore an abundance of heavy jewelry around both wrists and huge golden earrings. She had to be Spanish, except for her brown hair. But not all Spanish, of course, are dark like the Moors. The girl seemed to sense that eyes were watching her. After a few moments she casually looked up, saw me, smiled softly and went back to her reading.

The next afternoon she was at the desk in the lobby when I went to get my key. I introduced myself. I was relieved; she spoke English, even with an American accent. She said her name was Zeina Amara and she was a dancer in a local club.

It was too early for a drink, so we had coffee in the hotel coffee shop. I asked her about herself. She was not at all secretive in those days. It was not that she did not want to be, but she became confused and began giggling. "You don't believe me, about being born in Morocco and all that!"

"If you want me to believe you, I will."

"Okay, so I'm not from Morocco. I'm from California, the same as you."

"I admit I'm from California. What are you trying to hide?"

"Be serious! Who wants to hire a Turkish-Arabic dancer from Glendale? Now Morocco, well, that's different."

"You're not with a group then?" I asked. She nodded. "It's not an easy road, traveling alone for a girl."

"Dancing is my ticket to travel. It's quite simple. I wanted to travel so I learned to dance. If I had a good voice, I might be a singer instead." She asked for a cigarette, which I gave her, and held out a light. The smoke got into her eyes and after two puffs she stubbed it out. Over another cup of coffee and long chats during the next few days, she filled me in on her background.

Between semesters at UCLA, she spent the summer traveling in Alaska selling advertising space for a travel guide. Now that she had a taste for travel, she did not want it to end with Alaska. She longed to see the capitals of the world, exotic places like Marrakesh and Kathmandu and Pago Pago. She wanted to meet and know strange and exciting people and ride on a camel and live on a houseboat upon a mist covered lake and lay back while being serenaded in a gondola and be carried up a mountain on a sedan chair. She wanted to do all these things. She was convinced if someone, women included, wants to do something badly enough, they can make it happen. She wanted to travel and she would. She considered working for a travel office, or with an embassy, or maybe an airline. But this was not the romance she had in mind. Karachi can be just as trying and boring as Peoria if you are stuck behind a typewriter in a stuffy office all day. No, it would have to be something else.

The arts! She would become a performer. She thought about dancing. The more she thought about it, the more fascinated she became with the wild idea.

The concept was not completely alien to her. While she was a Placement Manager at Ad Employment Agency in New York, she shared a flat with a young Greek girl. Through this companionship Zeina was to find her new life, although she was unaware of it at that time. Usually after work the two girls met, went for a show or movie, and afterwards visited some Greek restaurants on the West Side. They were mostly small restaurants, with good food and authentic music. Some had live bands and hired belly dancers.

Zeina became intrigued by the music and dancing. She had never seen anything like that before, other than on television or in the movies. But this was real, alive and pulsating. Soon she picked up some of the basic steps from the dancers when they were free between shows. Sometimes they encouraged her to come up on stage. This was nothing unusual, for customers were often called up onto the stage. These people always brought laughter from the audience. But with Zeina it was different; she showed signs of talent; she had the spirit. For her the audience clapped in rhythm, and she began to like it. She felt very proud when one of the managers said, "Any time you want a job, you have one here. "

Zeina was fascinated by the unique tempo of the drums and the spinning skirts and the whirl of faces in the audience, and she thought about what the manager had said. "If I could learn to dance, to really dance, and dance well, I could work just about any place in the world," she said to herself. She began serious training as a belly dancer. Six months later she was good enough to hit the open road, and so convincing was she in her new role that many Greeks who came to the restaurant believed she was Greek, or at least Arabic. But Zeina knew she could not push her luck too far in the beginning.

She would stay away from the Middle East for a few years. She decided to start her new career in Mexico City and then travel down through Central America to Panama. After Panama she would go to South America, and later to Asia. She had it all worked out, and nothing was going to deter her from her aim. The truth is, it did come true, all of it. But there's the unpredictable that one does not take into consideration before setting one's goals. She got her wish, but she was coping with a big and mighty world.

There was not much more she had to tell in Panama. She was enthusiastic; she was filled with love for life; she was curious about everything and everyone; and she was very naive. And our lives were to cross a dozen times, with both pleasant and tragic effects.

My first big mistake in our relationship was taking her for granted. But then I never thought I would see her after Panama. She was someone who happened to be there at that time. But I was to learn that no one treats Zeina lightly.

When she heard about my trip to the San Blas Islands, she became very interested. "I've always wanted to do something like that," she said, "Can I come?"

I should have said no and made it final. I was looking forward to spending some weeks with the primitive Indians and did not want to alter my plans at this late stage. Instead what I said to Zeina was the trip would be difficult. That was like feeding fuel to a fire.

"I don't care. I want to go."

"But what about your job? I don't know when I will be back, or I may go down to South America."

"I have a week left on my contract. I won't renew it. You said it would be a week before you arranged everything."

She was determined but maybe she would change her mind. After a week anything could happen. She might even forget.

We became rather good friends in Panama, not intimate friends, but we found each other's company pleasant. The fact that I was not one of the many back-stage charleys hanging around the stage door might have had something to do with it. With me Zeina was always serious, but with others she flirted and joked, and at times was even a bit naughty. Her zealousness often got her into trouble, and then she would come running to me for help. I was to see this pattern over and over again for the next ten years. In Panama, for example, she would phone my room at 1:00 AM and in a hushed voice asked if I could come down to the club and meet her at closing time in an hour. I would dress and rush down to the club, and there she would be with all her admirers. She would immediately introduce me as her boyfriend, take hold of my arm and off we would strut.

"What did you do that for?" I asked.

"Do what?" she said innocently. She never gave me a direct answer and always managed to change the subject.

Rich playboys, and those who wanted to be, often wined and dined her lavishly until four or five in the morning, and once she brought one of the more persistent fellows back to the Colon with her. But instead of going to her room, she knocked on my door. When I opened it, she threw her arms around me and left the poor devil standing embarrassed in the hallway. I could not understand her motives unless it was some pathological desire to reign supreme over men in general. Zeina, mind you, was not any kinder with me. The night she brought the playboy to the hotel, for example, I closed the door and she threw herself on the bed. She motioned for me to sit beside her. She began talking excitedly about the night; her jewelry gave a metallic ring as she moved about on the bed; and her body radiated with the intoxicating scent of strange perfume. I could feel the veins in my neck pounding and my throat run dry. Her voice was far and distant. She spoke words that lost their meaning. Then suddenly, as though the curtain dropped and the play was over, she leaped up from the bed and went to the door. She threw me a kiss and said, "See you in the morning." She fluttered out of the room leaving the door open. I wanted to murder her.

Zeina did not forget the San Blas Island expedition. "When do we go?" she asked when her contract was nearly up. I half expected that she might have given up the idea of joining me, so I worked out a little prank with the bush pilot which would certainly make her change her mind. As I look back, it really wasn't a nice thing to do. One afternoon a few days before I was to depart I took her to the small landing strip on the outskirts of Panama City.

"You see, there are no landing fields on the San Blas Islands," I said, as the pilot dragged out a parachute and began strapping her in. "The only way we can get in is to parachute," I continued. She made no comment. "Now we have to carry all our gear with us when we jump." I took her camera bag, which she always carried, and slung it over her shoulder. "There will be other bags, of course, you understand."

She looked absolutely pathetic, standing there, and I did everything to hold back my laughter. There she stood with the brown parachute sagging down to her knees, a camera bag over her shoulder almost choking her, and a look of eagerness in her eyes. "Yes, I understand," she said. "Now, will you show me how I get the chute to open."

The pilot and I no longer laughed. We had to tell her it was a joke and she could not come. She was livid with anger. If looks could kill we would have been dead. She tore off the parachute and stormed off the field. For the next two days she did not come to my room; she no longer sat on her balcony and avoided me if she saw me in the lobby. I missed her intrusions and felt remorse, and even considered taking her with me, but then I discovered she had checked out of the hotel and flown to South America. But Zeina had her revenge. The pilot flew me across the mountainous isthmus to the islands but bad weather closed in and we could not find the landing strip. Matters went from bad to worse. We could not regain sufficient altitude to climb above the range to reach Panama City. We were overweight for the return trip. One of us had to go, and I couldn't fly the plane. I bailed out over the coast, my first and last jump, ever. Zeina was sure to hear about my misadventure from friends and I could picture her gloating over it when she opened her mail in some hotel lobby in South America.

Two years passed before we met again. I was spending the summer in Jerez de la Frontera, a small wine-producing town in Southern Spain, when the concierge brought my mail. There was a letter from Zeina Amara in Madrid.

"I would like to see you," she wrote and gave the address. There was no explanation. What did she want? How did she know I was in Jerez? What was she doing in Spain? I caught the night train to Madrid.

I had forgotten how striking she was. She was more mature now, and more sure of herself. Her hair was tied up and held by a huge comb. She looked very sophisticated, hiding behind a pair of dark glasses. When she saw me she threw her arms around my neck like we were old lovers. She was warm and flowing, and if there was any malice about the incident in Panama, she never showed it. It was pleasant being with her again. She knew from a magazine publisher in New York that I had gone to Tahiti to live and that I was in Spain for the summer. I was rather flattered that she had gone to the trouble to find me. I didn't ask but I knew after a few days she would tell me everything that I wanted to know. Something was eating away at her.

There in Madrid I came to know Zeina, and fell in love with her. I even know the place, and the moment. It was in the caves of Old Madrid. The mood of Madrid had a lot to do with it. Centuries before, notorious figures of the underworld hid out in the subterranean caverns, linked by a network of tunnels to other parts of the city. Once the caves rang with pistol shots, where today they ring with the sound of a *buleria*. Everyone becomes high and happy and claps in time to guitars and castanets. The benches are wooden and deeply carved. There are alcoves and balconies, all crammed with people. When someone orders a drink they can also order a guitar, and when they begin to strum, everyone joins in. The caves resound with singing and clapping until the madness becomes uncontrolled, and someone will leap upon a table top and stomp his heels in a spirited flamenco.

Not until much later did I see Zeina dance on stage but I did see her do a wild and frenzied flamenco in the caves of Old Madrid, and when the Spaniards were about to leap up on the table and join her, she threw herself into my arms, shouting, "I am so happy, so happy." It was after one of the abandoned nights of dancing and singing and drinking wine that she returned to my hotel with me. For three days we remained there in my room, having our meals and wine sent up, and here she poured out her soul. She was in love with someone else. She told me the story, in complete detail.

Zeina Amara had been a success in South America. Within a few months her reputation had spread. She was a new discovery from the Middle East, a dancer who had escaped from the harem of a powerful Bedouin chief. She received top billing in all the great cities, Bogota, Buenos Aires, Rio de Janeiro. She hired her own musicians, perfected her dance and learn to speak Spanish like a native. She traveled in the best circles, was dined in the best restaurants. And she fell in love with a wealthy son of an industrial family in Brazil. He was mad about her. He showered her with gifts, bought her anything she desired, and would fly a thousand miles to have dinner with her. In Rio he offered her a penthouse overlooking the bay. He wanted her to give up her work, her dancing world, and she would have servants and the latest automobiles and chauffeurs. Oh, it was tempting. He was also married. "We were together almost a year after I found out," she said, lying there with her head on my arm in a hotel in Madrid." He could never get a divorce. Nor would he let me go."

Life for Zeina in South America became hell. Her lover became possessive and had her followed everywhere she went. Finally he began putting pressure on club managers who then became reluctant to sign new contracts with her.

She was a prisoner in her own flat; she had to get away. In an Ian Fleming type scheme, her friends helped her make good an escape to New York, and then on to Madrid. "I had to talk to someone," she said, "and I knew you were in Jerez."

"But why me?" I really didn't want an answer. When we were so happy in the caves I considered asking Zeina to return with me to Tahiti. The problem was I earned barely enough money from my writing to keep myself out of the poor-house. She was well aware that I could not keep her in the style to which she had grown accustomed.

"Oh, it could be so different, if only you were rich," she said. Once again she went her way and I went mine.

Our next meeting was in Tahiti a few years later. It was a mistake. After I left Spain we corresponded. I kept it friendly, for I did not want to go through any more agonies with her and was careful of what I wrote. She was cheerful in her letters and always enclosed news clippings about herself. She was dancing in all major cities of Europe, and for a few months joined a group which toured Russia. At first she seemed happy, and then I began to note a tone of discontent. I believed she was becoming bored with Europe. She wanted a challenge. She decided to turn to the Far East. Her agent arranged a contract in Manila, and she wrote saying she could organize her flight across the Pacific to make a few days' stopover in Tahiti. Would I meet her? Not much could go wrong in three days. I cabled her in Rome.

I met Zeina at Faaa Airport at the outskirts of Papeete. She looked radiant as ever. Her dress was simple, an ankle-length Mother Hubbard she had acquired in Honolulu, and in place of her expensive jewelry she wore shell necklaces and bracelets. She still had that perpetual youthful look and the air of helplessness about her. That had not changed. A half dozen eager men carried her luggage and handbags and pushed doors open before her. When she stepped through the glass door at customs and saw me, she introduced me as her boyfriend and they quickly vanished. She may have been dressed differently but she was the same girl I had met in Panama years before.

I was quite content living in Tahiti then, before the French turned the islands into a nuclear testing ground. I had a house, where I spent six months, and the rest of the year traveled in Asia. And I was happy with a Tahitian girl who shared my reality with me. Her name was Lea.

For a long time Lea had wanted to visit her family in the neighboring Tuamotu islands, and I had finally agreed to let her go. Two days later Zeina flew in from Honolulu. The timing was perfect.

Zeina fell in love with Tahiti, and I enjoyed the three days with her. Then the next thing I knew she canceled her flight and moved it ahead a week. I didn't mind, really. It gave us another week of fun together.

Several days later she gave me the news. She had cabled Manila and requested a month's delay in her contract. Manila had agreed. " Just think," she said, throwing her arms around me, "we have another month together."

Zeina might have been happy, but what about Lea? Lea was coming back from the islands in another two weeks.

I had to think of something. Lea was an island girl, sweet and loving, but capable of splitting a coconut in two with one swing of an ax. "You should visit the other islands," I said to Zeina. "There you will find real Polynesia."

"Come with me. "

"I can't. I must write."

Zeina left on the trading boat that brought Lea back to Tahiti. And that night Lea came close to killing me.

I should have known I couldn't keep things from her, not on Tahiti where gossips travels faster than the wind. She spent the afternoon running around the town, chatting with friends, and at sunset we had drinks at Viama's and watched the sun set over Moorea. Lea usually sipped a Hinano when it was hot but now she drank a double whisky. When we left Papeete to drive home she wanted to take the wheel. She was just excited about being back, I thought. She was cautious driving through town but when we reached the open road to the west she pressed down the accelerator: at that moment I became aware that she knew about Zeina. She said two words in French, "Jamai plus—never again—and at 70 miles per hour turned the wheel and drove off the edge of a cliff.

I was conscious of the headlights reaching into the black empty night, and then like a skier landing we struck the soft talus at the base of the cliff. The impact blew the doors open, and we shot forward into an entanglement of creepers and twisted vines, which slammed the doors shut and held them firmly in place as we came to a jolting stop. A half dozen husky Tahitians swinging machetes took twenty minutes to reach us. Lea was shaken with cuts on her forehead and hands. My right arm was broken below the elbow. Doctors in the hospital in Papeete set the bone but were fearful that chips had broken off. They placed me on a plane for Los Angeles for further medical treatment.

Zeina's trading boat encountered rough seas, lost its rudder and floated idly for a week before a tug boat towed it back to Papeete. Lea was waiting for Zeina, and I understand for the next week, until Zeina left, they were seen constantly together. By the time I resumed to Papeete, Lea had run off with a French naval officer to Martinique in the West Indies. And not long afterwards I gave up living in the islands. The French were slowly turning Polynesia into an army depot, with Papeete their headquarters for the nuclear testing site in the low archipelago to the east.

I went to Singapore where some months after leaving Tahiti, I read in the newspaper about a scandal in Manila. The playboy son of a high-ranking political leader, a young man in his mid 20s and known for his antics, was charged for kicking in the door to a dancer's hotel room, whereupon a struggle ensued and he broke her arm. The irate father made an out-of-court settlement for US$10,000. The girl, the report said, was Zeina Amara, an Oriental dancer from Morocco. First my arm in Tahiti, now hers in the Philippines. I couldn't resist the temptation of sending her a cable.

When I met Zeina again, she was the last person on earth I ever expected to see. But I must explain from the beginning the strange circumstances that brought us together.

As long as I can remember, I had wanted to explore the northern reaches of Afghanistan, along the route that Marco Polo followed 700 years ago from Persia to the Pamirs. In The Travels of Marco Polo, I had read the author's description of Balbaar, founded by Darius in the third century. And there was Murghab on the Soviet border and Mazar-i-Sharif, the terminus of the great camel caravan route. Farther to the north was the mighty Hindu Kush mountain range, marking the narrow corridor where the borders of Afghanistan, Pakistan, Kashmir, China and the USSR met. I wanted to see it all and set my plans. I outfitted a sturdy four-wheel-drive vehicle and loaded it with fuel and food. My companion for the ¡journey was an Englishman I found hitchhiking across the Persian desert. He could not drive but he could keep me amused for hours with great sea tales.

Not far from Herat in the west, the road ended, and for nearly 800 miles we had to follow caravan routes to reach the Hindu Kush. We crossed the floor of great valleys where the dust was axle deep and nomad tents stretched as far as the eye could see. When we attempted to approach these camps women sent their dogs after us and kids pelted us with stones. Some days when dusk fell we had to drive into the night, as hungry wolves followed us along the ridges above. In one village while we slept our food chest was stolen, and we had to rely on buying whatever food we could find. There were lean pickings. Cholera struck northern Afghanistan that spring, and village after village was evacuated.

News of the epidemic reached the world, with reports of thousands dying in the north. When I failed to make contact in Kabul after two weeks, it was feared that I was lost or a victim of cholera. My obituary ran in the *New York Times*, and several newspapers around the world printed the story from the wire service. The report said that there was still hope and a rescue party was about to leave in search of me near the Hindu Kush. Zeina was in Singapore when she read the news. She was on the next flight to Kabul, and somehow she managed to be aboard the first vehicle that set out to find me.

Our hope in the north was to reach Mazar-i-Sharif, but when we arrived at the gates we could not enter without proper medical clearance. We managed to cross the Hindu Kush, and with luck found a partially-built Russian road that led to Pul-i-Khumri. From there it was desert track again. It took all my failing strength to hold myself behind the wheel and to keep from falling out. I had to tie myself in. And when I looked at my English companion, I wondered if he would survive. His face was burnt from the sun and caked with dust, and his lips deeply cracked and bleeding. He no longer had witty stories to tell. Then in the distance, I saw a thin line of dust. A vehicle was coming our way! I began to imagine things. I even thought I saw people waving. I stopped the jeep and tried to step out, but I forgot I was tied in. I fumbled with the knots. The approaching vehicle stopped a few yards away. At that moment I passed beyond dreams, beyond feelings and emotions. I was beyond life itself. I was in another place, another world. World? Coming towards me, through swirling clouds of dust, was a beautiful creature in white. She had to be an angel. Her arms were outstretched and she called to me—"Steve, Steve." It was Zeina.

We moved into the Kabul Hotel where I recovered. After we left Afghanistan we toured India, Pakistan and up to Nepal by jeep. We spent three months on the road. Zeina usually picked up work in the big cities along our route. She did it mostly for a lark, for the excitement, for she did not need the money. The contract was usually for three or four days. It was at the Kabul Nandary where I first saw her dance professionally on the stage. The Nandary was full to capacity, without even the barest standing room. The lights dimmed slowly until the auditorium was black. The crowd settled down. Slowly, ever slowly, a drum began to beat in the magic of total darkness. It increased in tempo, very quickly, and stopped abruptly on a solid beat. A dim, orange light above the platform cut like a dagger into the darkness to reveal, like a tigress ready to strike, lovely Zeina, motionless and waiting, with heavily-painted eyes and masses of hair tumbling wildly over her shoulders. She dropped a hand and a drum began. Another drummer joined in, and another, and still another. The sound became deafening and the mood frenzied. It was wild and savage and beautiful. And that night Zeina danced again, for me alone in our hotel room at the Kabul.

Traveling with Zeina was an adventure that knew no bounds. Something was always happening. Her years on the road as a dancer did not jaundice her spirit or her love for travel. Everything interested her, nothing escaped her eyes, and her curiosity and disregard for convention was forever getting us into trouble. "You must listen to me!" I would rant, and she would say, "Yes, dear," and do what she pleased. I remembered warning her about the Tahitians, that one did not lead a Tahitian man on like one would a Latin and then turn a cold shoulder. One night we were with friends in Quinn's Tahitian Hut when the place was really unhinged. The

Zeina on elephant back, Thailand, and Angkor in Cambodia.

bamboo walls pulsated and the wooden floor swayed with the rhythm of the music. It was wild. Suddenly a lithe Tahitian vahine did a sexy tamure dance, while everyone clapped and shouted. When the dance finished Zeina appeared in the circle. The crowd went mad, and she pulled a huge, half-drunk Tahitian sailor from the crowd to dance with her. It was the highlight of the evening. When Zeina finally stopped, the Tahitian did not want to stop. A small riot started, and I almost got my head cracked trying to drag Zeina out of Quinn's.

It was somewhat more serious when we left Kabul in my jeep. We set out early in the morning and by late afternoon had crossed the Khyber Pass and were in Pakistan. We were only a few miles into the country when we came to a fresh-water spring. At a water catchment nearby, several women in bright nomad dress were washing clothes. We were low on water and I decided to fill our canteens. I warned Zeina not to mingle with the women. But as I was filling the canteens I looked and there she was sitting with them, chatting in sign language. Almost immediately a man came running across the field. When he stopped to pick up a stone, I could see rage in his eyes.

He rushed to me, knocked the canteen out of my hands, and turned on Zeina, grabbing her by the arm, snapping her to her feet. He drew back a hand to strike her with a stone. I leaped and caught his arm as it came down and knocked him to the ground, breaking his grip on Zeina, who ran back to the jeep. I followed in close pursuit, for now a half a dozen other men appeared and all began to hurl stones. One or two slammed against the side of the jeep as we sped away.

Zeina did not do things deliberately to get us into trouble. It was mostly through her innocence, like the time we were in Durbar Square in Kathmandu. We parked the jeep where street vendors sold various fruit. Zeina never could resist sampling local fruit wherever she went, and in Durbar she filled a paper sack with a dozen varieties. Nor could she resist animals. She loves them all, and at the risk of her own safety she always stopped to pet strange dogs, monkeys, goats, cows and even an elephant once. She would never heed my warnings. As we were walking across the courtyard in Durbar, she threw the peelings of the fruits she was eating to several goats that followed her, stopping now and then to pet one. On to the scene came a big bull, as mean as any I have seen including in the plazas de toros of Spain and Mexico. The bull sniffed the air, and when he saw the goats having a feast he came forth like a locomotive. Everyone rushed out of the way, except Zeina. "Oh, look at the nice cow," she said and fed him a banana peel. I expected her to be tossed and trampled but she wasn't. The bull kept sniffing at the bag she carried, moving closer and closer. Finally it was obvious that he was not going to settle for more peelings. He wanted the bag and everything in it.

Zeina, somewhat concerned, now sidled back to the parked jeep and squeezed into the front seat, thinking it might deter the bull. Not him. He pushed his nose in after her, and she hastily slid across the seat. But the bull kept coming, pushing his whole body into the jeep. Zeina leaped out through the other door and into the street. The bull was really angered now, and with Zeina still clutching the bag slowly backing away, the bull kept after her, pushing the vehicle like a small Tinker toy. The jeep was well on its way to being demolished, and it might have been if it were not for two porters from the highlands — certainly not Hindu — who dropped their loads and beat the beast off with sticks.

"And where were you?" Zeina demanded angrily when it was over.

"Watching!"

"Why didn't you do something?"

"I was laughing too hard." She did not speak to me until that night, and she still did not learn.

Zeina's vocation was dancing; Her avocation was gems and antiques. She became an expert on both. Her dealings were profitable. After years of traveling around Asia, she knew where to find the best buys and more important where to sell.

She knew, for example, with the war escalating in Vietnam and more service men coming to Asia, GIs would be in the market to buy gifts for girlfriends and families back home. Precious stones were included. But they would not want large expensive stones. In Ceylon and Burma she bought small rubies and sapphires and sold them to the stores in Bangkok and Hong Kong, the two main R&R centres for servicemen on leave. She knew a bargain when she saw one. I remember in Kathmandu we were rummaging around in an old shop, and I asked the keeper to look in some of the boxes he kept on the shelves. From one he pulled out an old necklace. It was a grotesque-looking thing. It had large animal teeth, bits of straggly hair, and some very fake, warped pearls separating the teeth. "Ten dollars," the keeper said, or what was the equivalent to $10 in rupees. An outrageous price, I thought. Zeina paid him the money, which annoyed me very much. I did not mind her buying it, but I hated to see her taken. Many months later when I saw her in Singapore she informed me that a dealer had offered her $500 for the necklace, and she refused. The pearls were real.

In Kathmandu I had an offer from the royal family to buy my jeep, which I accepted. The price was good, but I had to take the cash in Nepalese rupees. "Never mind," Zeina said. "You can buy gems and make a profit."

"I don't know anything about gems," I said. She offered to teach me.

I was not a good student, being more interested in Gurkha knives and tiger skins and wild boars' teeth than in gems, and in the end Zeina borrowed the rupees. She spent them on gems and antiques and things like prayer wheels which were inexpensive then. These she shipped to Singapore. I was convinced the money was wasted. She quadrupled the investment.

After our Indian venture, Zeina went off to Japan for six months, and for the next two years she performed in most of the capitals of Asia. Sometimes I met her and we spent days and weeks together. I have some fine memories of those times. Imagine travelling to Angkor Wat with a belly dancer. Picture cycling with her side by side down a jungle path that leads to those splendid ruins and there is not another soul for miles. And suddenly great temples appear, and bridges of stone, and soon an entire city in ruins, eroded, eaten by jungle. The beauty becomes overpowering. And among these ruins, Zeina danced, wild and savage, and for me alone.

We discovered similar beauty at the Taj in Agra, and on river steamers on the Ganges. We rode by elephant back during the day in the Kazaranga Game Reserve in Assam, and slept by night under a mosquito net listening to the strange and fascinating sounds of an untelling jungle. We rented a houseboat in Kashmir and lived in a sleepy village in Bali. And always after some time together, we parted.

Nothing, not Angkor Wat, nor the Taj, nor the Chao Phraya nor the Ganges, not a thing is permanent. And so changes in people's relationships do come, and most often unnoticed. I knew that it had ended when one day Zeina said, "How long do you intend to travel?"

"How long? How long? Forever."

"But don't you want to have a house, somewhere you can call home?"

"No," I heard myself saying, knowing it wasn't true, but I did not want it all to end. It wasn't what Zeina wanted to hear.

When we were apart, both Zeina and I lived our own lives. Her private world became closed to me, not like it was in Spain when she revealed everything. Things were too deep and meaningful to her now. In me she saw her escape, but not her life. She seemed to be happy and content, and was filled with zest and enthusiasm. And why not? She had everything she wanted, a career she could handle, money, adventure, travel. When things became boring, she made a change. Her one mistake was believing that I would always be there waiting, that I would welcome her back.

I had not heard from her in three or four months, not a

message, not a card, when a reporter, Jim Mathews, came in from Vietnam and told me she was dancing there. "She's making quite a splash," he said.

Soon the rest of the world beckoned and Zeina Amara left Asia. Word of her escapades drifted back, as did an occasional letter or postcard from her. That was all.

Capt. L.T. Firbanks, San Browne's Cavalry, rests while on a wild boar hunt in India in 1925. He apologized for not wearing his hat in the photograph

Chapter 7

Colonel Firbanks
A tale from the British Raj

A motor trip that I really enjoy is the drive down the Malay Peninsula from Penang to Singapore. I like to do it at a leisurely pace, stopping in small villages for lunch, spending nights in cool mountain retreats like Maxwell Hill or Cameron Highlands or perhaps putting up in old English-style resthouses in Malacca or on Pangkor Island.

Not having made the trip for a few years, I made plans to do the drive again. I decided to fly this time from Bangkok to Penang and there rent a car and drive to Singapore. I was packed and on my way to Don Muang Airport in Bangkok when a friend whom I have known many years, Roy Howard, handed me a book to read on the plane. It was a paperback, *Plain Tales from the Raj*. Roy is English, an expat who has lived many years in Asia. He had nothing but praise for the book.

"You've got to read it," he insisted. "You won't be able to put it down."

He was right. I wasn't able to put it down, which was unfortunate, not that I read the book but that I waited until I was in Penang to begin it. I was in the AVIS Car Rental office at the E&O Hotel and while the pretty Malay girl was having trouble locating a car, I opened up the book. I was hooked from the first page, and I wasn't able to enjoy my motor trip for the next few days. All day long I couldn't wait until I checked into a hotel at night to continue reading. I thought about the book all day.

Maybe it was the setting of *Plain Tales* that most fascinated me, the very countryside through which I was driving. Or perhaps it was the people who made up the stories. *Plain Tales* was taken from taped interviews of some 60 British Raj, all survivors of the British colonial period in India and Southeast Asia. These old Asian hands spoke poignantly about their lifestyles that have long since disappeared. They talked about their coming to Asia, and what it was like back then. They talked about how they lived and worked, and they told how they played. The book was filled with wonderful photographs, pictures that evoked all kinds of romantic images: Sam Browne's Cavalry at Rawalpindi, British troops on the Grand Trunk Road, Lord Wellington standing over a tiger he shot, and many more. I must admit, although I was anxious every night to begin reading where I left off, I did enjoy my motor trip much more after reading the book. The resthouses where I stayed were remnants from the British past, and I was reliving the past. When I had a stingah in the Tudor-style Selangor Club in Kuala Lumpur, I was in another era. All I needed was a solar topee to make it complete.

A few weeks later I was invited to lunch at the home of Captain Don McGuigan, a chief pilot with the Singapore Airlines. Don has been flying for the airlines for more than 20 years, and having spent all that time living in Singapore, he knows the local scene quite well. After the meal we sat back and in the conversation that followed I began telling him about *Plain Tales*. Before I got beyond mentioning the title he stopped me. "You really liked it?" he asked. When I assured him that I did, he quietly got up and walked over to the phone. He made a call. It sounded like someone he knew well. He hung up the phone and then asked me to follow him.

Don and his wife live in Crescent Flats on Meyer Road, one of the older colonial districts in Katong. We went a few doors away and there we stopped at an apartment on the ground floor. Don knocked and presently the door opened. An elderly gentleman stood there, tall, slender, distinguished. He wore shorts, knee-length, his shirt open at the neck, sleeves rolled up. When he spoke, it was with a definite British accent: "How good of you to come, old chap." Don made the introductions: Colonel Firbanks, retired. Then Don added, "It's Colonel Firbanks here whose photograph you saw in *Plain Tales*."

What a great introduction. To be so wrapped up in a book and then to meet one of the characters in the flesh. I remembered the photograph, and now Colonel Firbanks pointed out the original one, framed and hanging on the wall of his apartment. "I loaned it to Charles Allen for the book," he said. It was a photograph of a handsome young officer in full dress uniform of the Sam Browne's Cavalry. Colonel L.T. Firbanks, from out of the pages of Kipling, was alive, well, and living in Singapore.

That first meeting was several years ago, and since then I have come to know Banks—the name we call him but not to his face—on fair terms. One of my great pleasures when I'm in Singapore is to call upon him, and then lose myself in an afternoon of reminiscing, or rather, listening to Banks reminisce. He's a marvelous story-teller. Sitting at his flat by the sea, with framed photographs and prints on the walls, the mood is set. The high ceiling fans buzz overhead, and his wife—a grand Asian lady—pours tea, and as you listen you find yourself slipping back into time.

Listening to Banks talk, of course, is much better than reading *Plain Tales,* for the man who tells the tales now is an officer who actually served in colonial India, a man who remembers every lasting detail with absolute clarity, almost as though that morning he stepped down from his polo pony and he is now relating not what happened years or decades ago but that very morning. You are in India in the 20's.

Banks first went to India with a cavalry regiment as a young lieutenant in 1922. He saw action on the northwest frontier, fought in the Burma campaign in World War II and was military advisor during the post war years. When he retired he settled in Singapore rather than return to England. He's been in Asia some 60 years. He has seen many, unexpected, changes during that time.

"Many chaps thought soldiering in India was dull," Banks said, "but it was not." He pronounces India as Injah, "There was much to do, with always something exciting happening."

Banks admits like everyone else in India in the 1920's, he never foresaw the coming world war. "No one did. Injah would go on as it was, forever."

India when Banks arrived was a country divided into many small independent states each under a Maharaja. They had their own government and military force. Some states were very powerful and extremely wealthy. The Maharaja or Nizarn of Hyderabad was in fact reputed to be the richest man in the world. There's a story about the Nizarn hiring an expert to appraise his jewels, and after the man had been at the job for a few weeks the Nizarn called him in and asked how long it would take him.

When the man announced that he needed at least six months, the Nizarn fired him. It was costing too much money. Records show that his negotiable wealth alone, that is, jewels, precious stones and banks notes, was estimated to be two billion dollars.

Each individual state had a separate treaty with the government in New Delhi and it was here that the British played an important role. The British sent advisors to the states. Lieutenant L.T. Firbanks' first duty when he arrived in India was military advisor to one of these powerful Maharajas.

"It was great fun," he recalls. "We had a marvelous time. It seems we were always inspecting forces or were on parade. You went with your own charger, groomed to perfection."

When you talk to Banks, after a short while you discover he had a great love for horses. He can explain in detail how to cinch up a saddle or what is the proper way to hold the reins while driving two teams of horses. "It was a costly affair maintaining horses," he explained. "We had to feed them grain, and the grain had to be shipped in from Australia. Newcomers to India always remarked how well-trimmed the countryside was. What they didn't know was that it was an army of stable hands that went out and cut grass for the horses. You usually kept two cutters on your payroll, and when you could afford it, you had more than one charger. In India we lived horses. We rode them on parade and when that was over, we played polo."

"What happened if you didn't play polo?" I made the mistake of asking.

"Good lord, man, everyone played polo!" he exclaimed. "Two things you did. You played polo and you hunted."

In Colonel Firbanks' day, every young officer was expected to bag at least one tiger. Banks emphasized when you hunted with a royal prince and he set you up for a shot at a tiger, you weren't supposed to miss. Banks begins to chuckle now as he tells the story.

"As a young officer, when you were with the Viceroy and you were after a tiger, he made sure you didn't lose face by missing your shot. When you took aim and fired, shots rang out on both sides of you. 'Good shot,' he would yell to you. 'You got him!' When you went up to the tiger, he had half a dozen holes in him, but no one said anything."

Banks also pointed out that tiger hunting could be dangerous. "I knew three officers who died hunting tigers. If you wounded a tiger you were expected to go into the bush after him. I remember one case in particular. Two chaps, both friends of mine, went tiger hunting. It was Sunday, mid-day, when they wounded a tiger. They had to go into the bush after him. But they made a mistake. You should wait, a couple hours at least. Overnight is best. With time the tiger becomes weakened from the loss of blood. But these two chaps were on parade the next morning and had to get back. So they went in. They spread out, about 20 yards apart. The tiger was waiting, and when they came in range, he charged at one of them. The man fell to his knees and fired. He missed and the tiger jumped completely over him, but he then turned and attacked before my friend could fire again. The tiger started mauling him, sinking his teeth into his shoulder. The other officer ran up and shot the tiger dead. He managed to get his wounded companion to the hospital but the unfortunate chap died on the operating table. A week later another chap in the 17th Rifles was killed by a panther. Would you believe, a panther. Indeed, hunting in Injah could be dangerous."

As I spent many afternoons talking to Banks I began to realize how our ideas and concepts can change drastically from one generation to another. We can't even imagine hunting for a tiger today but not so many years ago it was not only accepted but envied. I grew up when boys my own age idolized Ernest Hemingway, not because he was a noted writer but for what he stood for.

Ernest Hemingway was macho, a soldier, boxer, bull fight aficionado, hard drinker, big game hunter. "It was good to know you hunted hard and that you killed clean and the brandy you drank afterwards burned going down and that was good too"—or something like that.

As kids we all wanted to be like Ernest Hemingway and Colonel Firbanks, big game hunters, and we all talked about which was the most dangerous game. Elephant? Tiger? Lion? Rhino? It was none of these we heard. The opinion of the professional big game hunters was that the most dangerous big game was the cape buffalo. When a buffalo started his charge, nothing could stop him, or cause him to flinch or to veer off. Either you killed him and killed him instantly or you never pulled another, trigger. I asked Banks about this.

"That's not so," he said when I mentioned the dangers of hunting for cape buffalo. "No, don't you believe it," he continued with a hearty laugh. "The cape buffalo is dangerous, certainly, there's no question about it; but there's a much more dangerous hunting sport than that!" I thought he was going to say tiger hunting but he didn't. "And that is pig sticking!"

"Pig sticking!" I exclaimed, somewhat confused.

"Indeed, pig sticking. It required great skill and courage. It was only a small step from polo to pig sticking. But you trained at polo first. We played polo all year round, with the peak tournament season in cold winter. If you could afford it, you had a second or even a third pony. And when you felt competent enough, you began hunting pig from horseback."

Colonel Firbanks has a magnificent collection of paintings of the sport of pig sticking in colonial India. Many are framed and hang on the walls in his flat. Others he keeps in artists' folders tacked away in closets and drawers. When Banks walks around the room, stopping in front of each picture, he points out detail and explains the action, and makes you feel the picture is coming to life. "You see," he said, pointing to a picture of two mounted riders charging after a huge boar, "the clothing we wore was important." Riders wore riding breeches, high leather boots and solar topees. They wore long-sleeve shirts with the sleeves rolled up. Banks continued: "Take the solar topee—I believe you Yanks call them pith helmets—there was no better hat for the tropics. It's a pity. Nowadays the only people who wear them are the doorman at Raffles or a few old trishaw drivers. They are cool, comfortable and not only protect you from the sun but in the bush they ward off branches and creepers. And furthermore, they float and you can carry water in them. They make good fans. They make a great receptacle to put your watch, matches and cigarettes in when you tuck in your mosquito netting for the night. And they look good. Better than these bloody baseball caps people nowadays wear."

He now pointed to the riding breeches the riders wore. "You wouldn't dare wear these godawful things they wear today, those things they call jeans. You wore proper breeches. They weren't very good in the mountains, not in the Northwest Frontier, but you couldn't beat them anywhere else."

I followed Banks back to the comfortable stuffed chairs in the living room. His wife poured us tea. He was sitting in the room talking to me but his thoughts were far away in India. He was on a pig sticking shikar.

"There are several things that made pig sticking dangerous," he began. "The main thing was the terrain. We tried to hold pig sticking meets in cold weather, when crops had been cut and the land was fairly bare. The jungles of the India subcontinent are not at all like those of Malaysia or Thailand. The Malay jungles are the worst in the world. They're hot and steaming and overgrown. You can't run in it;

you can't even walk in it; you certainly can't ride in it. In India you can see long distances, and there was every game imaginable. We had many different kinds of hunts, known as 'shikars'—for pea-fowl, deer, partridge, duck. It was not unusual to bag several hundred ducks in one day."

Banks went on to explain that although the countryside was bare in the cold season, you couldn't always see where you were charging with your mount, and you had to go at a gallop to keep up with a wild boar.

"If your horse put a foot into a hole or hollow and stumbled," he said, "you had a problem, and that was the spear. It was dangerous because it had a heavy lead weight at its base which made it awkward handling. And there was always the likely possibility that the boar would turn on you. The first rule of pig sticking, like tiger hunting, was never to do it alone. We did it in groups of threes."

Pig-sticking shikars were weekend affairs; Banks laughed when he said they usually began on Thursday and ended on Monday. Often as many as 30 or 40 people made up the camp, wives included, although women never hunted. Officers took two horses; they rode one and lead the other. The women usually followed in motorcars. They set up camp at the edge of the jungle.

The hunt was done from horseback, each rider with his weighted, five-foot long spear in hand. The beaters, as many as a hundred, set out before dawn. The horses were groomed, some with their legs bandaged. Each rider sharpened his own spear. They adjusted the chin straps on their helmets. Again Banks stressed the point: "You never rode without your helmet, your solar topee." Then he added, "They were damn good weekends, old boy, damn good!"

Banks now stood up, with his arms extended as though he were leading his horse by the reins. "You are dismounted, all three of you," he explained, dropping the imaginary reins. "The senior officer is in charge. He gives the commands. You must be very quiet; you keep your horse still." The hum of the ceiling fan overhead seemed to fade and you are in India. Banks continued.

"The beaters have come into sight. They are spread out in a line 300 or 400 yards ahead of you, less than a hundred feet apart. Then there's a shout. Something in front of them stirs in the bush. Suddenly you'll see the boar break," Banks stands up to his full height. "The senior officer now gives the command — 'Mount!' At once you mount, and then he gives the next command, 'Ride!' and off you charge as fast as your mount will carry you. You now try to beat the other two riders. But the trick is, as you approach you have to determine whether it's a boar or a sow. If it's a sow you raise your spear over your head, which means NO GO."

I was curious and interrupted Banks. "What happens if you stick a sow?" I asked.

He gave me a look of disgust. "Good lord, man," he said, irritated, "you never did that. It was a disgrace, old chap, a real disgrace. Not only that, but you were fined 50 rupees at the club."

Banks explained that riders tried to hit the boar in the shoulder so that the kill would be instant. If they nicked him a glancing blow, the boar then might stop, turn and charge the rider. Once the charge began, the beaters withdrew to the background. Horses had to be well trained. "You always had to face the risk that once you stick the boar he will bolt, in which case you were likely to be thrown from your horse." Banks sat down in his chair again. "The only thing that would save you then was the other riders. They had to be prepared to come to your defense. When you had the lead they rode on your flanks in a position to cover you."

The fight was not over. "The worse thing that could happen," Banks continued, "was when a wounded boar went into deep cover. You had to go in after him. A wounded boar was extremely dangerous. If he charged and you couldn't get out of his way, his tusks might go right through your boot and tear the underbelly of your horse wide apart. To protect your horse as much as possible, you bandaged his legs. But one thing you never did was get off your mount. Never."

I made another mistake by asking Banks if they ever carried side arms on the hunt for protection. I remember him mentioning carrying a .45 when he was on patrol in the Khyber. But hunting and war were two different things under the Raj.

"Good, lord, my man," he protested. "You never shot him! You never, never shot him. This was the sport. You were out to kill the beast for sport, after all. You weren't out to murder him. Nor did you eat him. The coolies did, but you didn't." I was just about to ask him about dining on wild boar meat, that in some cuisines it was a delicacy, and I was glad I didn't.

Banks was back in the field. He leaped up from his chair. The fight was on again. "The most exciting thing, the most exciting moment was when you were at full gallop, coming up along side the pig and then he charged. There can be no greater thrill. This was the moment you waited for." He stood looking out across the room. "You held your spear under your arm and depended upon the pig's charge to drive the spear into his shoulder. If you didn't get the pig on the point of your spear he could do injury to both you and your horse."

Banks has a dozen anecdotes to back up his stories. He told about one instance where a rider being charged by a boar head on didn't connect with the pig right and as they passed each other, the man was carried clean out of the saddle and ended up on the ground, holding the butt of the spear with a dead pig on the other end. He tells of other cases where the rider wasn't so lucky.

The largest pig-sticking meet in India was held in the Fall each year on the flat alluvial plain of the Ganges near Meerut. Teams here came from all over the sub-continent and competed for the Kadir Cup. It wasn't only British officers who rode but Indian princes and Maharajas as well. Charles Allen describes one of these events in his book *Plain Tales from the Raj*.

"One of the sights of dawn," he wrote, "just before starting the first beat, was the regular sight of all the chaps standing around holding their spears up and sharpening the blades to razor sharpness with a small stone. Immediately when a pig broke the meet was on."

Banks will tell you that the sport of pig sticking has all but vanished from Southeast Asia. Hunting, of course, is no longer a sport for gentlemen, and perhaps, even if it were, the cost of training and maintaining polo horses for this particular sport would be too costly. All that remains is the memory.

Aside from the paintings of India's lost sport of pig sticking that hang on the walls in Colonel Firbanks' flat, there are dozens of framed photographs taken during the colonel's military service in Asia. One that always catches my attention shows mounted soldiers passing in review, and the caption beneath reads: "Governor of Rawalpindi at the races, escorted by Sam Browne's Cavalry, 12th Frontier Force, Capt. L.T. Firbanks, 2nd in command, 1931." If you ask Banks about the photograph, or any of the others that hang on the walls, he takes great pleasure in explaining them and telling his guests about India and her glorious past. Aside from tales about hunting wild boar and tiger, he can take you on a chase after Pathan bandits through the Khyber or give you a feeling for what it was like fighting in the jungles of Burma during World War II. And he can talk at length about reshaping India after the war. But best of all, Banks likes to talk about the hunt, especially pig sticking. "It was a bloody good sport, bloody good," he will tell you. Then he will smile and add, "But then maybe hunting cape buffalo was good too. I never hunted them." He'll reflect for a moment. "The truth is," he will continue, "the truth is they were all good, and they are all gone. Who ever thought that would happen? But it did, you know."

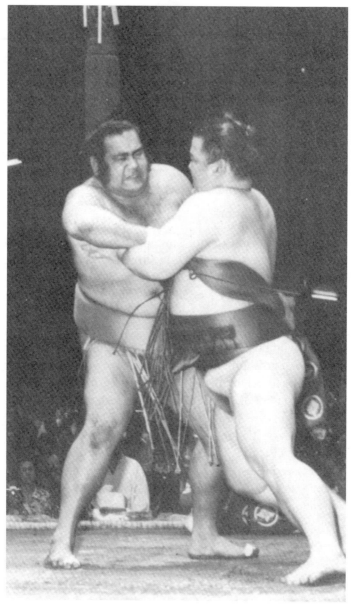

Jesse Takamiyama, he may have had a Japanese name and looked Japanese, but he was a kid from Hawaii who made a name for himself in Japan.

Chapter 8

Jesse Takamiyama
The kid from Hawaii who became a sumo wrestler

Try to imagine a sumo stadium in downtown Tokyo on tournament day. The only comparison I can think of is the blood-thrill excitement of the bullring in Madrid or Mexico City. The stadium on this day is filled to capacity, and the anxious audience awaits the arrival of the top sumo gladiators. Tension is high, enormously high. It is the final fight of the season, and the main event is the very last match. The match will be the struggle between two top wrestlers for the championship. Takamiyama is pitted against powerful Fujizakura. But to me it is more than an ordinary event. Takamiyama is non-Japanese, the first time in the sport's 1500-year history that an outsider has achieved recognition and acclaim.

Takamiyama's real name is Jesse James Kuhaulua and he's not Japanese. He's an American from Hawaii. The day before the match I went to his stable and met him, and after watching him train, I developed a great respect both for him and the game of sumo. Then just before the fight I stopped in his dressing room, so by now I was feeling the full agonies of the prefight, waiting, waiting with ten thousand others. As I looked around I noticed I was the only foreigner in our section — a stranger and foreigner among thousands of Japanese fans. Whose side were they on? The feeling I had was one of uneasiness.

The time arrived for the appearance of the gladiators. Wearing their elaborately-embroidered tunics for the opening pageantry, the champions assembled around the ring. They were introduced in turn, Jesse by his fighting name Takamiyama. The light glistened on his jet-black hair, fashioned into the traditional wrestler's topknot. They left the ring and sat themselves upon cushions in the first ranks. The first match began.

The referee, after a number of false starts, gave a signal

and two plump-bodied gladiators, near naked, locked in battle that lasted but fleeting seconds. The match was over, the prize was given, and two more contestants took their turn. Finally it was the last match. Jesse and Fujizakura entered the ring. Now the ritual began.

First they rinsed their mouths with water to purify their souls. Then they stamped their feet, often raising them sideways to the full height of their bodies, to frighten away evil spirits, and when a 350-pound man stomps it can frighten away just about anything. Then they raised their hands and held out their palms to show they were not carrying concealed weapons. Finally they scattered salt to purify the ring and insure against injury.

The entire stadium grew intensely still. Minutes before, the Japanese were pouring tea and opening bottles of beer and sake. Now all eyes were on the ring, a circle four-and-a-half metres across with no ropes or barriers. Jesse and Fujizakura took the 'get ready' position, by squatting and supporting themselves with one hand on the mat. They glared fiercely at one another. No sound. At first nothing happened. The two giants stood up to their full impressive heights, swung their arms and fumed their backs and slowly ambled back to their corners. They each took a handful of salt and tossed it into the ring. There is meaning and purpose to what they did. They were trying to psyche-out their opponent in a kind of 'cold-war' technique.

Three, four, five times they repeated the performance, but then, at the sixth, with the signal from the referee, they charged. Suddenly these two bulls of human flesh hit with a walloping force that could be heard in the streets outside. And like enraged bulls in a battle, they interlocked, pushing, tugging, purling with all their brute force and weight, gripping at one another's aprons until one subdued the other, until one forced the other or any part of him out of the ring. As suddenly as it started it was over. Jesse threw his opponent from the ring. The crowd went wild. In the next instant the frenzied Japanese fumed to face me. My cheers for Jesse froze on my lips. I thought for an instant I'd be massacred in one shattering banzai charge. The audience must have all been Fujizakura fans! Hands, thousands of hands it seemed, thrust out at me. Relief! It was not in anger but in joy. Everyone wanted to shake my hand. It was almost as though I was the hero. I'm sure had I let them, they would have picked me up and carried me triumphantly around the stadium. I felt ten feet tall. I shook their hands on Jesse's behalf. I was sorry to see the season end.

Jesse James Kuhaulua, better known in the professional sumo world as Takamiyama, or Tall-Looking Mountain, is the biggest sumo wrestler in Japan today. He is the first non-Japanese, the first *gaijin,* to achieve this position. An American from Hawaii, he is in his mid thirties, stands six feet four inches tall and weighs 370 pounds. The 'poor boy' from Hawaii came penniless to wrestle in Tokyo in 1964. He is now a veteran and a legend in his own time. He did what no one believed possible. He could not speak the language, could not eat the food, suffered terribly from the cold, and was hammered, punched and beaten until he acquired the fighting spirit of a true Japanese warrior. A dozen times he was on the point of quitting. When tears came to his eyes from the torture he received in the ring, he claimed it was sweat, and fought that much harder, as his superiors continued to whip him across the legs with a cane. But in his own room at night he would cry into his pillow. He wanted desperately to go home. He was tired of the humiliation, the fear of getting into the ring each morning. He debated with himself whether or not to give up. But he continued, alone, in the frightening world of the samurai. He wondered then, if he could possibly achieve success, and if so, would it all be worth it. There was only one way to find out.

Jesse James Walani Kuaulua was born on June 16, 1944, in Hawaii on the island of Maui. His ancestors were pure Hawaiian and he recalls his grandparents speaking nothing but Hawaiian when he went to visit them. "Many people today think that I have Japanese blood," Jesse said, "but it is not true, although I do consider it a compliment. No, I am one hundred per cent Hawaiian."

The Kuhaulua family was poor. They never knew the luxuries that most families do. When Jesse was growing up and wanted to watch television he had to go down to one of the local stores and peer through the shop window. From the very beginning he pitched in and helped support the family. The only time he had money to spend was when he saved his lunch money by not eating.

At the age of 13 he stood 6' 1" and weighed 260 pounds. He enjoyed hard work and never shied away from it, but what he enjoyed most was sports. He longed to join the track and football teams in school, but an unfortunate accident prevented him from doing so. When he was in the second grade in elementary school he ran across the street without looking. A truck hit him and sent him flying twenty-five yards. Both legs were badly injured. He spent six months in hospital and was later confined to a wheel chair. It was touch and go whether or not he would walk again. But sheer determination, especially when he saw the other children playing, made him abandon the wheel chair and force himself to walk again. But when he returned to school he was unable to keep up with the other kids. His legs tired quickly and pained him. He failed to make the junior high school softball and track-and-field team.

In his freshman year a sympathetic coach accepted him on the high school football team. Although he could not run for any real distance, he did exceptionally well as a tackle. He was then 6' 2" and weighed 280 pounds.

To strengthen his legs the coach encouraged Jesse to lift weights and practice sumo, a sport which was popular among the Japanese in Hawaii. Jesse joined the Maui Sumo Club, and during his first year of practice was picked as one of the seven men to represent the club in the inter-island tournament. His team did not win the tournament, but Jesse never lost one of his own matches.

Gradually Jesse spent more and more time at sumo and begin to enjoy the sport for its own sake. In the summer of 1961 three Japanese sumo instructors arrived in Hawaii to work with the wrestlers there and to promote understanding of sumo abroad. They staged a number of exhibitions in which young wrestlers were invited to participate. Jesse was one of them. The instructors were impressed by this 17-year-old boy from Maui. They admired his dedication and seriousness. Taken completely by surprise, Jesse was invited by them to go to Japan and take up the sport seriously. He was the only one to whom they made the offer. Jesse was elated. Having known many Japanese in Hawaii and their customs, he longed to visit Japan one day. Now here was his chance. But his mother reminded him that he had not finished school, and being the oldest son, he was needed to help support the family. Jesse was saddened but he also respected family life and traditions. He knew his obligations. The instructors left without him.

Jesse graduated from high school and began working for the Maui Pineapple Company, loading fruit cases into trucks and on trains. His interest in sumo, however, never waned. Whenever he had the time, he practiced with the club, usually once or twice a week. But at that stage never did Jesse consider taking up the sport as a profession. He enjoyed it, true, but now that he was 19 he had a job to perform. That was what he believed in February 1964. By the end of the month his whole life changed.

What Jesse did not know was that when the three Japanese instructors returned to Japan they took with them photographs of him during exhibitions. In Japan they showed the photographs to a noted sumo promoter named Takasago who was a former grand champion and head of one of the most successful schools in Japan. Two years later, in February, 1964, Takasago arrived in Hawaii with 10 top sumo wrestlers to give exhibition matches. He remembered Jesse and requested that the Maui Sumo Association permit him to participate in the exhibitions.

Jesse arrived in Honolulu and was given his first taste of tough competition. "It was like a Little Leaguer trying to strike out Willy Mays," he wrote in his autobiography *Takamiyama*. The Hawaiian wrestlers struggled hard against the pros, including Taiho, one of the greatest grand champions in sumo's long history. The irony of his story is that in the years to come Jesse fought against these men, including Taiho, and won. But now he was a green recruit slamming away with all his worth. Takasago watched the matches carefully, and with his trained eye could see that Jesse had something to offer. He had that vital quality— determination. After the first day's exhibition, Jesse was taken to meet Takasago, and without hesitation the great master invited him to Japan, on a five-year contract, all expenses paid.

As excited as he was to accept the offer, Jesse knew he had to check with his family, and he told Takasago so. Jesse returned to Maui but his mother did not welcome the news. She wanted him to stay at home and work rather than attempt a wild and uncertain career as a wrestler in distant Japan. He was the eldest son and the family needed him. It was that simple. Jesse reluctantly accepted her decision. Everyone, the Maui Sumo Club, the Association, Jesse's friends and coach pleaded with her, stating that Jesse would make something of himself. In the end she unhappily agreed to let her son go to Japan and become professional. Within a week Jesse had left his home for a new land and a life he had not imagined.

The young Hawaiian had never known winter, and the only snow he had seen was on the summit of Mauna Kea. He was unaccustomed to cold, and in February, 1964, Tokyo was in the midst of one of her worst winters. He was ushered from Tokyo Airport to his new home, an unheated wooden building where some sixty wrestlers trained and lived. His first impressions of Japan were the bitter cold and the uncomfortable life. He shivered constantly and thought he would never get used to sitting in that agonizing cross-legged position on the floor. After four days he left Tokyo to join the stable in Osaka. But instead of improving, life got worse. The real nightmare was now to begin.

The first thing Jesse had to learn was etiquette and humility. He was taught that the sprit of sumo begins and ends with etiquette. A wrestler who has slammed his opponent on to the mat will help him up, then bow when leaving the ring. This is totally unlike the hatred and disrespect fighters display in boxing.

Most people unfamiliar with sumo make the mistake of comparing it to western boxing or prize fighting. Boxers slug it out until, supposedly, the 'best man' wins. But is that a sure test? What happens when a fighter is not in his top condition the day he is scheduled to fight? It may be one of his off-days, and everyone has his off day. With sumo it is different. Six tournaments of 15-day duration each are held annually. Fans thus enjoy 90 days of their favourite sport. On all of these ninety days the 10,000-seat stadiums are filled to capacity. And many millions more — in homes, bars, hotels and restaurants — sit glued to television sets. If a wrestler has a bad streak, he can attribute it to his training. He must train harder for the next tournament.

Ranks are set by the Japanese Sumo Association in a listing called a banzuka. The banzuka is used by spectators much as a track score card. The top wrestlers, the grand champions, come first, their names printed in progressively smaller type in order of rank. An official banzuka is issued after each of the six Grand Tournaments of the year, three in Tokyo, and one each in Osaka, Nagoya and Kyushu. Promotion and demotion depend upon a wrestler's performance at each, or meet. Jesse had to start at the lowest rank of the lowest division. He had to win a series of lesser bashos before his name was even entered on the banzuka. He did incredibly well from the beginning. He won the first eight bashos easily and obtained the necessary points to be placed on the banzuka for the tournament in Tokyo the following May. But what it really meant was that his competition would now be keener, which meant work, work, and more work. For the first time he wondered if he could keep up the pace. Each promotion would mean harder training. It was never ending.

Jesse was showed no favoritism. He was treated no differently from the other low-ranking wrestlers. The climate which bothered him at first now seemed the least of his troubles.

His most difficult problem was one of communication for he could speak no Japanese. He had his ears boxed continuously for not understanding. He had to study the language constantly to save himself from beatings.

Then there was the problem of food. The meals served in the stables were nothing like those served in restaurants. Jesse found it near impossible to stomach the wrestler's basic diet. The first meal of the day was a communal lunch at 11 a.m. It was a protein-rich mixture of either meat, chicken or fish which together with vegetables was cooked in a receptacle the size of an outdoor laundry tub. The stew, if it could be described as such, was highly nourishing, especially when accompanied by a dozen bowls of rice and half that many bottles of beer. The alcoholic intake of most wrestlers is phenomenal. They consume not only vast amounts of beer but saki as well. The legends of great imbibers in the past is endless. One wrestler in his prime, now a coach, sat down at one meal and in the course of an evening drank 59 quarts of beer, almost 15 gallons. It is fairly common for a 350-pound giant to knock off ten quarts of beer with a meal.

The top wrestlers are served first in the stables. Lower ranks must wait until everyone else has had his pick of choice morsels. What is left is theirs, and it is always from the bottom of the pot. Some wrestlers buy extra food to supplement their diet, but Jesse had no money to buy anything. It took him almost a year before he became accustomed to the strong taste and smell of sumo stew. Training was not the only agony Jesse had to endure. He had daily chores that were never ending, including cooking and preparing meals, serving the senior ranks, washing stacks of dishes, pots, pans, doing the laundry, cleaning the many rooms of the stables, putting away the bedding and running never-ending errands for the higher ranks.

The real hell for Jesse, however, came during training. His legs were his weakest point, and the senior wrestlers never let him forget it. They put him through endless exercises to toughen them. The most strenuous was an exercise in which he had to sit on the floor and spread his legs as wide as possible. Ideally until they were almost perpendicular to the body. Jesse then had to lean forward and touch his chin and chest to the dirt. Unless he could come up with dirt on his chest, he was in for trouble. When he could not get his chest down far enough, two 350-pound giants sat on his shoulders. The pain was excruciating.

He had no time for himself. He awoke at 4 a.m. and was in the ring at 5 a.m. to begin exercising. The first round was to loosen up and work up a sweat. Then he went into the ring, taking on one opponent after the other, seeing who could last the longest. More exercises followed, including butting and ramming a solid pole. More ring work; lunch, then whilst senior wrestlers napped, Jesse began his chores. Back into the ring for three or four more hours' hard work. The evening meal was at five, and further chores followed. The lower ranks could not nap during the day. Not until eight or nine could Jesse lay his tired head down on a pillow.

Jesse was pushed to the limits of his endurance. Older wrestlers and the stable boss forced him to go on and on, often giving him a good whack with the end of a cane. And when they still weren't satisfied, they hit him on the back of his legs with bamboo sticks. Trainers would even spit at him and throw salt into his mouth. This was not because they disliked him, or because a gaijin was attempting to break into their time-honored sport, but to make him angry and stir up his fighting spirit. Often his legs were so painful he could scarcely walk and his body ached. And rather than let him rest, they pushed him into the ring to fight or feel the cane.

When he did anything wrong, anything, he was certain to be beaten. During his first two years he could not move without permission from the senior wrestler he was assigned to serve. But it wasn't only the top men he feared. He slept in a room with five other wrestlers, and when they went out at night, he lay there shaking, awaiting their return. He could catch hell for the slightest thing. But he never once complained and always responded with 'hai,' or yes.

Nor could he escape humiliation. Once when his stable was returning from an exhibition, he was slapped violently across the face by a senior wrestler because he failed to ask permission to sit down. He did not mind the blow as much as the shame he felt in front of other wrestlers and a crowd of well-wishers. Another time when one of the younger wrestlers mislaid a hat owned by a senior, they were marched to a school yard and in public put through rigorous exercises and beaten across their backs with boards. They carried the bruises for weeks.

Some of the scars Jesse received were permanent. He had ear trouble and asked for a few days off. Instead he was given additional training during which the other wrestlers concentrated on this ear. It was slammed so frequently he ended up with a full-blown cauliflower ear. Far more serious was the injury he received to his throat. In one match he was struck in the neck which damaged his vocal cords. Since then he has been able to speak only in whispers and often loses his voice completely. It is possible that an operation might restore his voice partly, but that would mean a year or more away from sumo. Jesse cannot afford the time.

More than once during these first two years Jesse almost quit. Once he wandered for hours around Tokyo considering his future. It never occurred to him that he had no passport— it was held by the Association—nor that he had no money. What concerned him was that he would let his friends down in Hawaii. They had supported him and believed in him. The Maui Sumo Club had all along sent him encouraging letters.

What would he say to them if he returned? To admit defeat in the ring was one thing; to quit altogether was another. He returned to the stable.

When Jesse's name was placed on the banzuka for the May tournament in Tokyo, he was given the name Takamiyama, or Tall-Looking Mountain. It was the boost his morale needed. He battered and butted his way through the next three divisions and captured the division championship. He was in the big league now. Competition was tougher. Success meant harder training. It was up to him now, and not someone bashing him with a cane to force him on.

Gradually, almost without his knowing it, after his second year Jesse became accustomed to stable life and its rigorous routine. He was beginning to enjoy his adopted country with its strange customs and ritual. But he was still an American, and as an American he was eligible for the draft. He had an exemption, which ended during the early months of his second year in sumo. Camp Zama near Tokyo called him in for classification. A two-year stint in the Army could ruin his career. Jesse flunked the physical exam. He was overweight. Three years later when the war in Vietnam was in full escalation he was called again but this time he was rejected because of the injury to his throat.

In June, 1966, the Sumo Association scheduled a good will tour and exhibition to Hawaii. As badly as Jesse wanted to go home, he now refused. He could not take the time from his training and he wanted to wait until he reached a higher rank. He did not feel that he was ready, and to select him because he was an American wasn't fair to those who were much more qualified than he was. He was adamant in this decision.

Pressure was put on him to change his mind. He stood fast, even when his supporters, the Veterans' Clubs, his high school, the Maui Sumo Club and even the governor wrote to him. Finally, the U.S. Ambassador to Japan made a personal plea to Takasago to make Jesse change his mind. He had no alternative in the end but to agree.

When he arrived in Hawaii, huge crowds fumed out to greet him. He was their returning hero. Suddenly the two years of torture, the ability to triumph over almost overwhelming odds, were worth all the effort. He was briefly united with his family, and on Maui an exhibition bout fell on his 22nd birthday. During the bout the top wrestlers decided to have some fun and began butting and knocking him around. They were quite brutal in their attempts to show that Jesse could take it. He accepted this in good humor, but the action suddenly stopped when one wrestler looked over to the front row where Jesse's mother was sitting and saw her crying. "If she had only seen what I had been through in the last two years," Jesse said later.

The Hawaii trip gave Jesse the confidence he so badly needed. When he returned to Japan he won tournaments for almost two straight years. He put everything he had into it. At last he realized there was no stopping him. If he could maintain the pace he was assured promotion into the top ranks in the Juryo or upper division.

His real break came with the New Year's basho in Tokyo. He was to fight a top-ranking wrestler for the first time. Newspaper reporters came into his dressing room to take his picture. "I knew then I had to make it," Jesse said. And he did. His name was immediately placed in the Juryo division on the banzuka. Now he was a full-fledged wrestler with a salary and with younger wrestlers assigned to serve him. Training, of course, would not cease, but no longer would he have to serve anyone else. No more would he lie awake at night, shivering, waiting for the senior wrestlers to come in drunk. And no more need he suffer the insult of being slapped in public. He was now to be called at all times by his name— Takamiyama-zeki.

Jesse was now receiving a salary but by no means did this mean he was rich. On the contrary, compared to most professional sports, the sumo wrestler's pay is poor. A top salary for a grand champion is seldom more than $20,000 a year, although in rare instances wrestlers have made more.

Rewards for the sumo wrestler are not monetary. They are the pride and prestige derived from succeeding in a survival of Japanese warrior cult. Sumo wrestlers in Japan are recognized and idolized wherever they move. They appear on television, in interviews and in advertising commercials. Their pictures stand out on posters. Their names are known everywhere. Banquets are held in their honor; wealthy business men invite them to expensive restaurants to dine, and then relish in seeing how much food they can provide their guest.

But a young wrestler needs money, especially when he enters the Juryo division. He must acquire overnight the trappings necessary to his new status. His support comes from patronage. A patron is vital. It could be an individual, a company, a club, an organization. Anyone who can support him.

Jesse was fortunate to have two patrons from the start. One was Pan Am, and the other the 442nd Veterans' Club of Hawaii. The Veterans' Club sent him the heavy, ankle-length apron made of embroidered silk, worn during the opening pageantry. At the bottom of the apron were the words "Go for Broke," the slogan of the old World War II regiment from Hawaii.

Being a foreigner in Sumoland, Jesse was always in the public eye, but when he became a Juryo his popularity spread throughout Japan. He was mobbed everywhere he went, congratulated, asked to sign autographs and given words of encouragement. For a 22-year-old country boy he had a difficult time accepting that he was one of the more famous wrestlers in the world of sumo. But he was, quite, definitely.

For a layman, or an outsider, it is most difficult to comprehend the innermost thoughts of a sumo wrestler when he faces his adversary in the ring. Often people have the impression that these grossly overweight, blimp-bodied gladiators are more figures of fun than fighters. What such people should do is go to a stable and watch them train, and they will swiftly change their minds. The dexterity they display and the speed with which they can move is incredible. Even Jesse was amazed when he went to Hawaii with a group of wrestlers who wanted to ride the surf. It was remarkable how these giant men quickly learned the sport. On a board they were as agile and quick of movement as the best experienced surfer. Sumo wrestlers may be mountains of flesh, but they have the speed and strength of fighting bulls.

What are the emotions, then, when two such men face one another in the sumo ring? Some of the most descriptive writing I have read on the subject comes from Jesse himself, in his book *Takamiyama*. He was a junior at the time, fighting in a bout against Tamanoumi, a grand champion. I will dispense with the preliminaries and commence with Jesse in the ring with a 290-pound giant. "I faced a mountain . . . sloping shoulders . . . protruding belly, and those pillars which are called thighs and legs on ordinary mortals . . . the ridges of muscles in his belly as he breathes . . . he seems invincible, a terrifying psychological advantage which he exploits to the full by gazing at me . . . I glare back . . . eyes only inches apart . . . huge mounds of muscle jut from his shoulders . . . he's mine today. I strain towards the moment when he will know it . . . the signal . . . this is it . . . I crouch down . . . I hear the crowd but sounds fade . . . we are alone . . . we lunge . . . collision . . . I jab a hand at his throat, shock from wrist to elbow, like straight-arming a boulder . . . but he is forced back . . . a thrust to my chest that is sure to hurt later . . . I thrust one more good push . . . I ram my hand under his chin forcing his body to bend like a drawn bow . . . his knees begin to bend . . . no man can stand this . . . he must fall . . . suddenly, impossibly, he spins to the right . . . I reach desperately for a grip, any grip . . . gotta regain balance . . . then I feel his forearm come down on my shoulder like a sledgehammer . . . I gasp and I'm breathing sand. The crowd roars . . . I stagger to my feet, each breath tearing at my constricted throat . . . I face my conqueror and bow . . . I long to be transported away, anywhere that is not here in front of all these people . . . as Tamanoumi bows and squats to receive the prize money I leave the ring . . . ."

Later in his dressing room Jesse learned that this particular bout lasted a total of 2.7 seconds.

The crowning glory in Jesse's career occurred on July 16, 1972, when he defeated Asahikumi and won the Emperor's Cup. That was eight years after he had arrived as a novice in Japan and after an eight-year struggle to reach the top. The reward Jesse received that day made it the most memorable of his life. The 'poor boy' from Hawaii, the 'Maw Marauder,' had against all possible odds, succeeded! When he entered the ring now he faced no growing opponent but instead the President of the Japanese Sumo Association. A bow, and then the President handed him the huge Emperor's Cup, the symbol of championship. Other prizes followed: banners, awards, more cups, congratulatory telegrams. As he was ready to leave, the tall and lanky American Ambassador to Japan, Robert Ingersoll, stepped into the ring. He had made a special trip to Nagoya to read a message from the President of the United States. Fighting back tears, Jesse stood in the middle of the ring and listened to the message. "Dear Jesse," the Ambassador read, "My personal congratulations . . . you have won the respect of your Japanese hosts . . . your performance has also won the admiration of your countrymen . . . the President of the United States."

A month later, Jesse went on a short exhibition tour to Hawaii. It exceeded his wildest expectations. The name of the Pan Am Clipper that carried him had its name changed to 'Clipper Takamiyama-go.' The day he arrived in Honolulu the Governor proclaimed it as 'Takamiyama Day.' And unbeknownst to him, Jesse found himself a state guest during his entire visit. He was welcomed by huge crowds at the airport and travelled in a motorcade to the state capital where the governor awaited him. Speeches followed. Then one reception and gala cocktail party after the other. He flew to similar gatherings on the main island of Hawaii and to his native Maui. Maui was not to be outdone by the officials in Honolulu. Their favorite son, their hero, had returned.

After three hectic days Jesse flew back to Japan, and more

training. He was now set on becoming an ozeki, the next highest rank, and second to grand champion.

Since winning the Emperor's Cup, Jesse had married a Japanese girl one-third his size, and he admits he will have to lose 100 pounds when he retires. But that will come when he can no longer maintain his status, when younger and more powerful gladiators take his place. And that day he knows will certainly come. In one tournament he failed to win the majority of his 15 matches which meant demotion. In the next tournament he was victorious and was promoted to the highest rank he has held since winning the Emperor's Cup five years previously. For the present, Jesse James Kuhaula, the Maui Marauder, still spends his time in sumo's upper ranks. He is a legend in his own time and one of the top money-makers in the sport today.

What impresses people most about Jesse is his immense size. When people see or meet him for the first time, they can hardly believe their eyes. He laughs when he thinks about flying. He is always assigned two seats. "People look anxiously at me before takeoff and then smile broadly, as if relieved, once we are air borne," he says.

What next impresses people is Jesse's mild manner. He is gentle and exceptionally polite and not the arrogant samurai he appears to be when in the arena. But the only real difficulty one has when meeting him is understanding him. He speaks in a low hoarse whisper.

Jesse has turned the handicap of being a foreigner into an asset. He is a national hero in Japan and with Japanese everywhere. And yet each time I see this giant of a man, each time I hear his name, I remember the time he was in high school in Maui and the Japanese Association invited him to Japan to become a sumo wrestler, and he had to ask his mother's per mission. The first time she refused, and he could not go. The second time, two years later, she relented. The world would have lost a great wrestler if she had not.

Chapter 9

F. Kurt Rolfes
The happy life of Tuan Kurt

All one has to do is spend ten minutes with Kurt Rolfes to become fired with his tremendous enthusiasm. It is infectious. One minute he will tell you about a fishing junket he has planned up a wild river in the central jungles of Malaysia, and the next he's talking about a forthcoming diving expedition at Pulau Aur. And in another breath he will mention something about journeying up the Rejang River to visit a longhouse in untamed Borneo or that he's trying to arrange a trip to visit Krakatau Volcano in the Java Sea. But it does not have to be adventure that captures one's interest when listening to Kurt. In a few days he's flying to Pattaya Beach south of Bangkok to photograph a bevy of bikini-clad girls for a German magazine. He's invited to spend a weekend at the Sultan's Palace in Perak; he has a story to do on the Sultan's golden Kris collection. Or perhaps if you are interested he can find you a seat on a helicopter to join him for a spin around Singapore harbor; he wants aerial shots of a new oil rig leaving a shipyard. And next month he has an assignment with an oil company in the Celebes.

For certain, Kurt Rolfes is bound to be doing something exciting and different. People who know him envy his life style. Photojournalism is his ticket to his happy life in Southeast Asia.

Kurt is often the topic of discussion among writers and journalists in Singapore. Not everyone believes that he has done everything he says he has. It could not be possible. And so the gossip starts. How many stories develop over a few beers among writers? How many rumors do they feed upon?

I remember the first time I heard his name mentioned. I was with friends, some of them journalists, at Bill Bailey's Coconut Grove in Singapore. The Grove in those days was the unofficial foreign correspondents' club. It had become rundown and seedy after Bailey died in 1965, but it did have atmosphere. Few bars still have cane chairs and ceiling fans, and there was old Bill Bailey's piano in a comer. The place has since been torn down, and replaced by a 14-story office building.

Few people went to the Grove in its declining years, other than journalists and writers. "See you at the club," they would say and there we would meet. There were four or five of us that night, exchanging views on everything from the escalating war in Vietnam to the changing skyline in Singapore. Soon we were talking about people, and Kurt was mentioned.

"You know him?" someone asked me.

"I think so," I said.

I did not know Kurt very well. I had met him about a year before, when he came from Vietnam for a few days' rest. He was not a person you could easily forget, not when he sported a 14-inch long handlebar mustache and had a pretty Chinese girl attentively hanging on his arm. He was tall, very good looking, and was always laughing. He had a nervous habit of twisting the ends of his mustache when he talked. When you stood close to Kurt, you noticed a faint scar down the right side of his face. Years later, when I asked him about it, he explained it was an automobile accident but I liked to think it was a dueling scar. It made him look very German, and very military, which he was.

I regret that we did not have more time to talk at that first meeting for I found him and his conversation rather stimulating. He returned to Vietnam the next day.

"I am certain I know him," I said at Bill Bailey's. "He's a combat photographer in Vietnam."

"No, not Kurt," another quickly replied. "He's an entertainer there. Folk singer. He has two round-eyed girls with him. American. They have an act called 'The Mustache and Us.'"

"Maybe you have someone else in mind," I said. "The Kurt I met said he was a combat photographer."

"The Kurt Rolfes I know was a photographer," a third man

said. "He was in the thick of everything. Wounded half-a-dozen times. Once a VC took a shot at him and Kurt would not be alive except his camera stopped the bullet. You know," he hesitated, "all the hell he took, I think it was just to prove himself."

"But he's German."

"American," I said. "He has an American accent. From upstate New York."

"I don't think so. He was born in a German interament camp in U.S. he told me. His father was a German officer."

"He has to be American. He came out East in the Peace Corps."

"That's not what I heard. He came on a raft."

"He what!"

"That's right. I know it's a fact. He and this old man. They built a raft and set out. It sank before they reached the Philippines and they were rescued."

"Someone said he speaks fluent Yapese. Only 4,000 people in the world know the language."

"He's a good diver. He joined us on a diving expedition to Shaman. One of his legs is chewed up. Some old scars. I asked him about it."

"What did he tell you? Sharks?"

"Nope. You'd never guess. It was a lion. I swear, he said he was maimed by a lion."

Everyone laughed. "Good old Kurt," they all chimed in, and then went on talking about someone else. I don't think anyone there really believed everything they heard about Kurt. He made a 'good story' in their minds, and that was all. It was not until later, when people got to know his work, that they no longer questioned him. He was one of the best combat photographers to come out of Vietnam.

I had a feeling after my first meeting with Kurt that I would see him again. He had indicated his intention of coming to Singapore for a long stay. He liked the town. He also liked boats, sailing boats, and he wanted to own his own. At the

Kurt F. Rolfes began his career in the Far East first as a Peace Corps volunteer in Micronesia, became a combat photographer in Vietnam, and after being shot at too many times, became an entertainer for the troops. After the war he moved to Singapore.

Kurt, top left, strums his guitar in Singapore. Top right, he gives his wife, Mae, a few pointers on taking photos. Bottom, from the jungle of Vietnam, outdoorsman Kurt enjoys a fishing trip on the Endau River in the jungle of the Malay Peninsula.

time I had plans to construct my own schooner in Singapore. "When I make my bundle," he said, "I'll be back." It was only a matter of time.

Our next meeting came quite by accident. Prince Tunku Bakar of the Johore royal family invited me and several of his friends to join him on a fishing trip up the Endau River in Malaysia. The Endau cuts a winding path through some rugged and unexplored primary jungle of the Malay Peninsula. Tigers and elephants come down to the river to drink, and in the Rompin area of the Endau there is reputed to be the last of the Sumatran rhino. And fish! The river has the best fresh water fishing in Asia. Tunku Bakar set a date and we met him at the Merdeka Hotel Restaurant in Mersing.

The Tunku and his friends were waiting when I arrived. He introduced me. Kenny Nelson was an Eurasian from Singapore. He was a professional guide for a jungle safari outfit in Johore.

Then there was Philip Liew, a scout who had gained his reputation during the Malaysian Emergency. He had incredible stories to tell about wandering tribes of Negritos in the jungles, and about seeing a prehistoric carving of a bull on a mountain top. There were half-a-dozen others there, all interesting outdoorsmen, but whose names I have since forgotten.

"We have a few minutes," the Tunku said. "We're waiting for one more person." We ordered more coffee.

Presently a blue sports car pulled into the parking lot next to the restaurant. "He's here," the Tunku said. "We go now."

I finished my coffee and when I looked up Kurt Rolfes was hurrying across the street. He still had his handlebar but it had been trimmed. He knew everyone at the table and shook hands.

"You're in from Vietnam?" I asked when we left the restaurant.

"Permanently," he said. "I'm having a ketch built in Singapore." He seemed very excited to tell me about it, but that would come later. For the moment, we had some rough traveling ahead of us.

We were two days up the Endau River when the monsoon struck late in the afternoon. It was early that year. Within a short space of time the river rose 15 feet. We could not negotiate the current and had to set up camp on the river bank. Tired and exhausted, everyone was prepared to bundle up in ponchos and await dawn. But not Kurt. "Give me a hand," he shouted above the downpour and pointed to a patch in the jungle ahead. He instantly began hacking out an area, which he covered with soft branches. He threw out a ground cloth and fashioned a lean-to overhead. Within half an hour we climbed into comfortable quarters and fell asleep listening to the rain.

We did not catch any fish on that trip; in fact, we didn't even cast a line, but Kurt and I became good friends and made many more trips into the jungle. We found any excuse to go exploring sometimes just to join our friends the Orang Asli on a fishing trip, other times to help the Malayan Nature Society in netting and classifying jungle birds. Once we outfitted an expedition to find that legendary stone carving which Philip Liew had seen on the mountain top, but within a few miles of our goal a tiger protecting her cubs chased us out of the jungle. It was the only time I saw fear in the eyes of Bujong, our Orang Asli scout. We did what came naturally. We ran. And when we reached the river bank we didn't stop there. We continued, arms and feet still moving when we landed in the river thirty feet below. Another time we had three wild elephants smash our camp, and then there was the discovery we made on the Endau which few people have ever believed. On a bank of the Endau above the Kimchin, Kurt photographed human footprints, or what looked like human prints, that measured 16 inches long. The tracks came down from the dark forest and disappeared into the river. The Orang Asli with us had an explanation; they were made by the "Orang Dalam," or the "interior people." Could their Orang Dalam be the Malaysian version of the Saskatchewan giant, commonly known as "Big Foot"? We never found the answer but we did discover that several such sightings have taken place in Malaysia over the last hundred years. Kurt was also instrumental in my organizing an expedition to search for a lost city at the bottom of Lake Chin. At the last minute he was unable to go.

On these jungle trips I got to know Kurt well. When you're in the jungle you spend a lot of time thinking, and in the evening around a comforting campfire, you give voice to your thoughts. From a jungle camp, upon a secluded sandbank far up river, civilization could be aeons away. All that exists is a log fire creating a circle of light upon dense foliage. That sphere becomes the only world you know, and all that is within it becomes intimate. And so you talk not in rumors or gossip but in truths. One tells things one would not nomally talk about. I am sure a man can say he does not believe in God, but unless he can openly deny the existence of God as he stands alone with his back against a dark brooding jungle on a black night, unless he can, then he is still a believer.

And so I came to know Kurt. And what everyone thought were rumors were really unconfirmed facts, about the internment camp, his speaking Yapese, the shipwrecked raft, the war in Vietnam as both combat photographer and entertainer, the camera that stopped the bullet, and, yes, even the lion. Kurt has lived an extraordinary life, and he is one of the few expatriates I know who intends to spend the rest of his days in Asia.

Kurt Rolfes was indeed raised in an internment camp. The place: Crystal City, Texas. His father was a German officer on a liner making a world cruise in 1939. The liner was in the Gulf of Mexico when France and England declared war on Germany. The captain immediately turned around and headed for Germany but in the Caribbean the vessel was apprehended by a British warship. Rather than surrender, the captain scuttled the liner and to escape the British, had his crew row their lifeboats to an American vessel that was standing by. The

United States at that time was neutral. The sailors were sent to San Francisco where Kurt's father met a young secretary. They fell in love and were married. Rather than go back to Germany, the ex-German officer requested political asylum, which was granted. But then came American involvement in Europe with the Japanese attack on Pearl Harbor. Nationals of both Germany and Japan living in the U.S. were sent to internment camps. Kurt was born in Forest Grove, Oregon soon after Pearl Harbor. The last three years of the war they spent in Crystal City, guarded by Texas Rangers.

After the war Kurt's father was sent back to Germany, and several years were to pass before he returned permanently to America. The united family moved to Oregon and it was there Kurt grew up.

Kurt showed a love for outdoors and an aptitude for two things early in his life. They were to play an important role in his future. The first was his flair for folk music which I will tell you about later; the second was his talent to take good photographs. He was still in high school when he started playing a guitar, and when he acquired his first camera, an 828 Kodak 'Pony,' he began taking and selling pictures.

Kurt learned fast, by accepting part-time jobs with local studios, and spending evenings and weekends handling portrait work and weddings, and learning techniques. Soon he was working as a 'stringer' for a major news agency, United Press International.

During his last year in high school the State of Oregon offered a scholarship in photography to the best high school photographer state-wide. Kurt won the contest hands-down and enrolled at the University of Munich, where he studied photography and art, design and sculpting. He later transferred to Syracuse University in upstate New York where he obtained a degree in public relations.

Somewhere between Forest Grove and Syracuse University young Kurt Rolfes fell in love with the South Seas. "I read every book I could get hold of on the Pacific," he said. "I read anything to do with the tropics. This was where I wanted to go. I knew I would get there one day, but I didn't know how. I had graduated by now and was looking for work. Then I happened to see an ad in the newspaper. It was titled 'The Peace Corps Goes To Paradise.' I read on. The Peace Corps wanted volunteers for the U.S. Trust Territory in the Marinas, Caroline and Marshall Islands. I joined immediately, not thinking about the difficulties of spending two years on a lonely coral atoll. It did not matter. I was going to the South Pacific."

The first tropical island Kurt saw was Molokai in the Hawaiian islands. He spent five months in a Peace Corps village learning the culture of the islands and how to speak Yapese. Day and night, for five months he studied an unwritten language only 4,000 people in the world know. His teachers were four Yap islanders who refused to converse in English. Kurt passed his course.

Kurt arrived at Yap island in the Carolines and loved it from the start. Here was the paradise he sought. He easily fell into the island life. Since no quarters were provided he built his own thatched house, but with a few innovations. He had an elaborate water catchment system and one of the island's few flushing toilets. He fumed enthusiastically to his job of running the radio station. It operated three hours a day. But more than anything, Kurt enjoyed the company of the Yap islanders, and he became involved in their feuds with the Palauans, their traditional enemies. He has some great stories to tell about the first fights that started between the two island groups. But then the U.S. Coast Guard arrived at Yap and sided with the Palauans who were working on the island. Kurt was soon at odds with the Americans.

After the first year Kurt became disillusioned with the Peace Corps and wanted to find a way out. He did not want to leave the islands, but if he announced he was quitting, he would be sent back to Washington. He had to find a way for them to ask him to leave. An idea came to him and he set the plan into motion. It nearly cost him his life.

It happened that on one of his frequent trips to Guam, Kurt met an old man named Frank Cushing. "He was a character," Kurt said. "When I met him I didn't believe a word he said. He said he was an ex-circus performer, a high diver, one of those nuts who dives a hundred feet into two feet of water. This was possible, of course, but when he told me that he was the only man in the world who had dived off the Brooklyn Bridge, the Golden Gate Bridge, and three or four others in America, and lived to tell the tale, well that was too much. As I said, I did not believe him, until on another trip to Guam he showed me his scrap book albums and sure enough there it was, all in print. News clippings. Magazine articles. Stories. Frank Cushing had done all he claimed. I was impressed, really impressed. And then he told me about a raft he was building. He was going to float from Guam to the Philippines. He was still an adventurer. I wished him good luck."

Back on Yap Island, sitting in the radio shack, Kurt was examining a copy of the Peace Corps regulations, when suddenly a line of print leaped out at him. "Peace Corps volunteers," it read, "are not permitted to go beyond the reef of their respective islands in any vessel not authorized by Peace Corps Headquarters." Kurt thought of Frank and his raft. If Frank would take him, the Peace Corps would have to discharge him. There was no other way. He wrote to Frank. The answer came back. Kurt was more than welcome to join the old timer on his half-mad adventure.

Kurt told no one about his plan! Any leak and the whole thing would blow up. When the raft was ready for departure, Kurt asked for a few days off and went to Guam. He moved aboard the raft.

The raft was constructed from 44-gallon oil drums and planks lashed together. There was a small cabin. The entire structure measured 22 feet. It was equipped with a radio, sextant and charts, time piece, two Johnson 40 h.p. outboards and steel drums of petrol and water, all carefully stowed aboard. News reporters and T.V. cameramen gathered around at the time of departure. Shortly, afterwards Washington was on the phone to Guam. "Who gave that Peace Corps volunteer authorization to make such a hair-brained voyage? Get him back!" It was too late. The raft had sailed.

They probably would have made it but for a freak typhoon that passed through the Philippines. They caught its tail-end, but this was almost enough to send the raft to the bottom of the sea. Their SOS reached Guam. The raft was sinking. A massive air-sea rescue was launched. The sinking raft was finally located 350 miles southwest of Guam. Dye makers were dropped and two U.S. Coast Guard cutters moved in. Sailor Frank Cushing and Kurt Rolfes were picked up from their raft, which was then put under tow, but with high seas running, it soon had to be cut adrift.

Kurt got his first wish. He was discharged from the Peace Corps, but it was not exactly the way he wanted it. He was given a one way ticket to Washington, with instructions to pickup any money due to him there. And he was broke. Unless he came up with a scheme he would be on the next plane to America.

"An idea came to me that night when I was sitting in a bar in Agana," he recalled. "A couple of Peace Corps guys came in from Ponape Island. They had two weeks leave and were heading for Hong Kong. 'Why Hong Kong?' I asked them. And they said, 'Something to do. Not much here on Guam.' I realized right there that few people knew anything about Guam. The problem was that there were no guide books, not a single one, written about the place. So I decided to write a guide book." Kurt never returned to the States.

He bought a ream of paper, folded the sheets in two and on the cover drew a map of Guam and printed the title *The Peace Corps Felt-Need Guide to Guam*. In the Peace Corps if something was considered essential, it was classified as 'felt-need.' Next morning Kurt started at one end of town and by evening had canvassed the entire business section of Agana. He sold ads, with the guarantee that every Peace Corps volunteer in the South Pacific would have a free copy of the guide. Kurt then toured the island, wrote what he thought was interesting, found a printer and published his book. Two weeks later he was $4,000 richer.

With money in his pocket Kurt explored the many islands of the Trust Territories, by tramp steamers, outriggers, schooners and cabin cruisers. After six months of frolicking around the islands he sailed to Japan and then visited Taiwan and Hong Kong. But once again he found himself becoming restless. He was slowly being drawn to the war that was raging in Vietnam. He applied for his old job as stringer with UPI, used the last of his dollars in Hong Kong buying cameras and film and departed for Saigon.

Kurt arrived in the war-torn capital in mid-1967, and found himself covering every major battle right through to the Tet offensive in February, 1968. He admits that it was largely curiosity that lured him into the battle areas. He had never been in a war, and was tired of people asking him if he had joined the Peace Corps to avoid the draft. No, Kurt wanted to see for himself what was going on. And, of course, he wanted to photograph it. It was one of the most bizarre experiences and the most tragic in his life.

Kurt remembers as a very green photographer he accompanied an NBC cameraman into a hostile area. As they approached the perimeter of the American defense, riding on the outside of a tank (with possibly a battalion of North Vietnamese Army lying in ambush) a few sniper shots rang out, and the tank commander gave the command 'Button Up,' at which time all the experienced personnel got into the cover of their troop carriers and tanks. Kurt and the movie cameraman, not knowing enough to take cover at the command, were left outside wondering what to do if they came under fire. Fortunately, the enemy pulled back and no further shots were fired.

Once outside the perimeter defenses, the tanks opened their hatches and the photographers scrambled inside. Kurt found himself crouched in a very small space alongside a 75mm gun and here he witnessed his first 'fire mission.' As the guns opened fire, the chamber filled with choking cordite fumes and as the breech slammed back and forth, barely missing him, the hot shell casings dropped straight into his lap. Kurt found himself in the archetypal cartoon situation of having to bounce the hot casings in his hands until they were cool enough to dispose of.

Kurt soon learned that survival meant knowing how to use guns. Most combat photographers learned how to use weapons and some actually carried them. On assignment he might be offered an automatic rifle, a sub-machine gun or, at most even a grenade launcher. Kurt made a point of learning to operate every type of American and enemy gun, and before long he could strip down an M-16 or a Chinese AK-47 automatic rifle like a veteran.

About a month after his arrival Kurt joined the Marines on a "search and clear" mission. Using giant Chinook helicopters, the marines would land in a selected area, clear out the resident population, and then declare the area a "free fire zone" in which they would shoot anything that moved. They were waiting for the helicopters to return one evening when it began to rain. Kurt wrapped his Leica fitted with a 300mm lens in plastic, stuffed it into his rucksack and continued shooting with two Nikonos cameras. The helicopters returned just before nightfall to lift them out of the area.

The chopper that Kurt rode was barely 100 feet in the air when there was the distinctive twang of a bullet. Everyone fell forward, and the UPI correspondent sitting next to Kurt fumed to look in astonishment at Kurt and then at a hole where Kurt had been sitting. Then came another shock. There was a second hole in the middle of Kurt's rucksack. When they landed fifteen minutes later Kurt pulled off his pack to find his telephoto lens had stopped the bullet which would have certainly put an end to his life. He was slightly wounded from flying fragments but otherwise escaped unharmed. For the next couple of weeks, he recalls, he did not pay for a single drink at the press centre.

Kurt was wounded twice more; the last time was at the battle of Hue. He was with a company of marines. "We were advancing into the town towards the Citadel," he said. "In three days we advanced only four city blocks, and of the 150 men who made the attack no more than 40 were able to walk back to the river when replacements came." Kurt caught shrapnel in his knee. "If it had not been for that last wound," he admitted, "I would probably have stayed on, and have been buried like a dozen other photographers I knew." Kurt was recovering in Danang, wondering why he was risking his neck for $10 a picture. It was true, his photographs were appearing in publications around the world but what was he trying to prove. He had been wounded three times, photographed most major battles, and seen what war was like first hand. And he didn't like what he saw. He was pondering these questions, trying to find an answer, when he went to the press centre that night for a drink. At the bar sat two very attractive American girls. They were destined to change Kurt's life.

The girls were entertainers and folk singers. They had just arrived and were looking for jobs. They had not yet registered their act. They asked Kurt what was the procedure.

"I got to thinking right there," Kurt said. "I did it in college so why not in Vietnam? We talked it over. They had their guitars. The next day I borrowed a guitar from one of the clubs and we had our first practice session. We formed a group and called ourselves 'The Mustache and Us.' Kurt had given up his camera for an electric guitar, at least for the moment. It was probably one of the wisest decisions he ever made.

Music was not new to Kurt. He had started playing guitar and singing folk songs when he was still in his teens. He had taken his guitar with him when he had gone to study in Germany, and nightly he had played in the coffee houses in Munich. Later he had put himself through Syracuse by playing and singing in college hangouts at night.

I had been to a couple of gatherings in Singapore when Kurt was there. I recall one incident where the host picked up a guitar and asked whether anyone there could play. Kurt politely replied, "I used to play a little," and took the guitar. He started playing and singing and at dawn the next morning he was still at it. He's good, with a style all his own. He had no trouble entertaining the GIs in Vietnam.

"I bought an electric guitar in Saigon," Kurt said. "We spent a couple of thousand bucks investing in amplifiers, speakers and that sort of thing. We practiced for a week and put a one-hour act together. Then we auditioned. We were accepted. We were told we could travel throughout Vietnam, make our own bookings, and could charge $400 per show. Our first night was in the Delta. They had not had a show there in six months. They were starving for entertainment. We did five shows that night. From then on it was all fun. We had a ball."

At the height of the war in Vietnam, entertainers could make a fortune within a few months. But the work was hard, night after night, and required constant moves from one camp to next. Sometimes they would travel through the night, and find, on arrival, half their equipment missing. They would then have to improvise. In the year that Kurt and his two female companions did the circuit, they travelled by C-47 transport plane, tank, minesweeper, helicopter, truck, jeep, by any means there was available. They covered the war zones from the Delta to the DMZ. Kurt made his bundle. He bid the girls goodbye, packed his gear and hopped a plane to Singapore. He had $40,000 in his pocket.

Kurt was on top of the world when he arrived. He had enough money to rent a furnished flat and set up a studio which would enable him to get back into creative photography. He could pick the photographic assignments now which he most enjoyed. And most important, Kurt could have his sailing boat built in Singapore. He found a shipbuilding yard, run by an Englishman, went over the plans and handed over $30,000 to complete the boat. He did not want to be tempted by so much money sitting idle in the bank. And whilst the ketch was being built, Kurt found pleasures in Singapore and Malaysia to the north. This was the period when I got to know Kurt Rolfes better.

Then suddenly, overnight Kurt lost everything. I was away from Singapore when I heard the news. I did not know all the details, but I understood that the yard had gone bankrupt. When I returned to Singapore I immediately called Kurt. He was excited to hear my voice and said, "Let's have dinner. I have something to tell you."

Kurt came to the restaurant smiling and waving, and on his arm was a very attractive Chinese girl. He introduced her as Mei. "We're going to get married," he said happily as a child on Christmas morning.

He didn't mention his bad luck with the ketch, and I had to bring it up. "I was sorry to hear what happened," I said.

"What happened?" he asked.

"Your ketch. I mean the shipyard doing bust."

"Oh that. Never mind. It's water under the bridge. I have something else going," he said and began telling me about the new assignment he had accepted. He would make his bundle back. Eventually he did.

One of the most interesting assignments Kurt took on was the comprehensive coverage of an Indonesian oilfield from geological and geophysical surveys to drilling operations. The assignment lasted a year and involved periodic visits to the sites, sites which included virgin jungle to offshore rigs. He spent four or five days a month shooting both stills and movies, each time making a five-hour flight over the dense jungles of Borneo, jungles so dense they could engulf, without trace, any helicopter unfortunate enough to crash. The trees here create an unbroken pall of foliage 200-300 feet high and provide cover for primitive headhunters and home of many venomous creatures. It was like being back in Vietnam, but of course, headhunters' darts from blowpipes were no match for the North Vietnamese arsenal. But nonetheless, it brought to

Kurt the excitement and challenge upon which he thrives. He needs a spell of wild adventure to enjoy the contrasts of the comparatively quiet life he leads in Singapore.

Kurt is married to Mei, the Chinese girl I mentioned and they have two children, Jacquie and Raoul. He owns his own penthouse on the 20th floor of an apartment building over looking the city. He surrounds himself with friends, people he enjoys being with. They vary from anthropologists and jungle trackers to roughnecks from the oil rigs. He is a legend in his own time.

Kurt reminds me of a cartoon I once saw of a white man sitting on the verandah of his palm-thatched house in the tropics. In the background two dusky maidens are carrying bowls of fruit. A reporter is interviewing him. The man is talking, and the caption reads: "I came out here to write, and now everyone is coming out here to write about me." This could well be Kurt. In a few years people will be coming to the East with instructions to stop and see Kurt in Singapore. "You have not seen Singapore until you're seen Kurt," they will say.

There remains one story about Kurt's past that I haven't told. It's about the lion that nearly chewed his leg off. Did it really happen?

"It was this way," Kurt will tell you. "I met Tarzan, you see, and he had this pet lion . . . ."

It's true. There was a man who legally changed his name to Tarzan, and he had a pet lion. In fact he had quite a few pet lions. He was a lion tamer at a miniature Disneyland called 'The Enchanted Forest' in up-state New York. Every afternoon he would take his lions into a cage and make them perform. Some would jump through hoops of fire; with another he'd stick his head into the lion's mouth. With Tommy, the pet lion, Tarzan would wrestle. Everyone loved the act and Tarzan was well known in the area.

Kurt was still in college at that time. He had taken a summer job as public relations officer in the town of Old Forge, which was a summer resort. Another town about 50 miles away, had a zoo which was opening up a new wing, and Kurt had the responsibility of promoting the project. He remembered Tarzan and his pet lion act. He would have Tarzan put on a show at the zoo. The town council agreed, Tarzan agreed, the owner of the Enchanted Forest agreed. Only Tommy the lion did not agree, but no one knew that at the time.

Kurt had to go along to see that things went smoothly. "It was about two o'clock in the afternoon," Kurt said. "We drove over to the Enchanted Forest and picked up Tarzan and Tommy the pet lion. He looked much bigger than I realized. He weighed about 450 pounds. We put him in the back of the station wagon and drove off. Tommy slept most of the way so it was no problem. We arrived at the zoo. Everyone was there. T.V. cameramen and directors. Reporters and photographers and several thousand people."

This was the kind of publicity Tarzan loved. He leaped out of the car rushed into the men's restroom, and returned wearing a leopard skin bikini. He looked the part, with his long black hair, flexing his muscles. Like a prize fighter entering the ring, bouncing around on his feet, holding his hands above his head. He worked his way over to the rear of the station wagon. He made a final bow, opened the door and pulled Tommy out. The performance lasted about 15 minutes with Tarzan rolling around on the ground with Tommy. They put Tommy back in the station wagon, and drove to the Enchanted Forest. They were almost home when Tommy, who was probably hungry, saw a white duck through the side window and made a leap forward into Tarzan's lap. Tarzan wrestled with him for a while and then tried to push him into the back of the station wagon. But Tommy wouldn't budge. Tarzan pushed again. Still Tommy wouldn't move. Kurt was sitting in the front seat. Tommy made one lunge and planted his jaws around the thigh of Kurt's left leg. He sank his teeth in and held. Kurt tried to free his leg by prying the lion's jaw apart. It was no good. "I had to do something," Kurt said. "One twist and he would tear my leg off. I wound up my right fist and hit him as hard as I could on the nose. The next thing I knew, he drew his head back and I fell out of the stopped car."

Ten minutes later, with Tommy locked securely in the station wagon, Tarzan carried Kurt into the town's infirmary. Tarzan was still clad in his leopard skin bikini, and Kurt, covered with lion's fur and his trousers leg half ripped off, was bleeding profusely. The doctor took it calmly as he stretched Kurt out on the operating table and began cleaning the wounds. "You never know about these," Kurt heard the doctor say to Tarzan. "You never know. Lions have a nasty kind of virus in their mouth."

"Yeah, I know," Tarzan agreed.

"Funny thing," the doctor continued. "About 40 years ago the circus was in town. Brought in two tamers bitten by lions. Did what I could. They both lost their legs."

"Yeah, I know," Tarzan said. "Same way my father lost his."

And Kurt listened silently as the doctor put 30 stitches into his leg. And as he lay there he made up his mind. If he didn't lose his leg, he would forget about adventure. He would go to the South Seas some day, but no adventure. If he only could have read his future.

Chapter 10

Boris of Kathmandu
A kingdom of his own

Have you ever returned from a trip to a foreign country with the feeling that you had really seen and done everything there was to do? I remember once I had come back from Taiwan, really feeling great. I had visited the Grand Hotel, had a Mongolian barbecue, saw the aborigines at Taroka Gorge, crossed the Central Mountain Range and went not once but twice to the National Museum. Then when I was back someone said to me, "You've seen the Lungshan Temple in the Wan-hua district, of course." I had to admit that I hadn't. "You hadn't," she snapped back. "But you haven't seen Taiwan until you've seen Lungshan." It always happens that way, and then you feel cheated.

When people in the know visit Kathmandu in Nepal, they find it is not the sights that matter as much as a person, a particular person. "Of course, you've met Boris," people will ask. If you say you haven't, it's the same old story. "Why you haven't seen Kathmandu unless you've met Boris:"

I went to Kathmandu, met Boris, and it backfired. I didn't know who he was. It was a bit embarrassing, not for me but for the people who introduced me. Even then, back in 1961, Boris had made a name for himself.

Getting to Kathmandu in those days wasn't easy. There were no international flights and if one wanted to travel by local airlines, it might take a month to obtain a booking. With no other choice I went overland, driving a Land Rover from Patna on the Ganges over the Tribhuwan Rajpath, the highest mountain road in Asia. In spite of the hardship, it was a grand trip, beginning in the rain forests of the low-lands and continuing upwards through banks of clouds, with blind curves and precipices dropping thousands of feet into gorges below.

There were few tourists in Nepal then, and as I remember, only two hotels, the Snow View and the Royal Palace. The latter was just that, a converted royal palace, and I didn't fancy driving up to the main entrance dust-covered and grimy. So I checked into the Snow View. Two days later a news reporter who had lived in Kathmandu for some years invited me to the Royal for a drink.

The Royal Palace Hotel at the time was considered to be one of the great hotels of the world. I did not know what the hotel had to offer by way of service, but I knew that the place was impressive. Built as a private palace for a Rana prince, it occupied a choice piece of real estate in Kathmandu on King's Way and was set back from the road in a beautiful formal garden, surrounded by great spreading trees. One entered the hotel by the portico at the head of a U-shaped drive. Porters greeted arriving guests and led them up wide steps past larger-than-life-size portraits of past Nepalese rulers to the reception area, and on to the splendid Regency dining hall with ceiling-high windows overlooking the garden, inter-spaced with more Rana portraits and lit by overwhelming chandeliers. But for all its regal splendor there were already signs of its probable future. The Royal was marked with cracked walls and missing plaster. Today in Kathmandu they speak of it as the 'now-decrepit Royal.' But it was quite another thing in the '50s and '60s.

I met the reporter with his friends at the Yak & Yeti Bar. I liked the place the moment I stepped in the door. It had a cozy atmosphere well-suited to Kathmandu. In the very centre of the room was a circular fireplace made of red bricks, with a heavy brass chimney flue and shield suspended from the ceiling. Comfortable arm chairs were arranged around the fire, and those who lounged there propped their feet up on the bricks. Nepalese waiters in white livery and scarlet sashes came running to take orders at the lift of a finger. I accepted a chair by the fire with the reporter and his friends.

As I was a newcomer to Nepal, they were all eager to tell me how Kathmandu had changed in the last few years, when suddenly my friend interrupted. "Wait a minute, there's Boris," he said and everyone stood up. Introductions were made and we shook hands. I was immediately intrigued by the man. Even then, in 1961, Boris was unusually rotund, yet he had unusually small feet for a man his size. He wore his hair brushed straight back, parted in the middle, a style that has been out of fashion since the '20s. In contrast to the gray of his hair, his eyebrows were dark and bushy. He was of average height. But I became intrigued when he spoke; his accent was heavy. You knew at once that he was Russian. I assumed that he was White Russian, for I had met and known other White Russians in China after the war. But a White Russian in Nepal?

Drinks were ordered and Boris sat down with us. I waited for a pause in the conversation, and when it came, I asked, "Are you here on holiday?" I was aware I had said something wrong the moment I spoke. Every head turned in my direction, with amused or shocked express-ions on their faces.

"This is Boris," the reporter said categorically. "You must know Boris!"

"I manage the hotel," Boris said without hesitation, and with a chuckle, and then while

Boris from Kathmandu.

patting his stomach, he added, "and I'm an ex-ballet dancer." His quick wit and ease of manner put everyone at ease.

Drinks were brought and Boris continued the conversation, keeping it lively and moving. He was in command of his audience, and when he spoke everyone listened. Judging by the greetings he received from people who went out of their way to nod when they either arrived or left, and by the respect he enjoyed from our small group, I began to wonder if he might not be a Russian count or perhaps even a dethroned prince. There are still a few who claim such titles and are found scattered about Asia. He conducted himself with an air of grace, and with a *savoir faire* that was not labored. Indeed, this Boris What's-his-name was a most interesting person.

He seemed keen, I remember, to talk about his experiences in Calcutta. He opened a club there called the 300. "In London they had the 400, and as Calcutta was the second largest city in the Empire, we called it the 300." Someone asked if he had much trouble running the club.

"Oh-ho," he chuckled, "that I did, at first." As he thought about it, the chuckle turned into a deep laugh, and like laughter in a schoolroom, it soon spread to everyone. He continued, interrupted from time to time with more bursts of laughter. "After a couple of bad experiences with drunks, I decided to hire a bouncer. I found just the man, the bodyguard of an ex-Viceroy, a Wazir from the northwest provinces. He was huge, about six four or six five. He had big shoulders, and wore a very bright red jacket with silver thread and shoulder epaulettes, and he had a very fierce mustache. But do you know"—his laughter grew—"he was the gentlest man I ever knew. He wouldn't harm an insect. But he was very useful as a figure. One day during the war three or four drunken American merchant sailors came in, pushed aside the man at the gate and entered the bar. I walked over and tried to talk to them, saying 'Look, you must know this is a private club. Nobody else is allowed and you will get me into trouble.' They didn't move, so I said, 'Okay, do me a favor, at least sign the book because that is the regulation.' They said, 'Bring the book!" I said, 'I can't; it's chained.' So one said, 'Okay, I'll go and sign.' I said, 'You all have to go and sign.' As they were standing there ready to sign the book, I called out, 'Zeffel Khan!' And Zeffel Khan strode across the floor in giant strides, chest puffed out. The men fumed around, took one look, threw away the pen and fell all over one another getting out of the door. Poor Zeffel, he didn't know what it was all about."

Boris was an amicable host that night. He kept us fascinated with his endless anecdotes, and was apologetic that his wife Inger was not with us to share our company. He spoke affectionately explaining she was away on holiday in Europe. Then he said, looking at me, "You don't believe that I'm an ex-ballet dancer, do you?"

"You haven't given me the chance to think about it," I joked.

"Well, I was, and a good one," he said and stood up. "Come, everybody, bring your glasses. I have something to show you."

We followed him from the bar and down a long corridor, and through a door which opened on to a landing. A winding stairway led upwards. It was like those secret passages you read about in castles in Europe. But this was real, and in the still semi-darkness, with a few too many whiskeys under our belts, we followed Boris up the stairs, making nonsensical banter as we climbed. At the top, one by one we filed into a room, while Boris, bowing slightly at the knees, held the door with one hand, and made a sweeping gesture with the other. "My private domain," he said.

One glance was enough to stagger the imagination. The room looked like a Hollywood movie set. It was in many ways elegant, and yet garish. There were divans and sofas, Oriental coffee tables and sideboards, many inlaid with mother-of pearl, Persian rugs and magnificent lamps, and a life-time collection of priceless antiques. On the walls hung fine oils and, above a carved writing desk in a far comer, were framed photographs. Boris crossed the room with a flourish whilst remarking on some antiques: "These cost me a prison term," and then stood by the desk. "You see, you see," he said jubilantly, "my younger days with the Ballet Russe." The photographs showed a youthful, and very much thinner, Boris, with a ballet company in Europe.

That was my introduction to Boris Lissanevitch, the last of a great line of hoteliers whose fame and reputation has perhaps exceeded that of the establishments they made famous. He has been the subject of countless newspaper articles and magazine stories; a book has been written about him; and thousands of travellers who have met him have carried away never-to-be-forgotten impressions. It is all too easy to imagine Boris in his heyday, the perfect host, standing with his attractive wife at the portico of the Royal Palace Hotel, greeting important guests as they arrived. And what illustrious personalities they must have been. Heads of state, ministers, religious leaders, kings and queens, princes and princesses, maharajas and rajas, sultans and viceroys, lords and counts, and so many, many more. And, of course, there were writers, playwrights, novelists, artists and actors; and finally, but most important in Nepal, the mountain climbers. Boris likes to tell how Sir Edmund Hillary and Sherpa Tensing arrived with their team and camped on his lawn in tents, but the following morning marched into the dining room and ate a gargantuan breakfast.

So much has been written about Boris, and so much said, that it is most difficult to separate the real from the legend. I have talked to others who have known him, and have listened to their impressions. But most helpful in discerning the facts about his life was a taped interview Boris made for an American writer, and friend, Steve Van Beek. The interview was conducted in Bangkok when Boris flew there and to other cities in Asia to promote his new Yak & Yeti Hotel in Kathmandu.

His family name is Lissanevitch and he was born in Odessa on the Black Sea in the year 1905. His father bred race horses, and his brothers studied at the Royal Naval Academy. They were commissioned into the Imperial Navy. When Boris was 12 he, too, was sent to the Academy to study. His term as a cadet was cut short as it was 1917, the year of·the Russian Revolution. The Bolsheviks, in one sweep of the ax, murdered the Tsar, the Tsarina and their five children. They then vented their wrath against the boyars. The White Russians, as they became known, made their mass exodus from Russia by the hundreds of thousands. They poured eastward, into Mongolia and China, and settled in communities in distant cities. Their lives, or rather their existence, was a far cry from former days. They were outcasts in cruel and alien lands. Their tragedy was their birth, from which there was no escape. They were to be chastised by the Japanese invaders of China, and later expelled by the red revolutionaries as they had been from their homeland. But nevertheless, they had to make the best of what they had. Some of them, professional soldiers, sold their services to the many warlords in China and became cavalry and gunnery officers and advisers. Some few obtained government posts, others took up their lives again as architects, lawyers and engineers. And many opened restaurants, ran hotels, or became saloon and brothel keepers. They spoke of their great estates in Russia, and poured drinks for drunken foreign seamen; they talked about gala dinner parties and attending the opera, and served cold borscht and sausages to foreign travellers.

Boris was one of the more fortunate. Through a friend of the family he was accepted by a ballet company where he trained as a dancer. The company was the famous Diaghilev Ballet Russe. With proper papers it was safe for him to remain in Russia. In 1924, when Boris was 19, the Ballet Russe moved their base to Monte Carlo. Boris was with them. He never returned to Russia.

"Those were some grand years," Boris said. "We toured all over Europe—Paris, Rome, Madrid, Barcelona. I had a wonderful time in Monte Carlo during rehearsals where we met the cream of the composers, painters, conductors, people of letters. Diaghilev came to rehearsal every day. I could have made a fortune had I picked up the little drawings that Picasso, Dali, Duchamp, Chirico and others were always sketching and throwing away; they were swept up with the trash."

When Diaghilev died in 1929, the Ballet Russe split up. Boris joined the Monte Carlo Ballet. From Europe he went on tour to South America where he spent several years. He returned to Europe in 1932, danced for various ballet companies on the continent and in 1936 went with a troupe to

Shanghai. He immediately fell in love with the Far East.

Throughout all his travels, Boris held a White Russian passport issued under Tsarist Russia. This became a problem after the revolution when there was no longer a White Russia. Travelling became increasingly more difficult. To obtain a new passport he had to establish residence somewhere, which meant remaining for several years in one place. He decided to become British and chose to live in Calcutta. When he arrived he had little money, and there was little opportunity to dance ballet in India. But Boris was never short of ideas.

"The first time I had visited Calcutta was in 1934. I met some very pleasant Indians and a few Europeans and had made quite good friends. After a show we had gone to a place, a sort of club run by an Australian lady. It was not exactly a red-light house but sort of a medium pink. And when I complained that there was not a decent place to drink after 11 o'clock in the second city of the Empire, one of them said: 'Why don't you open one?' So on the way back, two years later when I decided to change my nationality, I started the club, which was the first in India where both westerners and Indians could join as members."

Boris tried to enlist in the British Army during the war, but being Russian, he was rejected. Instead he was given a job in the Censor's Office. He continued to run the 300 Club, met an attractive girl named Inger, and they were married.

Boris engaged in several business ventures in and around Calcutta. One was a distillery in Cooch Bihar, north of the city. It was doing well until the separation of India and Pakistan. All the sugar cane plantations were in Pakistan and Cooch Bihar was practically cut off from all sources of supply. Boris had to close down, but the time spent was not entirely wasted. In 1951 he was invited by King Tribhuban of Nepal for a visit. Club manager, distillery, politics, they all had a part to play in Boris' future. The year 1951 was an exciting one for Nepal.

It was then that Nepal opened her doors to outsiders. The Rana family—the ruling aristocracy who had usurped the powers of the king and had turned Nepal into their private estate — were the ones who forbade visitors to enter the country. The mountainous terrain made it easy to enforce the ban. It was not until India achieved her independence after World War II that the king's revolution succeeded, the Rana prime minister resigned, and the country began to emerge from obscurity. King Tribhuban regained power, and in the same year invited Boris to visit Nepal. "Like the man who came to dinner," Boris said, "I never left."

When Boris and his wife Inger went to Nepal it was completely untouched. There were no roads from India—the first one wasn't built until 1956—and travellers had to be transported over the Himalayas by sedan chair. There were 12 cars in Kathmandu at that time, and they, too, came over the mountains from India on the backs of porters. There were exactly seven tourists to the country that year.

Boris saw the possibilities. "I knew I had to persuade the king to develop tourism. The king asked, 'Who would visit Nepal? What is there to see? The prime minister goes to Calcutta and spends two days walking around New Market. That's what tourists want to see.'"

Boris first interested the king in letting him move his distillery from Cooch Bihar to Kathmandu. "The Nepalese drink raksi," he explained, "and their system of manufacture was the one used by Adam when he made his applejack in Paradise. What they produced was so potent and so full of alkalides and fusel-oils that it knocked you out for a couple of days."

The king then gave Boris the Royal Palace to manage as a hotel on a trial basis. It was Nepal's first hotel, and was subsequently to become one of the world's most famous, an achievement that is Boris' alone. "When I think of what faced me," Boris said 25 years later. "It was one of those palaces which was very badly built. It was made with brick and cow dung and it was badly cracked. I had to spend a lot of time and money repairing and repainting."

But not all was rosy in the Himalayan kingdom. Boris had an uphill struggle all the way. Troubles really began when his benefactor and friend, King Tribhuban, died in Switzerland in 1955. Boris lost much of the support he had. In fact, soon after the king's death, he was arrested.

"I had already started the Royal," Boris said, "and one day about forty people with machine guns came in and presented me with a bill which claimed I owed the Nepalese government 175,000 rupees and 15 pisa, payable at once." When Boris had started the hotel he had closed down the distillery. Now a few petty government officials were claiming compensation for all the time it had not been in operation.

"They took me to the tax office first where I spent four days," Boris said. "Then they put me in police headquarters. There was a room there where Inger could come and visit me any time of the day. But my back started acting up, an attack of sciatica, so they put me into hospital. They found me a little room with a verandah and squeezed in a bed, and gave me a 'thunder pot,' you know, a chamber pot, and the first time I sat on it, it broke. Anyway, I stayed on and even had my birthday there, with about 40 guests, including several ambassadors. I was in for 70 days that time."

Boris was arrested a second time a few years later, after a reporter for the Daily Telegraph in London misquoted him in their color magazine. The paper was running a series on the most interesting hotels in the world and number two was the Royal. The misunderstanding came over the antiques Boris had collected.

"It was really ridiculous," Boris said. "I had given a paper to the prime minister, at his request, on what should be done to promote tourism. One of the main points was unless they stopped the stealing and exporting of all antiques, nothing would be left in two or three years." When the officials read that Boris had his own collection, they arrested him. He was held for 72 days before he was finally released.

Boris is enthusiastic about the new Yak & Yeti Hotel, which

he insists is even better than the Royal. A stone's throw away, the new hotel is yet another refurbished Rana palace, the Lal Dubar, or Red Palace. The old Yak & Yeti bar has become the Chimney Lounge, but the decor is much the same, and so is the mood. If Boris has his way, the new Yak & Yeti Hotel will one day soon be home for the world's rich and famous.

There is one question people never tire of asking Boris — Why Kathmandu? What is the attraction?

Boris admits he has been in the East more than 40 years, and when you stay that long, you cannot return to Europe happily. "But there is another reason," he admitted. "It has to do with ceilings! I've gotten used to ceilings 18 feet high. In Calcutta, the club was in a very old house and the ceiling was about 18 feet high. And when we moved to the Royal in Kathmandu, it was a palace with very high ceilings. The same for the new Yak & Yeti that also has high ceilings. Now when I go to Europe I get claustrophobia. I just cannot live anywhere without tall ceilings."

And so Boris Lissanevitch, hotelier, raconteur, bon vivant, and ex-ballet dancer of the Ballet Russe de Monte Carlo, stays on in Kathmandu.

Homer Hicks, the old man from Zamboanga, with his wife and daughter.
Homer came to the Philippines as a US soldier prior to World War I, fell in
love with the country and its people and never left, or ever returned to his
home state of Texas, even for a visit. He was captured and held prisoner by
the Japanese during World War II and severely beaten. The date on the
photo shows 1958. He was an avid fisherman and ran his own machine
shop in Zamboanga.

Chapter 11

Homer Hicks
The old man from Zamboanga

The first time I saw the Old Man from Zamboanga he was sitting alone in an open-front cafe called The Diner on Guardia Nacional Avenue. He had a table near the street but I had not noticed him when I entered. Only after I unfolded my newspaper and ordered a San Miguel did I see him, sitting on the edge of his chair, leaning both arms over a walking stick. He stared vacantly at people moving in the street.

Had the time been different, he probably would not have held my curiosity. But now I was surprised to see him there. He could not have been a tourist. There were few tourists in Zamboanga in the fall of that year. Muslim rebels were up in arms against the government. I certainly was unaware of the situation when I arrived in town that morning. We had sailed my schooner up from Sandakan in Sabah, Borneo, and not until I anchored outside the seawall did I hear about the trouble.

Seated in The Diner I eagerly scanned the papers for news, but each time I looked up, my eyes fell upon the Old Man. He had not moved. I was soon more interested in him than in the paper. What was he doing here? Who was he? I judged him to be about 70 years old. He was squarely built and one could easily imagine that he was a powerhouse in his younger days. But he was old now, with gray hair closely cropped, and he wore thick glasses with one lens darkened.

My thoughts returned to the newspaper when suddenly there was a rumpus in the street. I turned to see that the Old Man was up from his chair and had separated two boys who were ready to swing blows at one another. The Old Man waved his stick and shouted at them in Tagalog. The way he spoke the language I knew he wasn't a tourist. The two boys reluctantly walked off, with the Old Man still scolding them. When he turned and saw me standing by the sidewalk, he said in English, "Just throw an arm-lock around their neck, like this"—and he proceeded to demonstrate how to apply an arm hold around an imaginary neck. "That's all, they'll stop."

"Can I buy you a beer, Old Man?" I asked.

"Hell, I've never refused a beer in my life, but only if you'll let me buy the next one." We sat down at the table and I ordered two cold San Miguels.

I immediately wanted to ask him about himself, what he was doing in Zamboanga, but thought it best to wait. "What do you think about the situation in Jolo?" I asked instead. "What will they do?"

Jolo is an island in the Sulu Sea, and a stronghold of the Muslim rebels. A few days before we arrived the rebels had assassinated 36 military men at a peace conference. The newspapers were filled with stories and photographs about the massacre.

"What will they do!" he shouted. "I'll tell you what they are going to do. They're not going to do nothing about it. That's the trouble. I'd put a stop to it. Give me a thousand troopers, no more, and I'd do something about it."

"How?" I asked, uncertain how the conversation was going to go.

"I'll tell you what I'd do. The same as we did in 1922. No, it was '23. You don't chase those bastards into the hills. That's what they would want. You wait by the trails for them to return. Then you ambush them. They got to come down from the hills. They cannot stay there for ever. That's what the U.S. Army did in 1923."

"Where are you from?" I asked.

"Texas," he shouted back. "Where else! El Paso, Texas. You know they wouldn't let Mohammed Ali fight in Texas. You know why? Because he refused to serve in the Army. Not in Texas he couldn't fight. I heard on the radio when he fought in Manila. I wanted to see him get stomped. He almost did."

He continued to talk about Texas, and as he did, he removed a battered tin cigarette case from his pocket. He carefully withdrew a fat, locally-made cigarette, popped it into his mouth and with his tongue pushed it back under his lip. He saw me watching. "Good tobacco," he said, "but only if you don't smoke it."

"How long have you been here?" I asked.

"Came out in 1919," he said. "Came out with the U.S. Army from Siberia. Been here ever since."

I motioned to the waiter for another round of beers. "Since 1919," I repeated. I could not take my eyes from the Old Man. He appeared a gruff old cobber, and obstinate, but I liked him. He was outspoken and to the point, and you could expect a direct answer from him. "When's the last time you were back in Texas?" I asked.

"Back! I've never been back," he growled. "I've been here 58 years. Not in Zamboanga. In the Philippines. I was eighteen when I came."

"But wouldn't you like to go back, just for a visit?"

"Hell, yes, I'd like to go back. But I'm on a pension. With all my daughters and grand daughters I can't even afford a trip to Manila. Sure I'd like to go back, but only for a visit. I want to be buried here in Zamboanga, next to my wife. She died two years ago. She was Filipina. We fought our whole life, but goddamn she was a good woman. Some men and their wives live together. Not us. We fought together. I thought she was gone when the Japs caught us in the hills after the war broke out. I didn't see her until after the war. They trucked us in from the prison at Santo Tomas, and we were getting down from the trucks, and Charley, that's Charley Hughes, Charley says to me, 'Homer,' he said, 'I think you're gonna be surprised. Somebody over there wants to see you.' I thought he meant my son. I never expected to see my wife alive after the war. But there she was. Then when I saw her we couldn't do a thing. Just looked at one another. God almighty! We couldn't move. We just stood there and looked. Hell, I've never cried. I never cried in my life. But damn your soul if I didn't cry then. Me"—he tapped his chest—as tears came to his eyes. "She saw me cry and she came running towards me, and then she kept jumping up and down, and I said, 'Damn, woman, what are you doing?' Then she looked at my hand." He held it up. It was broken behind the knuckles. "She was there when the Jap interpreter slapped me. No man slaps a Texan. I laid him flat with one punch. Man, did I clobber him. He went flying over backwards. I can still see it. They grabbed me, the whole squad. They put my hand down on a stump and the sergeant brought his rifle butt down. Then they busted my instep so that I couldn't run away. And there's my wife looking at my hand, and she says, 'Why did you have to hit that Jap? They could have killed you.' She knew better than to ask me that. Three years and we don't see each other and we start fighting five minutes later. But damn she was a good woman."

The afternoon slipped by so quickly I hardly noticed the time. For that matter, I was even unaware of the cafe where we sat, the people who passed, or the empty beer bottles on the table. I was like a sleepless child at bedtime who keeps saying, "And then what happened? Tell me." But quite suddenly, without any warning, he stood up. He stuffed his cigarette box into his pocket.

"Sure nice talking to you," he said. "Time for me to go. My daughter expects me at five. Maybe I will see you again. I usually come here in the afternoon." We shook hands and he turned to leave, but as an after-thought he said, "Be careful. Wouldn't walk the streets at night. People do, but they take a chance. I remember in 1928 they had five policemen in Zamboanga and they never had any trouble. But it's different now. There's a war on." He gave a slight wave and disappeared into the crowd on Guardia Nacional.

I sat there for a long time thinking about the Old Man. He had to be over 40 years old when the Second World War started. In my mind's eye I saw him defiantly standing in front of the Japanese squad, after they captured him and his wife, and I saw that arrogant Texan slam his heavy first into the face of a five-foot-tall bespectacled Japanese interpreter. And I saw the horror as his captors worked him over. I wondered what had happened after that. The tale was only half told. How had he possibly managed to survive as a POW? I returned to my schooner as the sun was setting over the Baslin Strait, and that night in the main salon, with the light of the gas lantern shining on the faces of the crew, I told them about the incredible old man I met in Zamboanga. I tried hard to imitate his manner, but that, of course, was impossible.

The next afternoon I found myself walking up Guardia Nacional. It was hot and I felt like a cold San Miguel, and it would be good to sit and listen to the Old Man talk about forgotten years. But when I reached The Diner he wasn't there. I sat and had my beer and waited but he never came. I was disappointed and wondered if something might have happened to him. The next afternoon I returned and there he was, watching people go by.

"You knew Manila before the war?" I asked when the beers arrived. "I heard many stories about Intramuros, the old Spanish city. Was it really beautiful as they say?"

"If you like museums. Sure it was nice. But so was all Manila. It was an exciting city. There was music everywhere. Hell, there wasn't a Filipino who couldn't sing or play an instrument. They sang Spanish songs mostly. And the women, they were lovely things. They still are, mind you, but then they wore cotton skirts down to their ankles and blouses with long wide sleeves. When you saw a knee that was something. No wonder my first wife divorced me."

"Your first wife!"

"The first one. She was the C.O.'s niece in Baguio. She didn't like my carousing. She wanted me to go back when my hitch was up in 1924. I extended once but they would not give me another one. I like the Philippines. I didn't want to go back. So I took my discharge. Anyway, after that we got divorced. I was torn up real bad, but it was the best thing that ever happened to me."

For the next two weeks every afternoon, for a few hours, we would talk. Or rather, the Old Man would talk while I listened. I never told him I was a writer, for I was afraid that would change things. It always does. When people know you write, they tell you only the things they think you should know, not what you want to know.

As time passed, and I kept making excuse after excuse to remain. I found myself being drawn closer to the Old Man. He was a man who had taken from life all its pleasures without regret. He was born into an age that knew not the automobile, electricity, telephone, radio, nor the possibility of flight. His life coincided with one of the greatest periods of technical development the world has ever know. He was part of it, and yet removed from it all. He had never been back to his native Texas, to America, but he was as Texan as the best of them. He had so much to tell, and there was no one to listen. This was the tragedy. This is why I felt so sad about the Old Man.

The Old Man was 76 when I met him. He was alert and his mind was quick. He could remember every joke he had heard, and some were pretty raunchy; or else he could make one up to fit the occasion.

The Old Man was in the Philippines at a time when a sergeant made $45 a month; an expert rifleman would make an extra $5. Life in the Philippines with the U.S. Army offered excitement and challenge. Something was always happening. The Americans had not succeeded any better than the Spanish— who tried for 400 years—to pacify the Muslims in the south. These Muslims, sometimes called Moros, are widely known as a fierce, brave and independent minority who follow Islamic law, social conventions and marriage ceremonies. However, it was not only the Muslims but a number of other island tribes who refused the American plea to surrender. With lethal bolo knives they continued a guerrilla resistance which often erupted. Reprisals were certain to follow. The U.S. Army and Filipino Regulars were sent in. The Old Man was amongst them. These are the stories he told so well, but there were others passed down to him that he likes to retell.

I could no longer hold back the clock. We had to leave Zamboanga. With trouble brewing in the Sulu Sea all commercial sea routes were cut temporarily, and it was for this reason that we were prompted to return to Sandakan in Borneo. My first mate accepted a charter to carry half-a-dozen passengers from the Philippines. But it did mean, if the winds were right and we could keep clear of the islands, we could return to Zamboanga a few weeks later on our way north to Manila. I went to say goodbye to the Old Man. He was sitting in The Diner when I arrived.

"Good to see you, good to see you," he said. I could see he was eager to tell me some episode from his past that would hold me for the afternoon, but I did not have the afternoon free to spend with him.

"I'm leaving tomorrow," I said.

"You're not!" he said.

"I'm afraid I must," I replied, and then explained about the schooner, that it was my home in Asia, and that I was a writer.

"Well, I'll be dammed," he said. "Hell, why didn't you tell me. I wish I had known."

"I didn't want say I'm a writer, then you might have—"

"Hell, I don't mean that. So you're a writer. Everyone seems to be a writer these days. I mean the schooner. Why didn't you tell me about the schooner. Hell, I love the sea. I had my own boat."

"I didn't know," I said.

"Well, yes. I'm a diesel mechanic. You have a diesel engine, haven't you?" I nodded.

"Good! I'll sign on. You need a good diesel mechanic, don't you?" He didn't wait for an answer. "I'll go with you." There was a long pause. I could feel myself choking up inside. "Hell, who am I kidding? I can't leave my family like that. They need me. Hell, if I were only younger"—he slapped the table with his open hand—"Why do we have to grow old? Somebody tell me why? Why? Why?"

I don't believe it was the thought of growing old that disturbed the Old Man; it was inactivity. He admitted he was active until he was 74, until his wife died. "But I still have a lot of fire in me," he said. And believing can make it so.

"Look, Old Man," I said to him, "I'll be back, and I'll tell you what, when I do, you come aboard. We'll have dinner and I'll take you sailing. You can bring your whole family."

His face lit up with a cherubic glow, and he nodded. "That will give me something to look forward to," he said and we shook hands and parted company. I did not look back as I walked down Guardia Nacional towards the waterfront.

Early the next morning we took on supplies, the passengers came aboard, and after we cleared immigration, we sailed westward with the high tide. With a six-knot current in our favor, we slipped quietly down the Baslin Strait, and when we passed the last of the islands, we turned southwest. The wind from the starboard quarter filled our sails and the miles quickly dropped behind us. Next morning the islands of the Sulu Archipelago appeared on our port like shimmering wafers on an unattainable horizon, and we kept a wide distance between them and us. It was a pity, for here were some of the finest isles to be found in any sea, and they were forbidden to us and all outsiders. But still, one has to admire the Moros for their determination.

Two weeks later we passed the same chain of islands, but now they were on our starboard. We entered the Baslin Strait at dusk and waited for the tide to carry us six knots in the other direction. At dawn we anchored outside the seawall and with morning coffee watched the sun rise east of Zamboanga.

There is something pleasant about returning to those places in the Orient that you most enjoy. I have always felt this way about Zamboanga. I find it one of the most exciting, if lesser known ports in the Far East, with Chittagong running a close second. Zamboanga is part Spanish, in both temperament and design, but with overtones of American influence, as one can easily see by the stone structure of the City Hall. The Hall was built by 'Black Jack' Pershing in 1912 to quarter his staff officers. The Spanish built the forts and parks and the main public plaza. Spanish and American, true, yet when you walk along the waterfront and on the streets of Zamboanga you know you are in the Orient. There's no mistaking that.

But I wasn't thinking about the glories of Zamboanga when I rowed ashore. I spent the morning clearing customs and immigration, and that afternoon made tracks to The Diner. It was a joyous moment to see the Old Man sitting there.

It took a few seconds for him to recognize me. "Hell," he shouted and tapped his walking stick on the floor. "You're back. We were worried about you. I just told my daughter this morning, I said, 'You know those boys are out there in the Sulu with all those pirates, and there's no navy to back them up.' And now here you are."

"Was it any different 50 years ago, with the pirates I mean?" I asked, pulling up my chair and motioning for the waiter to bring two cold San Miguels.

"I remember the time in 1922. Nope, it was '23. We went down with an infantry company of 250 men to Jolo, and—"

I was back, and it was as if I had not left.

But now as I listened to the Old Man I tried to piece his story together in one logical sequence, from some sort of beginning. It was a most trying undertaking. His anecdotes could be as much as 50 years apart. But nevertheless, he had a way about him that held my full attention. Listening to him retell his life's story was much like seeing an old photograph come to life. If you have seen some of the old photographs in the National Museum in Manila you will know what I mean. There is one in particular that stands out in my mind. It shows a flat car on a side track outside Manila. It was taken in the early '20s. U.S. Infantry soldiers and Filipino Regulars are sitting, standing, and some kneeling on the car. The enlisted men are wearing breeches, wrap-around leggings, jackets with high collars and campaign hats. The officers are wearing polished boots and Sam Brown belts. I found myself staring at the photographs, studying the expressions on the men's faces, and soon I could not help feeling compassion for these men, for I knew that most of them, so filled with life and desires when the photograph was taken, were now long gone. But as I listened to the Old Man, the photograph began to move, and for that one instant while he was talking, I was there. It was real now, a blacksmith shop in Texas, a wood-burning train crossing Siberia, quelling revolts in the Philippines, fighting the Japanese, independence and living a rambunctious life with women who believed in him—and all told with a profligate abundance of detail.

The rigorous, rugged life in Texas is what shaped young Homer Hicks. He had little formal education, but then at the turn of the century few young men did, unless born to a privileged class, which Homer definitely was not. At 12 years of age he began working in a blacksmith shop, swinging a 10-pound hammer 10 hours a day. He never complained, and had not the Great War come along, he might have spent his life in Texas. But life was to have another meaning for him.

One afternoon the town came to a stop when one of those new, fancy, horseless carriages chugged down the main street, sending horses pulling at their reins and chickens and dogs scampering for cover. People came out of the shops and children fell in line running behind the vehicle. Young Hicks, who stood tall as a full grown man for his age, laid aside his hammer and stepped out into the street. As though destiny had pointed a finger at him and said, "Now," the automobile suddenly stopped. It came to an abrupt halt directly in front of the blacksmith shop. Children stopped in their tracks, and those who were watching the spectacle stepped back, suspecting that the machine might give one last shudder and explode. The only daring person to come forth was young Hicks. As if a magnet were pulling him from the crowd he approached the machine, wiping his hands on his apron, and stood looking down at a contraption he had never seen before, except in advertisements. But he had been curious. He read all the ads about the mechanics of combustion engines. He understood, or believed he understood, the principle of the magneto. "Can you fix it?" he heard the driver say, and without looking up at the man, he nodded.

"It didn't matter if I couldn't fix it," he said 65 years later in Zamboanga. "I just wanted to get my hands under the cover and see what it was all about."

Twenty minutes later the machine ran, and thereafter the blacksmith shop carried a sign above the door AUTOMOBILE MECHANIC AVAILABLE. Homer Hicks' love for machines and his innate ability to understand and work with them was to play an important part in his life.

Homer Hicks joined the army during the Great War to fight in Europe; he was sent to Siberia. It was a time when every major power in the world was maneuvering politically and sending its armies and navies to ports like Vladivostok and Port Arthur. Sergeant Hicks was assigned to train guard on the Siberian Railway but was soon spending more time working with the engineers and mechanics in the locomotives than riding in the caboose with the others.

After Siberia his regiment was sent to the Philippines by troop ship, with a stopover for refueling in Hong Kong. The Navy crew was given shore leave but not the army regulars. Sergeant Hicks was not about to be kept aboard. When darkness fell, he slipped aboard a bumboat, and at four the next morning was picked up roaring drunk in Wanchai. His punishment was reduction to rank of private and 14 hours in the crow's nest. The punishment would not have been that bad," he recalled, "but we hit a full storm. I had to ride it out."

Few soldiers lost their ranks and were promoted more times than Sergeant Hicks was during his stormy military career in the Philippines. He never stepped out of his way to avoid trouble. Trouble for him meant excitement; trouble meant being alive. He professed not to be a religious man, but he did believe in fate. Fate always got him out of trouble. There was the time he was drinking with his buddies in a bar on Mbabane Street in Manila, and in walked a lieutenant whom no one liked, officers included. A fight started and Sergeant Hicks hit the lieutenant. If brought to court martial he would have had to face twenty years hard labor. But it so happened at the time an engineer was needed for the rail line to San Fernando. Sergeant Hicks was the only man available. He was made to apologize to the lieutenant—"The hardest thing I ever had to do"—and became engineer on the Philippine railroad.

After a year on the railroad, he was called to initiate another service, a transportation run to Baguio. When the Americans took over in the Philippines, they decided to build a cool summer resort in the mountains there. There construction of a road through these mountains was an engineering feat. The Army Corps of Engineers labored four years to complete it. The road was open only a few years when Sergeant Hicks began driving convoys through its rugged mountain passes. He became so intrigued with the summer resort that when he was discharged from the army he began his own private transportation company between Manila ans the resort at Baguio. Hard drinking and hard living put an end to the company and his short-lived marriage. He became bankrupt and his wife divorced him.

He was emotionally broken up by the divorce. Now that he was out of the Army, and had lost all his money in the company, he did not have the means to return home. Nor did he want to stay around Manila. He went south to the island of Negros and opened up a machine shop on borrowed money. "It was primitive," He said. "But there was no competition, and machines were coming to the islands. I made enough to get back on my feet."

In 1928 the Old Man moved operations to Zamboanga, met a Filipino girl, got married and for 10 years lived a good and happy life. But then 1938 and the shadow of doom fell across the islands and the south Pacific.

In 1935, General Douglas MacArthur became military adviser to the new government in Manila with headquarters in the Manila Hotel, but when tension began to mount in the Pacific, the U. S. Congress called him back to active duty and gave him command of the U.S. and Philippine Armed Forces.

A year after the outbreak of war in Europe in 1939, the Japanese invaded French Indo-China and followed with the signing of the triple alliance with Germany and Italy. It was evident that Japan would strike. But where? When?

News about the surprise Japanese attack on Pearl Harbor did not reach the Philippines until the day after the bombing, on December 8, 1941. Almost simultaneously, Japanese planes began to bomb various parts of the islands, including Davao, Baguio, Tarlac and the major air base at Clark Field north of Manila. Within two days most of the American defenses were destroyed and the naval base at Cavite City was reduced to smoldering ruins. On December 21, the Japanese invaded northern Luzon and began their advance to Manila. Without air support the Filipino and American troops were forced to retire to Bataan and Corregidor.

Homer was offered a field commission in the U.S. Army, which he accepted, and became a communications officer in Mindanao. In March, President Roosevelt ordered General MacArthur to leave for Australia, and General Jonathan Wainwright became commander of all forces in the islands. Soon after this Bataan fell and Corregidor was overrun. This marked the end of organized resistance against the Japanese.

Lt. Hicks was sitting in the communications shack with his earphones on when news of the surrender was announced. General Wainwright's voice came over the air. "It was enough to make tears come to your eyes the way he talked," the Old Man said. 'This is General Wainwright. I order all armed forces in the Philippines to surrender to the Imperial Japanese Army. This is beyond my control. I repeat, this is beyond my control.' He spoke like he had a revolver pointed at his head."

Lt. Hicks had instructions from General Short to blow up the communications shed and the motor pool if the order to surrender came. "I let the men go into the hills with whatever they could carry, and then with ten cases of dynamite I blew up the camp." Lt. Hicks then loaded his wife and son into a 32-foot tug boat he had made ready for the occasion and sailed to Bukas Grande where he burned the boat and took to the hills to join the guerrillas.

"There were three of us, my wife, my ten-year-old son, and me. We had a make-shift camp in the jungles, with food and supplies. There was no way the Japs could have found us, but when I opened my eyes one morning, there they were, standing over us. I did not know it then, but in the village an informer had turned us in. He had sold his information for ten pesos. The guerrillas knocked him off as he sat in a toddy shop drinking." The three prisoners, after the Japanese had broken the Old Man's hand and foot, were dragged down the mountain to the village. "They loaded my wife and son with all the other women and children on to a ship at dockside. I tossed my wife my billfold with all the money I had, and that was the last I saw of her and my son until after the armistice."

Before the War, the Old Man had hiked through many hills and mountain trails of Mindanao. As a mechanic he was called to repair machinery at missions and government stations. Sometimes it took him days to reach the destinations on foot or by muleback. He came to know the countryside better than most natives. The Japanese command was keen to make use of his knowledge of the island and his command of Tagalog. "When they wanted to contact a guerrilla force they sent me out. Their method was simple. They lined up half-a-dozen missionaries and their wives and said, 'If you don't return, we shoot them.' I knew they would. The guerrillas wanted to come down and take the post. They could have, easily. But what was the use. I told them that the prisoners were fed and given what medical treatment was available. But in the hills they would be hunted, the old men and women. The Japs would not give up until they caught every one of them."

On October 20, 1944, US Forces under General MacArthur landed on Leyte, and by the end of November, nearly a quarter-of-a-million troops were in the Philippines. Japanese resistance was ebbing. Guerrillas came down out of the hills and jungles and joined the advance. By July 5, liberation was complete.

Lt. Hick's field commission never was confirmed. All records were destroyed by his own hands when he blew up the post, and the officers immediately above him were killed in the fighting. There was no retribution for Homer Hicks, no compensation for his service. He was penniless and broke when the Japanese were driven out, but he was not defeated. He seriously considered returning to Texas, but he no longer had either relatives or friends there. There was a sister but she had moved north to New England, and he had not heard from her in more than 20 years. By now he had lived almost 30 years in the Philippines. He would wait a few more years, until he was financially able, and take his wife on a visit to see Texas. She died before that dream could come true. He started a business again in Zamboanga after the war, and he was able to raise a son and two daughters and see them all married.

"There's not much else to tell," he said, and I could see that his thoughts were now upon his wife.

"Yes, there is," I said. "There's one more thing you can tell me." His mind returned to the present. He listened. "You can tell me if my schooner sails better with a beam wind or a quarter wind. We go sailing tomorrow and in the evening we shall have dinner aboard."

The next morning I had the crew turn to, cleaning and polishing the schooner, especially the engine room, and invited a few friends on board to add company. The Old Man arrived in great spirits and refused a helping hand from the dinghy up the ladder. "What do I look like, an invalid?" he shouted to the mate. He walked along the rails and stood at the bowsprit. He stared up at the rigging, pulled at the halyards on the fife rail, and he went below and lifted the engine hatches. His mind was not in the past now but in the future. He remained silent all the while, and all eyes followed his movements, waiting for him to pass comment, to make some judgment. It was unlike the Old Man to be so taciturn. He went back on deck, stood at the taff rail, and looked out upon the sea. He said one word, "Youth," and raised a fist to an imaginary being on the horizon. "To be young again," he continued, "to be 50 or 60!" He turned now and saw us looking at him. "What do you run here, a dry ship? You haven't even offered me a San Miguel."

We did a short sail with all canvas billowing, and the Old Man staunchly gripped the helm, feeling the wind and the motion of the sea as he turned the spokes to ease the helm. He would not relinquish the helm, even when the wind stiffened and we came about on a tack, and only when we dropped anchor at the seawall did he give up his position.

We had dinner early that night, just as it became dusk, and soon afterwards the Old Man announced he had to leave. He got me aside, shook my hand, and said, "Don't live in the past.

Aboard the author's schooner

That's the secret. Now is important. I enjoyed the Philippines before, sure, but hell, I enjoy it now. Maybe I'll never make it, but I long for one last look at Texas. That's the kind of hope that keeps a man alive. Son—" he placed a hand on my shoulder—"this is one of the best days I have had in years."

"When I see you again, Old Man, that will be the best."

"I'll be waiting," he said, as he climbed into the dinghy and two crew rowed him ashore.

Chapter 12

Jeff and Robin
Two sailors who may be kings

One thing you have to admit about Jeff and Robin is that they have perseverance. Real perseverance! You may not agree with their lifestyle, few people would, but they have a stick-to-itiveness that few of us have. Asia is their adopted home, and they are as much a part of the scene as is the expatriate rubber planter in Sumatra or the British skipper working a tug boat in Hong Kong. There is a difference, however, and that is the extreme to which these two men go to find contentment in Asia.

Jeff and Robin are beachcombers, of a sort. What most travellers would spend in one evening for a hotel and dinner in a restaurant, they will live on for a month. They manage to do it so cheaply because a long time ago they concluded that to live the way they wanted to in Asia meant finding a solution to the cost of accommodation and transportation. What they needed was a mobile home. Now, in Hong Kong, they had seen the carefree sampan dwellers living in the typhoon shelters. No rent; no taxes. In the Philippines it was the blond-hair, brown-skinned Bajaus. They came and went as they pleased. At Batu Pahat on Malaysia's west coast, the local folk have taken to living on the rivers in houseboats.

Was this not the way to do it? they reasoned. They would become sea gypsies. The fact that they knew nothing about the sea or how to sail didn't deter them in the slightest. They pooled their resources, a total of US$500, went to Bali and bought a Bugis turtle-catching sloop. And ever since, some eight years now, they have been loafing around the ports of Southeast Asia. There are few men who can boast they have sailed among the forbidden isles and fabled seas of Indonesia. They have, and their tales are startling.

Those who have read the daring adventures of Daniel Dravot and Peachy Carnehan in Rudyard Kipling's *The Man Who Would Become King* will know Jeff and Robin. Kipling's two heroes ventured into Kafiristan in northeast Afghanistan to seek fame and fortune and to make themselves kings in a foreign land. Jeff and Robin sailed into Indonesia, to this day a partly forbidden land, and found not fame and fortune but contentment. While Kipling's yarn, I am sure, is fiction, Jeff and Robin's escapades are real. Furthermore, Jeff and Robin are still there, somewhere doing their thing.

I first saw their frail little craft with its grass-top cabin and patched sails crossing the sand bar at the mouth of the Chao Phraya River some eighteen miles south of Bangkok. I was aboard my own schooner, sailing up from Singapore, when we overtook them. With unfailing determination their tiny craft was beating against winds and current. When I saw them, I was reminded of Conrad and his description in his novel *The Shadow Line*. "One morning, early," he wrote, "we crossed the bar, and while the sun was rising splendidly over the flat spaces of land we steamed up the innumerable bends, passed under the shadow of the great gilt pagoda and reached the outskirts of town." Nothing had changed, and that's what was so remarkable about it all. "There it was, spread out largely on both banks, an expanse of brown houses of bamboo, of mats, of leaves, or a vegetable-matter style of architecture, sprung out of the brown soil of the banks of the muddy river."

Through this Conradesque world we sailed, and by afternoon had anchored in a small klong a few miles south of Bangkok. Three days later Jeff and Robin came drifting up the canal with the incoming tide. They had little or no wind and with each change of tide they were forced to anchor. But nevertheless, undaunted by their slow progress, they arrived in good spirits. "We made it!" they said calmly stepping ashore. "We made it!"

The significance of their arrival had little meaning to those who watched the tiny craft drift up the canal. It wasn't until I learned their story later did I understand their excitement at reaching Bangkok. It took a long time to get to know Jeff and Robin, after many Mekongs and sodas under the awning on the afterdeck of the schooner. They never volunteered information. But once you asked, they never hesitated to tell you what you wanted to know. They kept no secrets.

Sailors Jeff and Robin are Australian born. They have family names but I have never heard anybody call them anything but "Jeff and Robin." When anyone talks about one of them, he may say, "I met Jeff the other day, you know Jeff and Robin. . ." They are both thin and a bit haggard, and I would guess around 30. Jeff might be a few years older.

Although he is quite thin, Jeff is sinewy. It's pleasant to watch him balance and swing nimbly across gang-planks from ship to ship. He has the agility of an old square-rigger tar. He keeps his hair long and wears a Moses beard. In fact, he looks like the young Moses Michelangelo painted on the ceiling of the Sistine Chapel in Rome. He has a long, almost aquiline nose, and he has penetrating eyes that can easily stare one down. When you talk to him face to face you get the unnerving feeling you are being hypnotized. You find yourself staring at your hands or feet, or fixing your eyes at some distant object beyond him. I have never heard him say a harsh or unkind word about anyone. He is reserved in action as well as thought.

Jeff and Robin sail the Spice Islands of Indonesia in a tiny craft, a converted Balinese turtle boat. They have no engine, nor other mechanical devices.

Robin is more outspoken and more gregarious than Jeff. He's spent years living in Asia, among foreigners and Orientals, but his accent is heavy Australian. "Ah, yeh, ah, yeh," he says, "she's right." His badge of freedom is his long, almost waist-length hair, which he so adeptly braids and conceals so one would hardly suspect its length. He has a boyish appearance, brown eyes and a skin that never tans. After years of living in the tropics he gives the appearance of having just stepped off the plane from Sydney in July, during their winter there. He's quite knowledgeable about mystic philosophy. He wears a small Buddha votive tablet around his neck.

When they have women with them, Jeff's preference is for Asian ladies. Robin prefers blond Australian girls; he somehow persuades them to come adventuring with them. These relationships may last for months. One Australian girl remained eighteen months.

Jeff came to Asia to study the craft of jewelry making. It was his trade in Sydney and he was en route to Afghanistan when he met Robin in Penang. Robin was a rock musician with a group in Bangkok. For two years he had played the clubs in the Thai capital, until one night his apartment was broken into and all his belongings were stolen, including his passport. He reported to the authorities the next morning, and found himself in jail until a new passport was issued. To obtain a new visa, he flew to Penang. There, Jeff met Robin and formed so compatible a relationship that they decided to tour Asia together for a few months. They travelled overland to Laos, and then on to Assam and India. Their expectations of a sea gypsy life had not at the time occurred to them. That was to come later. Jeff went on to Afghanistan, and Robin returned to Bangkok.

The open road made a profound change in Robin. He no longer felt a desire to continue with the group in Bangkok. He craved excitement, not the sedentary life that musicians must accustom themselves to. He was undecided what to do when he heard about a converted Thai salt junk that was sailing with a cargo of timber from Pattaya to Singapore. The skipper-owner was a young American, a self-made trader who had been operating up and down the coast for several years. He agreed to take Robin on as crew to Singapore. The voyage took five weeks, and Robin fell in love with the sea. He probably would have stayed on the junk, but the owner found himself booked on drug charges in Singapore. Robin checked off the crew.

Robin was standing on the quay near Anderson Street Bridge, overlooking the pulsating Singapore Harbor, when who should come along but Jeff, just in from Afghanistan, with his recently-acquired knowledge of jewelry and a bag filled with a sample collection. Robin could talk of little except his sea voyage aboard the junk. Had the setting been anywhere else, he probably would not have been so convincing. Beyond them, anchored in the inner roads, were ships from many nations: freighters, tramp steamers, Chinese junks, Rhio barges, ocean liners, cruise ships, yachts, sampans, each with a story to tell, each with an adventure to relate. "There, out there is your world of freedom," Robin said. "A world without regulation and authority. When the law gives you a hard time, you lift anchor and sail off. Where? Any place you like."

Jeff did not need much prodding. "I really did not want to go back to Sydney," he said. "So I said to Robin, 'What are we waiting for?' We sold everything we owned. We had $500 to put down on a boat. We headed for Bali."

The type of sailing boat they had in mind was out of their price range. They had to settle on a 28-foot Bugis working boat. It was a rough hewn boat, but seaworthy. The Balinese fisherman who sold it insisted that it could hold fifty turtles in the bilge. Robin likes to tell how these daring Balinese seafarers would remain at sea for weeks on end in their little ship, until they caught their quota. They captured turtles by harpooning them, and kept them alive by shoving chewing tobacco into the injury made by the harpoon.

The turtle boat was rigged as a sloop, with a traditional

Bugis design, dating back hundreds of years. There was, of course, no engine, and no fancy gadgets like winches. Nor was there a head or a galley. A wooden bucket served as the toilet, and a charcoal burner on the stem was the galley. Bunks were the bare wooden floor, covered with mats under the grass roof. All gear was stowed in the bilge under the floor boards.

They paid their $500, took possession of their sea gypsy home and sailed to a small island near Benoa to prepare for their maiden voyage. They had no choice but to follow the wind to the north. However three months passed before they were able to leave as they both became infected with hepatitis. They were so crippled by the illness they could barely lift their heads to feed themselves. The air under the roof became superheated in the unrelenting tropical sun. After the first month they were scarcely more than skeletons with flesh over bones, pulpy yellow skin and bulging eyes that burned. The Balinese brought them fish, fruit and water, and they recovered but recuperation was painfully slow.

When they gained sufficient strength to attempt their voyage, Robin went into Denpasar to recruit a young New Zealand couple for crew. The man professed to be an accomplished yachtsman with knowledge of navigation. But he proved to be neither a sailor nor navigator, and jumped ship at the first island. The young girl, Nancy, came aboard as ship's cook. "She was seasick the moment she stepped aboard," Jeff laughed. "She not only didn't cook, she didn't even get up. We ended up feeding her. She was so sick she could not leave with her friend when he jumped ship. We were stuck with her. All we could do was hope she didn't die on us."

Their intent was to sail along the northern coast of Java, cross the South China Sea to the Malaysian east coast and eventually work their way up to Bangkok. Once they reached Bangkok they would decide their future. Bangkok was to be the deciding point.

Since they knew no celestial navigation, nor did they have sextant or time piece, they had to remain close to land. It was slow going, often following the contour of a land mass rather than chancing it across open and unknown seas. "We reached a group of islands north of Java," Jeff explained. "We anchored in a sheltered lagoon. The people were really nice; they took us in. It was a beautiful existence, fishing with them on the reef, gathering wild fruit in the hills. We learned a lot about native folklore and craft, how to weave mats, sun hats, baskets. But I guess we overdid it."

"What did you overdo?" I asked.

"We stayed too long. We kept missing the right monsoon."

"How long did you stay?"

"A year and a half!"

For eighteen months they lived upon their idyllic tropical isle, outcasts, far removed from a world of time and authority. They lived simply, taking what pleasures they could find. Passports, visas, sailing permits—they were unconcerned about them. "The only law we had to follow," Robin admitted, "was Muslim law. As long as we abided by their rules, we were welcome, at least by the islanders. When a government boat came around, we made ourselves scarce. But eventually we had to leave. It was getting late in the season again."

It was, indeed, late. They were but two days at sea when the northeast monsoon struck. It came with sudden fury, with monstrously high seas and fierce head winds. They had to turn south and run helplessly before the wind, like blown chaff in a grain field. Unable to stop, or alter course, they shot past their island paradise as though she were a cloud out of reach. At the full mercy of the wind they were headed for Java, and Java meant trouble. Thirty-six hours later with the wind still driving them, and without rest, they saw in the flashes of lightning the silhouette of a promontory. If they could only seek shelter behind that rise of land!

"We disobeyed the first rule of good seamanship by trying to make a landfall at night. Logically we should have stood off shore for the night, but we were not thinking logically. We were too exhausted. The lights kept getting closer. We figured they must be fishing traps, the kind of kelongs you see around Singapore, with lights to attract fish. If we could tie up to the pilings until morning we would be safe, we thought."

The north coast of Java where they attempted their landfall is flat land. What they saw were not fishing traps but the lights coming from a village a few hundred yards inland.

"When we realized our mistake it was too late. Suddenly breakers were crashing all around us. We could not come about. The surf picked us up and carried us head on towards the beach. Water came swirling into the boat." As they were telling the story they began to laugh. "Poor Nancy," they sighed, "She almost got washed out of the cabin. That was the only thing that ever got her up. We had always joked that the boat would have to sink for her to get out, and now it was happening."

Jeff quickly threw out two anchors from the bow, hoping to turn the craft into the oncoming seas, but Robin working at the tiller could not get her to swing. Suddenly there was a shattering thud as she struck bottom, once, twice; each succeeding wave drove her further on to the beach. Their luck had not run out completely. They encountered no reef, no knife-like coral. There was a gradual fall to the beach, and it was all soft sand. Furthermore, the tide was falling. Within an hour they were high and dry. Too exhausted to survey the damage they fell asleep in the debris-strewn cabin.

When thin shafts of yellow light filtered down through the torn grass roof, they realized the sun was up. Like awakening from a bad dream they lay there, and slowly they became aware of voices outside. Then it dawned on them that they were not at sea, but washed up on a strange beach. It was not a dream.

"When I sat up and looked out from under the roof, I saw a sea of faces surrounding us," Jeff said. "They had already begun to fumble with the rigging and began untying knots. Their sea god had washed a treasure ashore for them during the night. They were startled to see a bearded white man emerge from the cabin. And they were equally surprised when they saw a blond girl and then Robin. But after a minute or so they began closing in together. They were hostile looking. Not one of them smiled.

Even when I tried to be friendly they would not smile."

"It was obvious they had no regard for us," Robin said. "They were going to take what they could. Maybe they expected us to stand back. But we were not about to do that. I grabbed my parang, my Malay knife, and Jeff got a boat hook, and we began swinging. In the melee someone grabbed Nancy by the arm and began to pull her over the side, but she broke free. We yelled at her to get inside, which fortunately she did."

"We just could not understand why," Jeff said, "on a couple of islands a hundred miles away we lived like kings with the people. They did not want us to go, and now we were being mobbed, fighting to save our skins. What really saved us was that the tide started to come in. It was not enough to float the boat, but enough to keep them away. They gathered on the beach, there must have been a thousand of them, and watched our every move."

There was little damage done to the little Bugis boat. When the tide reached its full height, Jeff and Robin leaned their backs against the bow and endeavored to push her out to sea, but she was now buried too deeply in the sand. They tried dropping an anchor and winching her out, but she still did not budge. Their alternative was to dig a channel down to the sea at the next low tide. But they would have to hurry, for each tide the boat sank deeper into the sand.

The Javanese no longer crowded the boat; they stood their ground, watching, waiting. They were amused by these strangers' misfortune. They giggled and pointed when Robin slipped and fell in the sea. They laughed and nudged one another when Jeff bashed his head on a boom. They were like spectators at a circus, with Jeff and Robin the entertainers.

The next morning the army arrived. "They are paranoid about spies," Robin said. "They insisted that the three of us accompany them to headquarters for interrogation. We knew there would be no boat if we left. We refused. They put us under arrest but we still would not go. Finally they agreed that Jeff could remain behind. We had Nancy pack up all her belongings. This was her chance to leave; it was too risky with a white woman with us."

Robin returned the next afternoon, jubilant as a song bird. At first Jeff couldn't understand—two army trucks loaded with soldiers were with him. "They came to help us," he shouted.

"Where's Nancy?" Jeff called.

"Right now on a bus to Jakarta. They let her go."

The two sailors lost no time in showing the soldiers what had to be done. As the soldiers were lining up, preparing to push the boat, a news photographer appeared. He shouted to them in Indonesian, and they began to push. He took a dozen photographs, and then shouted again to the soldiers. The photographer put away his camera and returned to the trucks. The soldiers followed him, dusted themselves off and climbed aboard, and both trucks drove away, leaving Jeff and Robin standing aghast next to their boat. The villagers now roared with laughter. Who were these funny foreigners on their shore?

For the next two days, at low tide, Jeff and Robin dug. They labored unrelentingly to dig a channel to the sea, and with each incoming tide the sand filled in their previous day's work. But they could not give in, and while the villagers watched, they fought their battle against the tide. "Then the afternoon of the third day a strange thing happened," Robin said. "A little old man broke from the crowd and came down to us. He was carrying green coconuts. He hacked the tops off with his parang and handed them to us. I could not help it, this single act of human kindness brought tears to my eyes. The people saw and they went silent. The old man returned to the edge of the crowd, and we sat down on the sand and drank the cool, sweet milk. It was refreshing."

"They were Javanese and spoke their own dialect," Jeff said, "but I figured they might know some Indonesian. I decided to give it a try. I walked up to the old man. 'Why do your people just sit and look?' I asked. 'Can they go away? If they want to stay, why not help us! We need help. All your people do is laugh. This is our boat; we have nothing else!'"

Whether or not Jeff was understood, they didn't know at first. The old man stood up and said something to the crowd, and all the men left. "They must have understood," Jeff said. "At least they were finally leaving us alone."

But after a half hour passed the men returned. They carried with them picks, and woven baskets to be used as shovels. Then from up the beach a group of fishermen came, carrying two coils of rope. Now the women and children descended in one mass down to the beach, and everyone began digging and shoveling. The fishermen tied the two lengths of rope to the bow, and at least five hundred men and boys took hold. In no time a hundred-yard-long channel to the sea was dug, and now the men began pulling. Someone began to chant, and others picked it up, and as they chanted and tugged, the sloop began to move. They were alive now with excitement. Almost effortlessly they pulled the boat into deep water, to meet the incoming tide.

As soon as it began to float the Javanese gave a loud cheer. Jeff leaped aboard and hoisted the main. The sail filled and the sloop gently heeled to port and began to move. Robin, half swimming and half running in waist-deep water, could not keep up. Jeff turned the rudder into the wind, and with the sail luffing, he pulled Robin aboard. He then turned the tiller away from the wind, and slowly the craft nosed her bow to open sea. Villagers lining the shore waved good-bye to them.

The promontory to the west stood fifteen miles distant, a six hour walk, half hour by jeep. It took Jeff and Robin three weeks of incredibly hard sailing to make the distance. Three weeks to sail fifteen miles. They had to clear the point, for to give in would put them back on the beach. It was three long weeks of agony. They started with no water and little food. When they were stranded on the beach, they jettisoned their water to lighten the load. They were able to catch some rain water, and they survived by eating flying fish that landed aboard at night. Once they cleared the point it was easy sailing.

But it was obvious they could not continue to fight the monsoon winds and would have to wait another six months for a favorable wind. Five days later they put into a small port. They had to anchor far from shore, and with no dinghy for transport, they had to swim and then wade through mud. The rains were incessant, and the road leading to the port fumed into knee-deep mud. "Even the horses got bogged down to their harnesses and could not pull their carts," Robin explained. And to make matters worse, Jeff and Robin were harassed by the police. Every week they had to report with their passports to headquarters in a village 20 miles away. It took a day to make the trip. First one would go, while the other waited on the slope, and the next week the other one would go.

"And always it was the same," Robin said. "They'd pick up a passport, look at the photograph, and then say, 'Ah, that's you,' while the other officers gathered round to look. Not once did they check our visas, which were now years out of date."

It may seem impossible that in our modern world where everything is divided into time, that two men could lose completely the very concept of time. Time had no meaning to them. Their only awareness of time when the monsoon changed.

Nor could they see that they were changing. Jeff and Robin were more Indonesian than they realized. They spoke the language with fluency; their clothing had long since worn out, and they wore only Indonesian garments, mostly wrap-around sarongs; they could climb a palm to gather their own nuts; and their diet was local food. They lived mostly on rice, spiced with chilis. And when times became difficult, they knew how to cook the bitter leaves of the papaya tree to stave off starvation. Still, they could not remain indefinitely on Java.

It was no small wonder then, when they were tired of fighting monsoons, they decided to run with the winds and sail to the forbidden Spice Islands. Instead of sailing westward along the coast of Java and through the Gaspar Strait to reach the east coast of Malaysia, they would sail east and turn north

through the Macassar Strait, between Sulawesi and Borneo to
the Molucca Sea. Only they could pull off such an adventure.
They were no longer foreigners in a foreign land. And so they
set out eastward. They were sailing not only forward upon the
tossing sea but backwards across centuries of time. Few
dwellers outside this vast region, and certainly no European,
knows much about these remote places, save, perhaps, for the
larger towns. Most travellers have never heard of them, islands
like Salayar and Pasi Telu, Taliabu and Mangoli, and Bechan.
No wire or wireless connects them with the outside world. No
tourist visits them.

And yet what is so absolutely astounding about these Spice
Islands is that Jeff and Robin came to know them so well.

It was this small cluster of islands in the Malay Archipelago
that sent Asian maritime kingdoms to war and eventually
sparked off the age of discovery in the 1 6th century, which
led Columbus to discover America and Magellan to
circumnavigate the globe. The Moluccas produced the spices
aristocrats craved. But even when trade with Europe flourished
and ports like Malacca became as important as Genoa and
Venice, the Spice Islands were still a mystery. Where were
they? No one knew for certain. From somewhere beyond the
sea came Bugis trading junks and Macassar schooners, their
holds swelling with their precious cargoes which they traded
for European goods at ports like Bencoolen and Malacca. They
kept their secrets, and no one knew if pepper grew on a tree or
bush or if cloves came from above or below the ground. To
this day the islands remain, for the most part, forbidden to the
outsider. Jeff and Robin in their tiny Bugis sloop held the key.
They discovered their earthly paradise. They did it the only
way possible, a price few modern-day adventurers would care
to pay.

And here Jeff and Robin's tale about the Spice Islands stops.
Why is it when something is truly deep and meaningful to
someone, he cannot talk about it? Could it be that superlatives
are insufficient to describe it? That no one would believe it?

Is it that these rare people do not want to share their secret?

"Were these islands really that lovely?" I asked.

"Yes." Silence.

"And the people, how were they?"

"Great." Silence.

"Come on, tell me, what was the attraction?"

"Everything." Silence. I finally gave up and changed the subject. They didn't want to share their secret.

From the Moluccas Sea, Jeff and Robin sailed north of Borneo and crossed the South China Sea to Trengganu on Malaysia's East Coast. They then followed the coast northward into the Gulf of Siam and entered the Chao Phraya—which was where I first saw them—and anchored in the small klong south of Bangkok. Six years had passed from the time they bought the Bugis turtle boat to the day they anchored in the klong. Six years before they reached their goal. That was two years ago.

Jeff and Robin have found they can make a little money by delivering yachts for their owners. I met them in Manila after one such delivery. "What will you do now that you are earning money? A bigger boat?" I asked.

"It sure would be nice," Jeff said.

"But it would not give us the freedom we have on our Bugis sloop," Robin said. They had made up their minds when they reached Bangkok that they would return to the Spice Islands. They can live well on fifty dollars a month, and they can see what no other sailors can see. They have learned to accept poverty, if the need be. And so they have sailed their Bugis boat down the Chao Phraya, across the sand bar, and headed south. They are out there, somewhere.

One day Jeff and Robin may change. One day they might find that perfect island in the Moluccas. If they do, they will know they have made the right decision. Their story is unfinished.

Chapter 13

Frans Schutzman
Twenty years at the Raffles and Manila hotels

Frans Schutzman is general manager of the elegant Manila Hotel. He has held the position ever since the hotel reopened her doors in 1976. Mr. Schutzman lives in grand style in a lavish suite on the second floor of the hotel. His executive office is a short distance away on the mezzanine. Unlike his suite, his office is simply furnished, but it looks impressive, with framed photographs of important people, decorative awards and trade honors covering the walls. The first thing that catches your attention when you enter the room is a Japanese watercolor of the sea which dominates the wall behind his desk. Along another wall are cupboards, paneled in Philippine mahogany, but you would hardly detect that they cleverly conceal metal filing cabinets until Mr. Schutzman starts pulling out drawers looking for news clippings and old photographs, to illustrate a story he tells you about his past.

At first when you sit across the desk from Mr. Schutzman, you can't keep your eyes away from the framed photographs and plaques. Even from a distance, you can recognize famous people who stand next to a younger and smiling Mr. Schutzman. But as the man behind the desk talks on, everything in the room—the photographs, the awards, the paintings— they all begin to fade into the background in a strange and magical spell that he casts with his soft spoken voice. "British intelligence had a plan," he begins, almost in a whisper. "They wanted me to penetrate the German S.D. in Rome." The pounding of a typewriter in an adjoining room blends into the drone of the distant past. "France had fallen," he continues, "and with my being Dutch, the British knew I had a better chance than other agents had."

By now even a telephone ringing somewhere beyond could not bring me back. It was like viewing a James Bond thriller on the silver screen, except for one very important difference. The man on the other side of the polished desk was not an actor before a camera. He was very much real and alive. But on the other hand, in his youth he had been a screen actor, aside from being a legitimate spy. He also had been a successful music publisher, and squandered away all his profits on good living. For excitement, he became a journalist looking for action in the jungles of Malaysia and Indonesia. The last profession left him frustrated and penniless without a job in Singapore. But a shameless, young Frans Schutzman turned his misadventure into a new career. He entered the hotel business. He not only entered the hotel business but in six short months he reached the top, as General Manager of the famous Raffles Hotel in Singapore, and since then, in some thirty years now, he has managed a half dozen of the world's top hotels.

But hotelier Frans Schutzman, outspoken and unorthodox, is an exception to all the rules that govern the hotel business. He symbolizes the old school where flair counted more than academic qualifications. He doesn't try to mask the means by which he achieved his ends. On the contrary, when the Manila Hotel reopened her doors in 1976 after being restored and

Born in Surabaja, the Dutch East Indies then, young Frans Schutzman, far right, poses with his older sister, mother and aunt.

Frans Schutzman was picked over 200 other possible choices to serve as General Manager, an irate Filipino hotel school graduate asked the panel, "Why am I, a Lausanne graduate, not the GM of one of my country's hotels instead of a foreigner?" Mr. Schutzman's answer was direct. "Why should you be?" he asked. "All your Lausanne certificate proves is that you have a rich father."

Should the truth be known, Frans Schutzman also had a rich father, but that was no help to him in Singapore. He had a knack for survival, coupled with the desire to have the best that life had to offer. He is one of the best examples of an old Asian hand that I know.

Frans Schutzman was born in 1915 in the seaport town of Surabaja on the island of Java in Indonesia, which then was called the Dutch East Indies. The Dutch had established themselves in the Malay Archipelago in the early 17th century and up until World War II maintained a flourishing trade with the Netherlands. The islands were invaded and occupied by the Japanese during the war who, in turn, were ousted by the Allies in the fall of 1945. But the so-called white man's burden in Southeast Asia was over. The Indonesians rebelled, threw out the Dutch and the Dutch East Indies became Indonesia.

It was under this Dutch colonial regime that Frans was born and spent his early years. "We lived in a grand house in the suburbs of Surabaja," he recalls with pleasant memories. "I remember the garden, with flowers, and the path where the servants walked with us every day." Then he sighs. "I went back three years ago. The house was still there, but it has become a mission of some kind. The garden was in ruin, a real shantytown."

The senior Mr. Schutzman was a businessman, an importer of Swiss watches for the Straits Settlements. For Dutch citizens living in the colony life was pleasant, but Frans' father was uneasy with the political unrest that followed World War I and decided to return to Europe with his family. They went to the Hague. Frans was five years old when they left Asia, but those formative years left a deep impression upon him. He grew up knowing that he would return one day.

After a year in the Hague the Schutzmans moved to Vienna. It was here in the Austrian capital that Frans grew up. He went to a German-speaking school and learned to speak Italian. He liked sports, especially rugby, and at 19 landed his first job— he became a music publisher. "It was a natural choice," he said. "Vienna in those days was a great place to live, and there was music everywhere, in the cafes, the hotels. People loved music." Frans began publishing English songs in German. His hit that made him a fortune was Jimmy Kennedy's "Red Sails in the Sunset."

But as a young man in Vienna Frans couldn't hold on to his money. "I blew it away," he laughs. "I loved to live. I guess way back then I took to fine hotels. I frequented them all, the best ones."

In search of a new career, Frans, now in his early twenties, left Vienna and went to Paris to live. He still had a little money left and in 1939 made what he calls his first big mistake by marrying a Danish artist named Marie Louise Jorgesen. Not long after, France was at war with Germany and Frans found himself in the French army. "They wanted me for my connections in Vienna," he admitted. The

As an actor in Rome

Schutzman family had been high on the social register with prominent European families, including the last Austrian chancellor who, since Frans had left Vienna, had been sent to a German concentration camp.

Frans was assigned to the French secret service. He was sent on his first mission to Vienna. Marie Louise was pregnant and he insisted that she be permitted to accompany him.

Working out of Vienna he made two missions to Berlin and the third to Rome. Marie Louise went with Frans to Rome where a few months later their daughter was born.

In 1940 Paris fell and no one was certain if Italy would join Germany. He was ordered to Genoa to report if Italian ships were leaving the harbor, which, if they did, was an indication Italy would not remain neutral. When it was obvious what was happening, he returned to Rome. "I was in a cinema with my wife when the announcement came that Italy joined forces with Germany," he said. "We went out into the street and everyone was cheering and shouting. All I could think was 'Oh, my god, now you've had it. With Holland invaded by Germany and now Italy joining with them I was automatically an enemy in Italy."

Early the next morning Frans and Marie Louis made their way to the Swedish Embassy. The Swedes assumed responsibility for Dutch citizens in Italy. Frans and Marie Louise announced they wanted to leave. "I didn't tell them what I was doing in Italy," Frans said. "I didn't trust anyone. You couldn't. I then said I wanted to get in touch with the British."

Contact was made but Marie Louise refused to go to England with Frans when the time came. She had fallen victim to the Italian propaganda machine. Everywhere were posters showing English ships sunk by German U-boats. There were photographs of women and kids in the water. She was convinced she would not reach England with her infant daughter. The Swedish Embassy managed to get her a safe conduct pass and she went overland to Denmark.

The British M3 intelligence network learned from the French that Frans was operating for them in Rome. They made contact with him and soon after he was on their payroll. He didn't go to England. "They instructed me to stay in Italy," he said. "I was more useful there than in the UK."

Frans received his orders. He was to try and penetrate Heinrich Himmler's highly secret S.D., the German super intelligence that spied on other Germans. "We knew that Himmler's key man in Rome was a poet who translated Italian books and plays into German. Since I had experience translating English into German, it wasn't too difficult getting a job in his office."

Frans worked on tedious translations and at the same time passed on information to the British M3. He lived lavishly but not to cast suspicion on how he obtained his money, he became an actor, working for the Italian cinema doing stand-ins and bit parts. The files behind the mahogany doors in his office hold photographs taken of him during those years. He was as handsome as a movie star—dark, suave, even Italian looking. When the war did end, Frans had an opportunity to continue in the film industry but he was restless. Nevertheless, Rome would see him again, serving in another capacity.

As soon as hostilities ended, Frans tried to contact his wife. He wrote to friends and friends of friends, everyone who might know the whereabouts of his wife and daughter. He finally located her, but he was too late. She and everyone else thought he had died in the war. A week before the letter had arrived, she remarried.

Frans decided to remain in Italy for a while, and made the "second biggest mistake" of his life when he married the daughter of an Italian senator. But the marriage wasn't meant to last long. Frans spent most of his time running back and forth to Milan. He had acquired an old German touring car, the camouflage paint still on it, and started a taxi service between Rome and Milan. It was the excitement he craved. "Today you can drive it in five or six hours," he said. "Then it took two days. " He collected 5,000 lira per passenger, and could carry five. It was easy money. "Everyone after the war wanted to travel. Those in the south wanted to go north, and those in the north wanted to travel south. Only there was no train service. All the rail lines were gone. And even the highways, most of them were in ruins. There wasn't a bridge standing. We had to ford rivers and make tracks across open countryside. But we always made it, with an overnight stop in Florence."

In Florence Frans always took his passengers to the same small hotel. "First-class hotels were occupied by the U.S. military," he said, "but that didn't matter. Some of the small hotels were good, and you were always welcomed back." The concierge at the hotel where they stayed was a little man with an exuberant personality. "As soon as he saw us, he threw up his hands and said, 'Mr. Schutzman, how are you? So good to see you.' I learned a lot about the hotel business from him. He taught me about the human element. Stopping in his hotel was like going home. It made you feel good, and that's important."

Frans remembers 18 years later when he was in Rome he took a trip to Florence." I had money then and I could have stayed in the best hotel in town, but I decided to go back to this small hotel. And would you believe, the concierge was still there, the same little man. He had grown white, and obviously had eaten a lot of spaghetti, but he still remembered me. 'Mr. Schutzman,' he shouted, 'where have you been all this time!' That taught me a lot about running a hotel."

When competition set in and his marriage was edging towards the rocks, Frans decided once again to move on. But he was looking for something new, something different. Then one day when he was reading the newspaper, an idea came to him. He had always longed to return to Asia one day and his plan might be the solution. "It was a brilliant idea, brilliant, " he said. Then he laughed, and added, "'But I must admit, it wasn't mine. I stole it."

At the time a well known but notorious bandit was living in Sicily. He was a kind of Robin Hood, and as a result, he was protected by the people. No one could get to see him. But one day, a determined young correspondent for the *Stars and Stripes* newspaper, Michael Stem, took his camera and notebook and went to Sicily. He got his interview. "It was a masterpiece of journalism," Frans said. "Newspapers around the world carried the story, with photographs of Michael Stem and the bandit standing side by side. What a sensation! That's when the idea came to me. There was trouble in Asia, in Indochina, Malaya, Indonesia. Civil strife, bandits in the jungles, everything. And nobody in Europe knew what was going on. I would find out and tell them."

Frans took a train to Copenhagen and went directly to the biggest newspaper in town, the *Politiken,* and arranged a meeting with the publisher Niels Hasager. "I announced to him I was going to Indonesia, and to Malaya. I was going to interview the government officials, and then go into the jungles and interview the rebels. What Michael Stem can do with one little bandit, I could do with all of Asia. The publisher took the bait. Fabulous! I was in business. He gave me letters of reference and I became a bonafide correspondent. I got passage on a steamer, the East Asiatic *Korea,* and sailed for Asia. That was in 1951. There was only one thing wrong, one thing that Niels Hasager and I didn't realize. Michael Stem was an American, and the Italians, especially the Mafia, liked Americans. I was a Dutchman, with a Dutch passport, and the Dutch weren't very well-liked in Indonesia. They just threw us out of the country and got independence."

In Singapore, Frans was warned not to go to Indonesia. He was certain to be jailed. He then tried to get a permit to enter the Malay jungles, hopefully to interview one of the leaders of the "Communist Terrorists." He went to the top, to see General Gerald Templer. Permission was denied. The Chinese Communists lumped all foreigners into one group—the enemy. They would surely kill him on sight.

Frans was stranded in Singapore. He had no money, no job, and no prospects for one. But he had to do something. He had remembered seeing the old colonial Raffles Hotel on Beach Road. He liked the place. It had a lot of charm. He would give it a try.

With a fresh shirt and a clean shave, Frans walked into Raffles Hotel and went to the receptionist, an Indian with a dark face and gleaming white teeth. Frans asked to see the general manager. "The guy didn't even bother to get up. He just sat there and pointed down the hall. It annoyed me," Frans said.

The general manager's name was Guido Cevenini. "The only reason he received me," Frans said, "was that I spoke Italian. " Mr. Cevenini listened patiently as Frans explained that he was broke and would like a job.

"A job, a job!" the manager exclaimed. "Impossible."

"Look I will do anything," Frans pleaded. "Wash dishes, sweep the floor, just name it. Any job. Just a job."

"You don't understand. A European can't do that. The British would never allow it. A clerical job at least, but we have no openings. I'm sorry."

"I have to get a job," Frans continued. "At any cost I have to get a job." He could see the manager was losing his patience. Frans had to try another tack. "Well, let me tell you," he said, "I heard so much about your famous Raffles Hotel, and when I went to the receptionist, he didn't get off his chair when I said I wanted to see you. And when I went down the corridor, there were cigarette butts on the floor, and as I passed the bar three or four waiters stood yapping away, all with dirty uniforms. I had to ask myself, was this really the famous Raffles I heard so much about?"

Cevenini became angered, and that was exactly what Frans wanted. "See here," he shouted, "did you come here to criticize the management of the hotel or to ask for a job?"

"Look, Mr. Cevenini, I don't criticize you or the management, but don't you have an assistant who can look after all these things?"

"I have an assistant," he said, pausing for a moment, "except he's never here."

"You see, you need someone. Give me a chance, one month only, with no salary. One month and let me show you want I can do for you."

Mr. Cevenini thought for a moment. "You know, a few

months ago we hired a headwaiter," he explained. "He is a former Foreign Legionnaire. He had no experience. I hired him to get him out of trouble. Would you be interested in the job as headwaiter?"

"Headwaiter, Mr. Cevenini. I told you I would wash dishes," Frans said. The manager shook his hand and explained he would give the Legionnaire a month. Frans should come back in a month.

"But I cannot wait a month," Frans said. "I must begin work today, now."

The manager was astounded. He had never confronted anyone quite like Frans Schutzman. He liked the brazen young man; he liked his spirit. He found Frans a room, paid off the Legionnaire and three days later made Frans Schutzman headwaiter of the Raffles. Frans was immediately fitted with a tuxedo and informed by Mr. Cevenini that the hotel was giving a St. George's Day dinner that very night. At his first function, Frans would have to carve what the menu called "Ye Olde English Roast," or to put it in Frans' words, "half of a bloody cow." Furthermore, it had to be carved at the table for none other than the Governor of Singapore, Sir Franklin Gimson. When Frans declared to Mr. Cevenini that he had never sliced roast beef in his life, the smiling manager sent him to the bar for a stiff double brandy. "By God," Frans recalled after it was over, "I was the greatest roast beef-slicer ever that night."

In her fascinating book *There Is Only One Raffles,* author Ilsa Sharp paints a candid picture of Frans Schutzman in those days in Singapore. She writes, "It was the beginning of a life-time career for a distinguished, and self-taught hotelier, who was at heart an adventurer, one might even say a buccaneer. He was to show his more piratical side six months later."

What happened six months later? Headwaiter Frans Schutzman was suddenly catapulted into the position of general manager. How did it happen? The same way he became headwaiter, by not taking no for an answer.

The assistant manager Ernest Smith was in England on home leave, which in those days of colonial service and slow steamer travel amounted to six months, when Mr. Cevenini suffered a heart attack. Frans called the chairman who instructed him to cable Smith in England and request that he come back immediately. Smith declined, as he was just beginning his leave, and the board appointed Frans joint manager with Smith. "That was not enough, " Frans said. He told the board it was unacceptable. They called another meeting and agreed to appoint Frans manager and Smith his assistant.

Frans was still not contented and asked for more. He asked to be made sole manager. To run the hotel properly, he had to have full authority to make decisions. The board met for the third time—Frans Schutzman was appointed General Manager.

Frans immediately set to work to upgrade the hotel and make it a success. Eighteen months after he took over, he paid a 25% dividend to shareholders, the first time ever. He moved Raffles from the red into the black. He found that 75% of the hotel's expenses went on food, the reason being that the staff was stealing food from the kitchen. They had quarters but were not given food, and consequently were dining on expensive roast beef, lobster and

Frans with Primo Carnera

Swiss cheese. Frans called in the hotel carpenter, had him build tables and benches, and had a cook prepare meals for the employees without cost or deduction to their wages. He fed them rice, vegetables and fish that they liked. When the board learned what he was doing they called him in and asked for an explanation. "Gentlemen," he said calmly, "you should ask me why our expenses have dropped from 75 to 30% and why we are making so much money now. I'll tell you why, because the staff are not eating up our profits."

In Frans' earnest program to upgrade the hotel and make it the most famous hotel in Asia, publicity played a big part. He discovered that Somerset Maugham had written in one of his novels that "Raffles in Singapore stands for all the fables of the exotic east. " He wrote to the author and asked for permission to use the extract in publicity material and in return he invited Maugham to stay at the Raffles when he came to Singapore. Maugham at first declined, saying he was "getting too old" and didn't think he would ever travel that far again. He changed his mind five years later.

Frans made the Singapore Sling one of the world's most famous drinks by sending the recipe to leading hotels around the world, with the remark "the drink that originated at Raffles in Singapore." He opened the Elizabethean Grill and suggested the construction of 400 more rooms which the board considered impractical. He couldn't do much about additions but he didn't hesitate to make changes when they were needed, like the time King Faisal of Saudi

Frans with King Fiasal

Arabia announced he was arriving and needed four large suites. Raffles didn't have any large suites, so Frans sent the guest on one floor packing to another hotel, at his expense, and immediately set his carpenters to work. They tore out walls and partitions, added glass doors, wall paper and curtains and welcomed the King when he arrived the next day.

Frans became a lifelong friend of many of the hotel guests. He dined often with the Sultan of Johore and Xavier Cougat. And his volumes of photo albums in his office contain autographed pictures of Ava Gardner, Gloria Swanson, Jane

Mansfield and Abbie Lane; Frans shaking hands with Lyndon B. Johnson, Ben Gazzara, King Khalid; smiling at the camera beside William Holden and many heads of state including President and Mrs. Ferdinand Marcos.

To upgrade the hotel, Frans made it a policy that all guests wear dinner jackets and ties should they desire to dine in the Elizabethan Grill. The move was also aimed to keep out dowdy soldiers who were coming in drunk and causing trouble. One evening, a Chinese banker brought a guest to the Raffles for dinner. They were not in proper dress so Frans refused them admission. Furious and humiliated, the Chinese banker bought a share into Raffles and, after four years, proceeded to become chairman of the board, and thereafter made Frans Schutzman's life as miserable as he could make it.

Another incident happened that was to lead to some changes at the hotel. Somerset Maugham wrote to say he was going on a sentimental tour to visit all the places that inspired his writing. Frans invited him for the second time to be the hotel's guest but the chairman refused saying Frans had no right to invite anybody to the hotel and that Maugham was rich enough to pay his own way. The invitation had already been headlined by local papers. Frans invited him anyway and paid the famous author's expenses out of his own pocket, and when Maugham left, he resigned.

Frans came to know Maugham rather well, through correspondence and their time together in Singapore. "I wouldn't call him snobbish as most people thought," Frans said. "He was more caustic. He had a very sharp tongue and he could not tolerate mediocrity." Frans told the story of how he took Maugham to the British Tanglin Club one Saturday night. Maugham's photographs were all over town, and of course, everyone knew him. But at the Tanglin Club the manager would not let him in. Frans had on a tuxedo but Maugham only had a dark suit. Frans explained to the secretary. "This is Somerset Maugham," he said.

"I don't care who he is," snapped the secretary. "This is a

gentlemen's club and gentlemen dress properly."

Frans maintained his composure. "I'm sorry," he said to the secretary, "but I invited him and I must take him in."

"Then you suffer the consequences," the secretary replied and stepped aside as they entered. A few days later Frans received a letter from the club. His membership was withdrawn and he was expelled.

Just before Frans left Singapore, after ten years with Raffles, he received a letter dated 16 March, 1960, from Villa Mauresque at St. Jeancap Ferratan on the French Riviera. It read: "Thank you for all your help and kindness to me while I was in Singapore. I was very much pleased and deeply touched by your thoughtfulness and all the trouble you took. Many, many thanks." It was signed W. Somerset Maugham.

Frans now had new worlds to conquer, but he always had a soft spot in his heart for the Raffles. "But having made my name at Raffles," he said, "I always wanted to add at least one more of the Big Five properties in the Far East to my credit — The Hong Kong Peninsula, Bangkok's Oriental, the Imperial in Tokyo or the Manila Hotel." He was well on his way to achieving that goal, but first there were a few stops in between—Cairo, Rome, Toronto and New York.

From Singapore, Frans went to manage the Nile Hilton in Cairo, where he spent a year, and then moved on to General Manager of the prestigious Cavalieri Hilton in Rome. Close to the Vatican, it was one of Catholic owner Conrad Hilton's pet projects. But business was not what it should be. Unorthodox Frans Schutzman got to work.

"We opened the hotel in 1963 with 400 rooms and no bookings. There was an ecumenical council of cardinals coming to Rome so I went to see the Secretary of State at the Vatican. I asked him if he could recommend us. He couldn't do it. It was not fair to others, he said. 'You have no special reason for me to recommend you,' he said. But I replied, 'Oh, but we do, father.' I had to think fast. It so happened that I remembered some discussion about the difficulties of the cardinals attending mass every morning, which they must do. 'We have a chapel,' I said, lying through my teeth. He was delighted, and suddenly the Cavalieri was booked to capacity. I immediately went to the chairman and explained we need a chapel."

"What do you mean, a chapel!" he screamed. We have overshot our budget by more than a million dollars and now you want to build a chapel! The chairman wouldn't hear of it. He threw me out."

But Frans Schutzman had to have a chapel. Disgruntled, he went back to his apartment and confessed his problem to his housekeeper. "Ingra," he said, "what actually is a chapel."

"Why, Mr. Schutzman, it could be anything, a simple room with an altar is enough."

"But an altar."

"Mr. Schutzman, an altar is no more than a table with a pure linen cloth covering it and a crucifix. It must be blessed by the parish priest."

Frans emptied a small function room, placed three banquet tables end for end, covered them with white linen and bought a crucifix. He then had his carpenters make a wood cross and tack it above the door on the outside. He called in a parish priest, gave him fifty dollars for the poor and had him bless the chapel. Soon after the Cavalieri had world publicity. It was the first hotel with a chapel. Frans recalls, it was one of the most beautiful sights he can remember, seeing the cardinals in their flowing red gowns, walking through the hotel gardens towards the chapel. The hotel engaged five buses to shuttle the cardinals back and forth to the Vatican.

Frans Schutzman now had as much business from the Vatican as he could handle, and so impressed was Pope Paul that he awarded Frans by making him a Knight in the Order of San Silvestre. Frans was also instrumental in obtaining for Conrad Hilton the Order of Malta decoration, quite an achievement considering Hilton was a divorced Catholic.

But despite Frans' achievements and success at the

Cavalieri, he and Conrad Hilton were to go their own ways. Again, Frans had to speak his mind. It happened when all the Hilton Hotel managers were summoned to Madrid for a cost control meeting. "They were all flown in first class with their wives," Frans remarked, "and I had to give up a very busy schedule to be there. When we arrived in Madrid our program of bullfights and flamenco shows had been lined up. I thought it all very foolish, as we were supposed to be discussing cost control. We could have done the same thing with a circular letter —and I told them so. I got my notice after that."

After the Cavalieri, Frans took a break from the hotel business and accepted the vice presidency of a major oil company in Texas and represented them in Europe. "The only kind of oil I knew, " Frans admitted, "was salad oil. But I learned." A series of strikes took the joy out of the job, so when the Hyatt Hotel boss Peter de Tullio asked him to open the Hyatt Regency in Toronto, he didn't hesitate.

Frans with Liza Minelli

Frans charged into the general managership of the Regency with the same fervor that he did at the Raffles and Cavalieri. He even succeeded when disaster looked inevitable, as it did with truffles, an unexpected tragedy. Frans learned that Alitalia was establishing a direct air service from Milan to Toronto. How could this help the Regency? What did Italy have that Canada didn't? He then thought about truffles, a delicacy in Italy, unattainable in Canada and America. He would fly truffles directly from the markets of Milan to the tables of the Regency. What a marvelous idea! The Hyatt Regency would have the first restaurant to serve fresh truffles on the American Continent. He would build a deluxe grill room, even call it

Truffles. He called in his architects and construction began. It had the Old World charm, a European castle look, with heavy wooden beams, colored glass windows, brick floors. The restaurant opened to coincide with Alitalia's inaugural flight from Milan, bringing a shipment of truffles. The shipment arrived, and there it remained in a custom's shed. Canadian law prohibited the import of certain foodstuffs from abroad, and truffles was one. The Regency had been informed that they could import truffles, but when it came down to it, no one knew what truffles were. "So I was struck with a restaurant called Truffles and no truffles," Frans laughed. "But it's funny how things turn out. The restaurant was a success even without them."

But the Canadian contribution to the Frans Schutzman legend came not from Truffles but from a very much publicized gala party he gave, not for heads of state or royalty or famous people from the stage or cinema, but for another entirely different group—for the local cab drivers of Toronto and their wives. It was a stunt he had already pulled in Rome. Instead of abusing the local cabbies' union for their politically-motivated boycott of his hotel, as advocated by the owners, he wined and dined them and won them over. The Toronto cabdrivers' bash was even a greater success. "Think about it, " Frans explained. "Visitors come to town and ask a cab driver to recommend a good hotel, yet few cab drivers ever saw the inside of one. And how can they recommend a hotel? All they can say is that a hotel has a nice driveway. " After the cabdrivers' party they all knew what the Regency was like inside and were keen to take their passengers there.

Frans left the Regency in Toronto when the Hyatt president sent him to manage the giant United Nations Plaza in New York, the only Hyatt International property in the United States. The Plaza required a prestigious manager, one who was aggressive and stubbornly competent. They found what they wanted in Frans Schutzman. But Frans did not find the Plaza to his liking, nor did he care for New York. "I was unhappy there," he said, "and New York is a sewer." Where diplomacy was required, again, Frans was outspoken. Where any hotelier might think the UN Plaza was the fitting pinnacle to a GM's career, Frans thought the opposite. "Why should I be punished by staying in New York because all you have in the company are boy scouts employed as managers," he told the management. When Frans was offered the position as GM of the Grand Dame of hotels, the Manila, half a hemisphere away, the Hyatt president became so angered he gave instructions to get the Manila Hotel at all cost and then to fire Frans Schutzman. He, of course, didn't succeed.

The Manila Hotel is one of the Big Five in Asia that Frans had had his eye on when he left Raffles. Even if he had been happy at the UN Plaza, he admits the Manila Hotel was an offer he would not have turned down. But Frans also realized a tough job awaited him at the Manila.

Built in 1912 by the U.S. Army in the Philippines, the Manila Hotel became the haunt of the rich and famous and its guest book reads like *Who's Who* in Asia. The hotel's most famous guest was General Douglas MacArthur who made it his headquarters. He had a private Penthouse on the fourth floor "equivalent to the presidential palace" from 1935 until the Japanese Imperial Army staff took over as new tenants in 1941. When MacArthur returned to the Philippines, as he promised he would, he literally had to blast the Japanese out of the hotel. Fortunately the solid foundations and the heavy walls, constructed by the U.S. Army Corps of Engineers endured.

The Manila Hotel went through its time of troubles during the pre-Marcos era when it was deeply in debt, due mostly to high-ranking government officials and ministers who ran up huge bar and entertainment bills for themselves and their horde of bodyguards and never bothered to pay the hotel. But in the mid-70's, President Marcos decided to so something about the Old Manila, as everyone affectionately called it. He wanted to preserve it as an historical site.

Frans Schutzman at the Manila Hotel with Sammy Davis, Jr., top, President Marcos, middle, and Gina Lollohbrigida, bottom.

The challenge was to reconstruct it, with an 18-story wing behind, and bring it into the modern age. In 1975, the hotel closed its doors, and at a cost of $30 million the old hotel was reconstructed and restored to its former glory. When it reopened in 1976, it was nearly five times bigger, infinitely more luxurious, and once again the Manila Hotel. Naturally, it required one of the world's great hoteliers to run it and Frans Schutzman was the obvious choice.

What is the key to his success? "To be able to pick and hold on to a staff, from the humblest bellboy to the highest executive," Frans said. This is no easy task. The GM of a large Asian hotel may have as many as 1,500 trained people working under him. When Frans picked his staff for the Manila he had to sift through thousands of applications, and once he hand picked someone, they became members of the family, which accounts for their almost fanatical loyalty to him.

"Service is everything," he maintains. "I believe in building up the reputation of a hotel on its performance, and for this the human element cannot be replaced by computers." He remembers taking over the Regency in Toronto. "The NCR and his assistant invited me to see the hotel's latest invention," he said. "It was an automatic bartender. The NCR proudly announced, 'We don't have to hire a bartender anymore!' He was right. There was this machine with a lot of little buttons, and by punching the right button you could get any cocktail you could think of. I studied the machine and all its buttons and I said, 'Gentlemen, your forgot something.' They jumped back in alarm. 'What drink did we forget?' I said, 'I'm not talking about a cocktail. I'm talking about the human element. What a man wants when he comes into a bar is to hear, "Mr. Brown, good evening. Is it going to be the usual?" People don't go into a bar just to get drunk. They go into a bar to talk, to be recognized."

Frans Schutzman realizes that the "good old days" are gone and that the modern traveler will not accept living in the past however nostalgic he may be. But he likes to be reminded of the past. And this is where Frans Schutzman excels. He is Asia's living reference book of characters. It isn't only the famous and illustrious he knew, those whom you can always read about in books and magazines. It was the expatriate, the retired British colonel, the con man, the war profiteer—all the characters who are collectively known as "old Asian hands." These too were Frans Schutzman's friends.

Any time I want to know about someone who lived in Singapore twenty or thirty years ago, all I have to do is go to Frans Schutzman for the information. "Did I know Bill Bailey," he exclaimed when I asked if he knew him. "Bill Bailey, what a beautiful character. He lived in this old colonial house. He got it cheap after the war because no one wanted it, said it was haunted. He put in a bar downstairs and called it the Coconut Grove. It wasn't the original Coconut Grove. That was along the East Coast Road. The Japanese shelled it when they took Singapore. So Bailey opened this new Coconut Grove. And he had this other character helping him, Johnny Johnson. He's still around, I understand. Now there was an artist, full of imagination. He could do anything. Well, Johnny would tend bar and Bailey would sit in a huge butterfly cane chair and spin yarns. I used to bring guests from Raffles. I would ask them if they wanted to meet Bill Bailey. This is what tourists really want, to meet interesting people. They wanted to sit next to Bill Bailey and have their pictures taken. He wasn't the real Bill Bailey, but no one knew that. He was an entertainer, and he knew people like Mary Pickford and Doug Fairbanks. He was a great story teller. Tourists would ask, 'Why can't he go home again?' And I would say, 'Because he's wanted for murder,' or something like that. Maybe I'd add, 'He killed his wife in bed with her lover.' All the tourists loved it, and so did Bill Bailey."

Frans Schutzman lived in Southeast Asia during the transition period, when the colonial era was passing and individual states were emerging. Was it better then or today?

"I don't live in the past," he said. "Don't get me wrong, I enjoyed places like Singapore when I was at Raffles, but living there could be miserable. There's no comparing yesterday to today. Singapore today can be a grand place to live. No one ever believed that would happen. The colonials used to say, 'Wait 'til we leave and then see what happens. The place will collapse.' But look what did happen. Singapore grew from a second-rate port to the second busiest in the world today. Asia can produce some good leaders. The most extraordinary one has to be Lee Kuan Yew. He proved that socialism can work with capitalism. Singapore is independent, and she doesn't have to dance a ritual for any other country. Lee built her into what she is today."

Most old Asian hands don't think about retirement. They intend to go on doing what they do, for as long as they can. Not with Frans Schutzman. "No, I will retire," he said, "and maybe take over a small place on the French Riviera. I won't stay too long here at the Manila. Maybe another 20 or 30 years." Then he winks, and adds, "That will make me a hundred."

Chapter 14

Brian and Zahara Hughes
The expatriate and the princess

Until Brian Hughes was called into the National Service when he was 18 years old, he had never heard of Malaya and certainly had no idea where it was. Born in Birmingham, England, he was an average child from an English industrial town who lived an average life and got into the average amount of trouble. Birmingham was his home, as it had been his father's and his grandfather's before that, and there was no reason whatsoever to suppose that Brian would not follow in their footsteps. His family was typical working class, council house people who believed in a strong Labor Government and in the socialist system. When Brian Hughes completed his National Service he would return to Birmingham and take up where he left off.

But in 1950 something happened. New recruits were sent to Malaya in Southeast Asia.

"Where's that?" one recruit asked Brian.

"You know where Malaya is," another spoke up with authority. "It's part of Hong Kong, stupid."

And so it was Malaya, later to become Malaysia, where the Army sent him, to a land he knew nothing about. Never in his wildest dream did he imagine he would be making this unknown land his future home and giving up the country of his birth; even more improbable that he would marry a lovely girl from this far-off land. But she would be no ordinary girl. She would be a Malay princess. Had Brian believed in fairy tales, he might have dreamed he was the young knight in shining armor who fought the dragon to win the hand of the beautiful princess. In this case, however, his shining armor would be a bush jacket and the dragon the narrow-mindedness of their peers. This is his and Zahara's story.

I first met Brian when I was motoring along the East Coast of Malaysia. The drive is one of the finest in Asia, along a curve of coastline that begins at Singapore and runs for a thousand miles to the Gulf of Thailand, through picturesque towns and fishing villages which have scarcely changed in a hundred years. The Malays along the coast are perhaps more traditional than in other parts of Malaysia. They adhere to Muslim traditions and customs, and their dress, habits and language are pure Malay.

It was no small wonder then, when I left Kuantan and headed north, that I was more than surprised to see a sign pointing to the sea. It read Titik Inn. In a cluster of trees there appeared a beach resort. Progress had come to the East Coast. I drove a few miles beyond the sign when I thought it might be pleasant to have lunch at the Inn. It had seemed to be located in such very agreeable surroundings.

Indeed it was. A dozen chalets were spread out on land shaded by overhanging trees, carpeted with green lawns. There were tropical flowers, a flagstone path that meandered through the gardens, and even a miniature of colorful local birds. Beyond the lawns and flowers and trees the sea unrolled upon

Brian Hughes and his Malay princess wife Zahara in their garden .

a white sandy beach. A bar and dining room were open to the breeze and the perfume of flowers was everywhere. Comfortable cushioned lawn chairs completed a most welcoming scene for a weary traveller.

At the time, the Inn had been open just one year. There were few guests. I took a seat at the bar and Brian walked across the lawn and came to introduced himself. He had been working in the garden and was dressed only in shorts. His beard was long and his hair covered his ears. He was tall and handsome in a casual way. He spoke in a very proper English accent.

Brian talked little about himself but at length about the Inn and his aspirations. His knowledge of Malay customs and tradition was considerable. He could keep a visitor amused. He knew the best places to watch giant leatherback turtles come up from the sea to lay their eggs; he knew of the legend of the mermaid of Cherating and where to find her grave. He knew many tales about jungle lore, about tigers that come down to feed on cattle and of rogue elephants and untamed jungle rivers. The hours slipped by and it was late afternoon when I finally left the Inn. I reserved a chalet for my return a week later. "My wife will be back from Kuala Lumpur then," Brian said. "She's the one who really knows the country. She's Malay."

I was in Kota Bahru having dinner with friends a few days later when I mentioned the Titik Inn and Brian Hughes. "You met Tunku Zahara then?" someone asked.

Tunku in Malay means prince or princess. "No I didn't meet a Malay princess," I said.

"Tunku Zahara is Brian's wife."

I was mildly surprised, as Brian had not mentioned that his wife was a Tunku, but then why should he? I was then informed that she was from the royal family in Negri Sembilan. Tunku Zahara and Brian had fallen in love when he was still in Government Service and after his contract was completed they had married. He had no job, and no local prospects of one, and she was now estranged from her traditional background. The young couple had some hard years together.

When I returned to the Titik Inn I hardly recognized Brian. He was without his beard and his hair was clipped short. "Once a year," he said. "Once a year I have a haircut and shave. I dread it."

He really did look different, more like a business man from Singapore on holiday than the dedicated expatriate that he was. We settled down to drinks on the patio when a stunning Malay girl descended the stairs from an apartment above. She was in a colourful ankle-length batik gown; her hair was tied loosely on top of her head. She had a lovely smile. Brian introduced us. "This is my wife, Zahara," He said.

After spending five minutes in her company, I could understand why Brian had fallen in love with her. Zahara was truly beautiful; she seemed to sparkle with inner life. She was incredibly alive and aware. Never had I met anyone so animated in her speech. This elegant lady could express herself with her eyes alone. Her English was faultless, with perhaps the suggestion of a French accent. It was difficult to place. Obviously she had been educated in the best of schools. When she talked it was always with enthusiasm. "Before dawn this morning I heard the giant finch across the meadow," she said, sitting on the edge of her chair, unfolding her arms like a great winged bird. "You can hear them miles away," she continued, and then hesitated—"You know it's so quiet here sometimes in the morning, you can actually hear the dew." Brian and I looked at her without saying anything. "It's true," she cried. "I can hear the dew in the morning."

Brian and Zahara keep few secrets and they talk freely of the difficulties they experienced in their early years together. Brian tells an interesting a story about a misconception he had about the Far East. It started when he was called into the National Service. "You are going to the Far East," they told him. "Disease is rife there; it is safe to eat only in the military mess." He was bombarded by documentary movies about VD.

"I was frightened to death of every woman I saw during my first few weeks in Asia," he said.

It took very little time for Brian to change his mind about the East. Malaya was everything that industrial Birmingham was not. There was sunshine almost every day of the year; there was no smog nor the dampness of England and the food agreed with him. He returned to Birmingham at the end of his National Service stint and studied civil engineering at Aston University, determined to get back to Malaya at all costs. His chance came at the end of 1957 when he answered an advert put out by the old British Colonial office. It was for an appointment with the newly independent Malaysian government. He was interviewed by a sympathetic and delightful old "Malaya hand" who pulled out all the stops to allow Brian to resume his interrupted love affair with Malaysia. So it was a final farewell to Birmingham and off to his Kismet. Back in Malaysia he one day saw a very beautiful Malay girl driving a sports car; he knew he had to seek her for his own. That was in 1958. A year later, they were married in the true Muslim religious tradition.

Brian's early life in Birmingham had in no way prepared him for the role he would have to play in Malaysia, nor did Tunku Zahara ever suspect she would have to physically work for a living. They could, of course, have left Malaysia and have taken up a new life in another country, but that would be admitting defeat. No, if they were to find happiness, they would have to solve their problems on home ground. There could be no running away. It would not be easy. Brian was without a job and his chances of winning over the royal family were remote. Their immediate problem was how to support themselves.

In a sense they were both romantics, hopeless dreamers.

They found some land on the East Coast, where the Titik Inn stands today, and tried their luck at farming. They built a house, fenced in the land, and started raising goats.

"But why goats?" I asked.

Brian explained that he misguidedly believed that goats are easy to raise, and with milk difficult to come by in Malaysia and Singapore, they would be profitable. "It was disastrous," Brian said. "'Goats, very sad, very sad. Have you ever been close to goats?"—he threw up his hands—"Don't answer. They're individuals, with minds of their own. And what I didn't realize is that their resistance to disease is very low. They will eat anything. Never did I think I would be sitting up with a sick goat with a cold all night. Colds were the worst problem."

Zahara laughed. "We didn't have to pay a gardener," she said.

"No, she's right," Brian said. "They kept the grass cut, and the leaves trimmed on the trees, and they finished off the flowers. But no one would buy our goat's milk. We ended up drinking gallons every day, and we couldn't sell a single pint."

Then came a new idea, a get-rich scheme. This time it was eggs. They installed modern coops and imported proper grain for egg-laying hens. Within a year they had a thousand chickens, Brian burned the midnight oil reading books and literature on raising chickens. He read that some farmers had discovered music makes hens lay better. He didn't have piped in music to offer so he did the next best thing. He sang to them. Each morning he went to the chicken coops and sang opera: Rossini's "Barber of Seville" or Wagner's "Tannhauser."

"It didn't do any good," Zahara said. "Brian became a fine baritone but the chickens didn't lay any better."

But finally the ledgers began to show a profit. Then the Thais started shipping eggs into Malaysia. Brian and Zahara lowered their price to seven Malay cents an egg, and were barely breaking even. The Thais on the other hand began selling theirs at five cents a piece, including shipping. "First it was goat's milk we had to drink every day," Brian laughed, "And then it was dozens of eggs to eat. We had fried eggs and scrambled eggs. And all that talk about cholesterol. We waited and you know, the price of eggs never did go up. We were ruined."

"What about the Inn? How did you get started?" I asked.

"Luck, it was pure luck," they explained. When they were trying to make a living at farming, the commonwealth Armed Forces were still in Malaysia, and service men went to the East Coast for recreation. "So many soldiers stopped to visit and we began selling cold beer. Business became so good we started a six-room boarding house. It was an instant success. We were filled every weekend," Brian then designed and drew up the blueprints for a large beach resort with private chalets. It took time, but they began building, and the Titik Inn emerged.

I stopped again, after a gap of years, to see Brian. His reputation as an inn keeper was spreading across Asia, but he had not altered his life style. "I still get a hair cut and shave once a year," he said. "And the Royal family has come to accept us. We are invited to many state functions."

Brian with his trombone

Brian claims that the real person behind all his achievements is Zahara; she deserves the credit. "Think what she had to give up to marry me. She could be living in a Palace, with servants and people bowing to her. She's the one that holds the place together, making sure there's oil in the generator, that the leaves are swept up, and the maids have changed the linen. And what would we do without our chief drummer?"

Tunku Zahara is the snare drummer with the Titik Jazz Ensemble. She's part of a group formed from expatriate planters, tin mining foremen, inspectors and school teachers whom Brian gathers to pay music from another era. They play such tunes as "When The Saints Come Marching In," "In The Shade Of The Old Apple Tree" end even "Clementine."

Brian himself plays the clarinet and slide trombone. He

discovered a Chinese banjo player who works as foreman in a tin mine. An English manager of an oil palm plantation plays coronet. He drives forty miles each way twice a week to play with the group. Others come from up and down the coast. Brian will go to any extreme to recruit a new player. A French planter came to hear the group one Sunday. Brian asked if he played any musical instrument. "I can play the helicon," the planter said. On his next trip to Singapore Brian visited a junk shop and found an ancient helicon which he bought. When the Frenchman showed up at the Titik, Brian presented him with the shiny but battered instrument. The man was horrified.

"Mon Dieu," he sighed, "I can't play one of these. I never thought anyone even knew what they were." But the planter did come through. He went back to his plantation and learned to play. He's part of the group today.

With all the pitfalls and obstacles removed from their marriage, Brian and Zahara have found their niche. Their pleasure in life centers on daily living. They don't have to go looking for excitement; it's there all around them in Titik Inn.

Epilogue

After the Facts

When *The Strange Disappearance of Jim Thompson* first appeared in print in 1978, it was published under the title *Asian Portraits*. Many critics found the name to be a misnomer; none of the people whom I wrote about were Asian. Nevertheless, the publisher continued to use the same title through half a dozen more printings, and it wasn't until Wolfenden Books published this new version that the name was changed.

The text to the original version has not been changed or altered. I have kept it exactly as it first appeared in print. I did consider updating the material but then I realized that when I wrote about these people, I was capturing a period of time. To make corrections would be like altering history, and I wouldn't want to do that, to change the past. Enough of that is going on in the world today. Instead, what I have done is write this epilogue telling what has happened over the years to those people whom I wrote about.

The most controversial figure in the book is Jim Thompson who appears in the first chapter. I have heard it said over and over that the world might never know what had happened to Thompson. I find this hard to believe, for new information comes to the fore constantly. It may be only bits and pieces, but put together and it begins to fill in the giant jigsaw puzzle. Recently well-known mystery writer Francine Mathews, who was once an analysist for the CIA, came to Bangkok to do research on Jim Thompson. After a month of probing she concluded that the real story of Jim Thompson has yet to be told. She wrote a fictionalize account of the disappearance in a novel called *The Secret Agent*.

Recently I began corresponding with a lady who was married to the Security Officer of the US Embassy at the time, and she wrote that she and her husband often dined with Jim Thompson at his home. Did she ever note anything unusual about him? Not at all. When was the last time she saw Thompson? The day before he left for Malaysia; she and two others from the embassy had lunch with him at the British Club. Anything unusual? No. How was Thompson feeling? He was a little annoyed. He had a new prescription drug for his illness, and it was making him dizzy. He might change it later. The next day he left for Malaysia. I added the information to my file that keeps growing and growing.

Theories and rumors about the strange disappearance go on and on. I was in Singapore when wreckers' hammers were putting an end to the old shop houses along Sungei Road, the area famous for its thieves' market. Most of the shops had already disappeared and even the rubble was cleaned up and the area flattened into empty fields. But there was one shop house that stood alone, an antique shop. I went in to browse around. The manager greeted me and we began a conversation. He said he does his buying on trips he makes to Burma and Bangladesh and to northern Thailand. We got on to the subject of Jim Thompson.

"Oh, yes, I saw him," the manager casually said.

"You mean you saw him years ago in Bangkok," I replied.

"No, recently, the last time I was in Burma."

"Jim Thompson, when you were in Burma?"

The manager then unequivocally declared that he saw Jim Thompson in a small village in Burma. Thompson was living there, an old man now, running a lucrative antique business, with no desire to leave.

Did he really see Jim Thompson? Or was the man another foreigner who resembled Thompson? Or was the manager opting for his own cheap form of publicity? Whatever it is, the point still remains-the Jim Thompson mystery continues. Unless some conclusive proof of his death becomes known, there will always be speculation and the mystery of his strange disappearance will continue.

In preparing this epilogue, I wanted to meet once again as many of the characters that I could. I spent a month or better traveling around from country to country in Southeast Asia. It was both a happy and a sad time. It was sad, for example, when I drove up the long winding drive in Port Dickson to visit with Mr. Perkins, the rubber planter in Malaysia, and I learned he had died a few years before. He was in his 90s when he passed away, and they say he was active right up to the end. He had taken a swim in the ocean in the morning on his last day.

When I arrived in Kuala Lumpur I planned to hire a car and drive down to Port Klang, and from there I would take a ferry out to Ketam Island to visit with Dr. Connie Strickland. Years had passed since I had received mail from her. In one letter she mentioned that a book publisher was interested in her life's story. That autobiography will never be told. Friends in Kuala Lumpur gave me the sad news that Connie Strickland had died suddenly the year before. *The Straits Times* ran her obituary and many people had nice things to say about her. But no one stepped in to take over her clinic on Ketam Island. Its doors were closed and Snowy, her pet white crow, was turned loose. I heard he can be seen each evening at dusk, fluttering around the clinic, waiting for Connie to return home.

In "Treasures Beneath Southeast Asian Seas" I wrote about several successful salvage divers living in Asia-Pat Hamil, Ian Chamberlain, Doug Tiffany, Sandy Lentz and Bill Mathers. Of course, that was years ago and the oil drilling business has changed greatly since then. Bill Mathers, like most of the others, went on to other things. Bill outfitted his own boat, *So Fong*, to do salvage diving, then got caught by the Vietnamese in their territorial waters, and was told he would be executed for spying. He was kept in isolation for nine months, and one day was led from his cell to an airplane waiting at the edge of the runway. He was certain he was being taken to another city to be executed in public. The plane carried him not to his death but to Bangkok and his freedom. The Vietnamese confiscated *So Fong* but that didn't deter Bill Mathers. He outfitted another salvage boat, and discovered a Manila galleon near Saipan in the Western Pacific. The discovery made him a millionaire and the story appeared in *National Geographic*. Bill is till out there, somewhere, doing the same thing. The tragic news in Singapore was about Sandy Lentz. Sandy and his wife lived with their two boys aboard their schooner in Singapore. Sandy left his family behind and took a yacht delivery job to South Africa to earn some extra money. He and his three-man crew never arrived. Their last radio contact came when they were 500 miles from their destination, but with seas running high and the wind velocity increasing. The weather bureau reported a typhoon with winds at 190 knots had crossed their path. Not even a trace of wreckage was found.

Diver Doug Tiffany is in Port Townsend, Washington, refurbishing a trim ketch-rigged yacht and is planning to sail the South Pacific again.

Whenever I was absent from Asia for a spell and returned, I always enjoy traveling up to Chiang Mai to spend time with my friend Theo Meier, the Swiss painter who settled there after leaving Bali many years ago. What a delight to lounge away the afternoons with Theo, sitting in his grand Thai house, drinking Mekong and soda with ice and fresh lime, and talking about the "good old days" in the islands. Maybe if Theo had started a new canvas, he'll talk about that. Then when evening fell, sarong-clad servant girls moved about as silently as shadows and lit a myriad of candles. There might even be the sound of a flute filtering up from the garden. When I was with Theo I could feel the soul of Asia right down through every pore in my body.

But those days are gone. Theo Meier die in a hospital in Switzerland. He went there hoping to be cured of cancer.

No person was more shaken by Theo's death than Prince Sanidh Rangist. It was Prince Sanidh who invited Theo to come to Thailand to live, and ever since they had been close friends. "Something went out of my life when Theo died," Prince Sanidh said when I saw him at Theo's house in Chiang Mai. Theo had died one hundred days before, and according to the Buddhist religion, we were gathered to pay our last respects to Theo. I had taken a taxi from the airport to Theo's house. I entered the gate into the compound and there on the wall of the guesthouse was a sign Theo had printed.

Gone to Europe. Be back soon. Theo

Many had gathered by the time I arrived, both Europeans and Thais, all friends of his, from diplomats to tutuk drivers. Standing on top of the stairs leading up to the house was Theo's widow, Laiad. She motioned for me to join her. She saw my anguish and took hold my hand as she led me past people sitting on chairs and on the floor towards Theo's studio. Hanging on the walls were Theo's paintings, many I hadn't seen before. It was all so strange, like the action on a movie screen had frozen and I was the only moving thing. Laiad pushed open the door to the studio and stepped aside to let me enter. The room was a private sanctuary. No one was there.

I was aware of a double bed in the very center of the room. Gone was Theo's workbench and easel. More of his paintings hung on the walls. What caught my attention was a framed photograph of Theo, taken many years ago. It was in the middle of the bed, propped up by a worn Balinese sarong rolled into a kind of ball. Laiad said something. Her English is not good. I didn't react, and this time when she spoke she pointed to the sarong. "There is Theo," she repeated. She pulled the sarong partly open revealing a wooden box. Theo's ashes were inside.

I couldn't hold back the flood of tears. I wanted to flee from that very room but I couldn't. I wanted to call out to Theo, but no words came, only more tears. No more pictures to paint, no more tales to tell. All the beauty he had found, all the joy he had known, all the greatness he had created, all were gone. A hand touched me on the shoulder. Prince Sanidh stood there. "He is gone," Prince Sanidh whispered, "and with him has gone something from our lives that can never be replaced." Prince Sanidh couldn't get over the death of his good friend, and a few years later he too passed away.

Although Theo gained fame in his lifetime, he was not wealthy. In fact, life at times was a struggle, but he didn't let the lack of money bother him. A few times, when he was destitute, he let paintings go for a few dollars. Prince Sanidh often came to Theo's aid, but Theo would accept no handouts. He gave Prince Sanidh a painting each time he received money. After Theo's death, Prince Sanidh showed me his storeroom filled with Theo's oils, some which were exquisite paintings. When Prince Sanidh passed away the paintings went into his estate, and someone certainly became wealthy. At a Christie's auction in Singapore in 2001, several Theo Meiers went on the block, and the hammer came down for S$115,000 for one painting. They say his paintings may fetch as much as quarter of a million dollars in another few years. I remember one time Theo saying he was so poor on Bali he painted on burlap bags.

Zeina Amara from the chapter "Travels with a Belly Dancer" is a story that should begin where I left off. Zeina realized her lifelong dream of traveling all over the world by visiting 130 countries, and working in many of them over a period of twelve years. She appeared on television, in theaters and nightclubs with her dance act in most of those countries; she bought for export (and sold to stores) art objects, antiques and precious stones; she sold refrigeration and took bids on lumber; and she invested in international markets. After she returned to the USA, she worked as a stockbroker for several years. She married in 1970, divorced in 1978, no children.

From 1979 to 1982, Zeina traded commodity futures, using technical analysis to make her investment decisions. In 1982, she discovered a way of making this method work for picking winning lottery numbers. She began publishing her lottery strategies in March 1983. Since then, her systems have won 74 first prize lottery jackpots worth over $97 million. Her books have been translated into French, German, Spanish, Dutch, Norwegian, Latvian, Japanese and Chinese, and are sold all over the world, as does her line of lottery software. She lives in Las Vegas, Nevada, and is writing a tell-all book about her years of travel and adventure.

I went to see Colonel Firbanks from "A Tale From the British Raj" soon after the book was first published. He was living in Singapore. "Glad to see you back, old chap," he said when he saw me. I was curious about something I read, about the Sikh revolt in Armitsar in the late 1930's. Before long he was giving me a firsthand report. When I returned to see him this last time, his wife greeted me at the door. She gave me the news that he had quietly passed away in his sleep the year before. I learned later that his collections of prints of "Boar Hunting with the Raj" were on display at the National Museum in Singapore. He will always be remembered.

When I began writing the chapter about Jessie Takamiyama, "The Kid From Hawaii Who Became a Sumo Wrestler," I was told by some critics that I had better hurry up, that by the time the book came into print Jessie would be a "has been." Six years later, I was in Japan and discovered Jessie Takamiyama was even more popular than he had been in the past. In fact, Jessie Takamiyama was a phenomenon. Sumo had never known anyone quite like him. He had just won his 600th victory and had secured his position in the Makunchi division in the next tournament. I wanted to visit with him again but he had left for Osaka. Jesse since then has retired, and other foreigners from Hawaii have taken over after him. But it will always be Jesse Takamiyama who paved the way for them. Jesse is still in the sumo business. He has a stable in Tokyo.

Kurt Rolfes is another phenomena. You always hear about that rich uncle that dies and leaves a fortune to an unexpecting heir. That's Kurt's story. The last I heard from him he was living in Portland, Oregon. It wasn't that he intended to give up living in Asia, it just happen that Uncle Archie died and left him an estate. Kurt, his wife Mei and their son Raoul went to Portland to see what the estate was, not intending to remain long. They got stuck, at least for a couple of years.

Uncle Archie passed away at the age of 92. He left Kurt his house on a hill, a 20-year-old Cadillac, a pile of rocks and a coin collection. The house is old, and is filled with surprises. The yard has apple and pear trees, and acres of grape vines. From their front window they have a view of Mt. Hood and the Willamette River, and as Kurt said, "the best feng shui I have ever seen."

It seems Archie was a collector for all of his 92 years and the house is a goldmine of collectibles. By profession Archie was a geologist and left thousands of rocks in closets and in the basement. Kurt contacted the Geological Society of the Oregon Country, and was given the task of classifying the collection. It could take Kurt years, and in the mean time, the Geological Society made him a lifetime member. The coin collection, when gathered together, weighed over 600 pounds. Kurt hasn't even begun to estimate its value.

Around Southeast Asia they are still asking the question "Whatever happened to Boris?" I presented Boris with an original copy of Asian Portraits when I went to visit him in Kathmandu. He was 76 and going strong. He then took me to lunch at his new restaurant "Boris' Bar & Restaurant" in a quite neighborhood ten minutes from city centre on the Dili Bazaar Road to the airport. Aside from running the restaurant, Boris was dividing his time between writing and tending his farm. His literary projects were translating *Russian Noblemen's Cookbook*, dated 1820 to 1840, and he was working on a biography titled *From Ballet to Belly*.

Unfortunately the two books go unfinished, and never will be finished. Boris Lissanevitch died before they went to press. A few years ago I went to Kathmandu and talked to his wife Inger. I found her so fascinating, the woman behind the man, that I wore a chapter about her in my book *At Home In Asia*. She had a completely different story to tell.

On my return voyage aboard my schooner *Third Sea* across the Pacific to Singapore, I made an anchor stop at Zamboanga in the southern Philippines. I wanted to see Homer Hicks again, the American expatriate who appeared in the chapter "The Old Man From Zamboanga." After we sailed out of Zamboanga a half dozen years before, I intended to write to the old man but I couldn't read the address he had scribbled out for me on a matchbox. Instead I wrote to the manager of the cafe where we sat every afternoon. The letter was returned. The cafe had been sold and the new management didn't know any Homer Hicks. Now when I returned I went directly to the cafe and spoke to the new manager. He was sorry but he knew no one by the description I gave him. I spent the next few days looking in other cafes, talking to whomever I thought might help me. Then I met Benny, a marine salvage diver. "Old man Hicks, I know him," he said and named the street where he lives. "But I don't think you'll recognize him," he added.

Benny drove me in his jeep to the outskirts of Zamboanga. We checked the houses, driving up and down narrow, deeply rutted streets with no sidewalks, where all the houses were unpainted clapboard. Benny stopped when recognized the house. He stepped out of the jeep and walked up to a gate in a picket fence and called out. A young Filipino girl, perhaps thirteen or fourteen, came out of the house. They had words, pointing to the house and then to me. Presently Benny called out to me. The girl swung the gate open and stepped aside. She motioned for me to follow her. Benny said he'd wait in the jeep.

The house was Spartan, with block walls and throw rugs on concrete floors. Once inside the girl called out, "Grandpa!" There was no reply. She called again, louder this time. When it appeared nothing was happening, she pointed toward a curtain covering a doorway. I pushed the curtain aside, and there reclining on a hard wooden bed with only a sheet covering it was a very old man, his back toward me. He wore only trousers, no shoes or shirt. The girl shook him by the shoulder. "Grandpa," she said, "there's someone here to see you."

Slowly the old man turned. He looked at me but his watery blue eyes were far, far away. He feebly sat up. His right side was paralyzed. I recognized him. "Homer, don't you know me?" I asked. He tried to answer but his speech was mumbled. "I'm the writer you met a couple of years ago, remember?" He looked at me across a vast distance. "Remember the schooner," I continued. "You came aboard." His face lit up. He stared hard at me and slowly the words came.

"Yes, yes," he said. "We were worried about you." He explained that he had a stroke, and not many people came to see him. He asked about the schooner. When I said I was anchored in the harbor, he became more excited. He wanted to know if he could see the schooner again. But soon he become weary and had to lay down and rest. He closed his eyes and quietly I slipped out of the room and out of the house. Benny was kind and he understood and didn't ask any questions. My heart was heavy as we rumbled down the potted street, and through tears I could see a cocky US Army private arriving for the first time in the Philippines. He wore breeches and wraparound leggings, his campaign hat pushed forward over his brow, and he sat with other soldiers on a flatbed railway car. That was ages ago. I saw him brawling in the bars and cantinas and loving all the young and beautiful Filipino girls, all of whom would be long gone now. I saw him in later years, his Filipino wife at his side, defying the Japanese soldiers who interrogated him, knowing that he would be mutilated. But Homer Hicks was a hard-drinking, hard-fighting Texan. He came to a distant land, fell in love with the people and never made it back home, even for a visit. And now he never would. Homer Hicks had lived life to its fullest. I'm sure if he had to do it all over again, he would do exactly as he had done.

In the spring of each year The Oriental Hotel in Bangkok and Thai Airways International sponsor the S.E.A. Write Awards in which top literary prizes are given to selected Asian writers and poets. The Queen of Thailand or one member of Thai royalty presides over the ceremony and famous writers are invited to give keynote speeches. They have included James Michener, Frederic Forsyth, Norman Mailer, William Golding, Vidiadhar Naipaul and others. During one presentation, American novelist Gore Vidal was invited as guest speaker. I too was invited and at a cocktail party before the presentations I was introduced to Mr. Vidal. "Oh, you're a writer who lives here," he said, "I just spent all afternoon reading a book *Asian Portraits*" He had found it in the kiosk in the lobby. I didn't tell him it was by book, but I was curious which characters interested him the most. Would it be Perkins the rubber planter in Malaysia or Jim Thompson from Bangkok? I suspected it would be the latter, as most people who come to Bangkok are intrigued by the mystery. But Mr. Vidal answered my question without my asking. "I wonder what ever happened to those two sailors, Jeff and Robin?"

Others have asked the same question, what did happen to Jeff and Robin who appear in the chapter "Two Sailors Who May Be Kings." They did sail back to the Celebes in their tiny boat. We know that. But what became of them can be anyone's guess. Maybe they have become kings on some forgotten island in Indonesia. Maybe they have found their secret, and if they have, they certainly wouldn't tell. Or maybe like Sandy Lentz they have disappeared forever and no one will ever know. Time may give us an answer.

What time has not changed is Frans Schutzman, the GM of the Manila Hotel. He retired from the Manila and went to Florida to retire. Until a few years ago he wrote every now and then, and seemed quite contended with life. Unfortunately I have lost contact with him in the last two years. He appears in the chapter "Twenty Years at the Raffles and Manila Hotels."

Brian and Zahara Hughes from the chapter "The Expatriate and the Princess" continue to live happily ever after at the Titik Inn. Occasionally they have to attend royal weddings and other such functions, but "only when we are compelled to do so," they quickly explain. Their desire is to lead private lives and they intended to do what they are doing now, always.

Southeast Asia, we all must agree, has changed since Joseph Conrad and Somerset Maugham were here, but I'm sure they would admit, it's no less exciting, and it's the people who make it what it is.

HS
Bangkok